The Practical Approach™ Utilities for Maple™

Springer
New York
Berlin
Heidelberg
Barcelona
Budapest
Hong Kong
London
Milan
Paris
Santa Clara
Singapore
Tokyo

Darren Redfern

The Practical Approach™ Utilities for Maple™

Maple V, Release 3

With 83 Figures
DOS Diskette Included

Springer

Darren Redfern
Practical Approach Corporation
230 Brunswick Street
Stratford, ON N5A 3M4
Canada

Library of Congress cataloging-in-publication data.

Redfern, Darren.
    The practical approach utilities for Maple: Maple V, release 3 /
Darren Redfern.
      p. cm.
    Includes bibliographical references and index.
    ISBN 0-387-14221-5 (softcover: alk. paper)
     1. Maple (Computer file) 2. Mathematics—Data processing.
   3. Utilities (Computer programs) I. Title.
QA76.95.R434 1995
510'.285'53—dc20   95-30384
                                                                                          CIP

Maple is a trademark of Waterloo Maple Software.

Printed on acid-free paper.

© 1995 Springer-Verlag New York, Inc.
All rights reserved. This work may not be translated or copied in whole or in part without the written permission of the publisher (Springer-Verlag New York, Inc., 175 Fifth Avenue, New York, NY 10010, USA), except for brief excerpts in connection with reviews or scholarly analysis. Use in connection with any form of information storage and retrieval, electronic adaptation, computer software, or by similar or dissimilar methodology now known or hereafter developed is forbidden.
The use of general descriptive names, trade names, trademarks, etc., in this publication, even if the former are not especially identified, is not to be taken as a sign that such names, as understood by the Trade Marks and Merchandise Marks Act, may accordingly be used freely by anyone.

Production managed by Natalie Johnson; manufacturing supervised by Rhea Talbert.
Photocomposed copy prepared from the author's LaTeX files.
Printed and bound by Hamilton Printing Company, Rensselaer, NY.
Printed in the United States of America.

9 8 7 6 5 4 3 2 1

ISBN 0-387-14221-5 Springer-Verlag New York   Berlin   Heidelberg

I would like to dedicate this book to my grandparents, Vera and Delbert Dupré, who have always been like a second set of parents to me. Their support and love made me realize many years ago that I could accomplish anything I put my hand to, as long as I had faith in myself.

Contents

1. Introduction   1
An Issue of Usability 1 • Maple and Our Utilities 2 • How This Book Is Organized 3 • Design Issues 4 • How This Book Was Created 6 • Your Input Is Wanted 6 • Future Editions of These Utilities 7 • Acknowledgments 7

2. Installing the Utilities   9
System Requirements 9 • The Contents of the Utility Diskette 9 • 32-bit Versus 64-bit Machines 10 • Reading the Files from the Diskette 10 • Installing the Library Files 10 • Testing the Installation 15 • Installing the Other Directories 16 • Advanced Installation Procedures 17

3. Getting Started with Maple   18
What Is Maple? 18 • Maple's Internal Structure 19 • Starting Maple 19 • Basic Maple Syntax 20 • Basic Maple Objects 22 • Maple Expressions 25 • Lists and Sets 27 • Calling Maple Commands 28 • Assignments and Equations 37 • The Use of Quotes in Maple 40 • Maple as a Programming Language 42 • Special Built-in Commands and Operators 45

4. **ListTools** — 49
   What Maple Has 49 • Utility Commands 54 • Examples 73 • Programming Tips 77

5. **ExpressionTools** — 84
   What Maple Has 85 • Utility Commands 91 • Examples 114 • Programming Tips 117

6. **PatternTools** — 135
   What Maple Has 136 • Utility Commands 138 • Examples 149 • Programming Tips 150

7. **ArrayTools** — 155
   What Maple Has 155 • Utility Commands 164 • Examples 178 • Programming Tips 182

8. **DrawTools** — 189
   What Maple Has 189 • Utility Commands 197 • Examples 235 • Programming Tips 240

9. **StringTools** — 247
   What Maple Has 247 • Utility Commands 250 • Examples 257 • Programming Tips 262

10. **IOTools** — 270
    What Maple Has 270 • Utility Commands 274 • Examples 295 • Programming Tips 296

11. **MiscTools** — 298
    Utility Commands 298

Index — 305

CHAPTER 1
Introduction

An Issue of Usability

Historically, high-level computational languages have been designed *by* researchers *for* researchers. Little attention was paid to the niceties of consistency across commands, or to design intuitiveness. Some years ago, this wasn't a big problem; the only people using these tools were advanced researchers or those who aspired to that position, people who were *willing* and *able* to put up with the inconveniences that a less-than-intuitive system presented.

Since these types of programs have become more mainstream through advances in available platforms, better pricing, and more aggressive marketing, their audience has changed dramatically. At first, there were increasing instances of undergraduate courses being taught with these tools. Now the market is expanding to encompass all levels of the academic and commercial sectors. To a large extent, however, the programs themselves have not evolved in the area where changes could make them easier for *all* to use and understand: the *language design* area.

Language design is a subtle science consisting of, among other things, naming conventions, parameter conventions, ease-of-use issues, and subject coverage. Proper treatment in these areas greatly improves the usability of language-based programs, and lessens their learning curves. For more information on how *The Practical Approach Utilities for Maple* take advantage of language design, see the section *Design Issues* on page 4.

Maple and Our Utilities

> Maple is an extremely powerful and thoroughly exciting product, and it is among the best and most promising software applications in its field.

There can be no doubts about the preceding statement. When I worked for Waterloo Maple Software answering technical support questions, I was told countless times by Maple users something similar to "Wow! Maple is fantastic—it solved my [substitute your favorite complicated problem here] in three hours, which normally would have taken me days or weeks to do by another method." Unfortunately, in many of these cases, the same people came right back and said, "The only problem is that it took me two hours/days/weeks to figure out how to take my results and [substitute your favorite data manipulation task here]."

While Maple makes difficult tasks easy, it may also—however inadvertently—make easy tasks more difficult than necessary. This is what we are trying, with this book and software, to remedy. In order to accomplish the task, we have provided a package of Maple commands that supplement and complement the basic product you have purchased. The basic areas covered are:

- list manipulation,
- string manipulation,
- array (matrix and vector) manipulations,
- general data structure manipulation, investigation, and transformation,
- drawing, transforming, and manipulating standard two- and three-dimensional objects,
- input and output (I/O) facilities,
- rudimentary pattern matching facilities,
- miscellaneous facilities.

In each of these areas, we have provided the tools you need to perform most of your day-to-day non-mathematical operations. All of these tools have been programmed in Maple's own Pascal-like programming language, the same language in which over 90% of Maple's built-in capabilities are programmed.

The fact that we have programmed the entire *Practical Approach Utilities for Maple* in Maple's own language leads to the inevitable conclusion that:

> Everything contained herein is within the capabilities of *any* Maple user to create, provided they have sufficient knowledge of the system.

It is our hope that these Utilities will benefit not only the beginning users of Maple, but those more advanced as well, by providing standardized tools for performing day-to-day tasks, designed and coded to optimize performance and usability. As is true in most other areas of life, simple, mundane activities often take up a large percentage of your allotted time, while brilliance and insight are often fleeting sparks. What we have attempted to do is make the simple tasks much more efficient, so that all Maple users have more time for what really counts: exploring the myriad of possibilities that Maple opens for you.

How This Book Is Organized

Chapter 2 deals with all the information you need to install *The Practical Approach Utilities for Maple* onto your computer system, in such a way that it works seamlessly with your copy of Maple.

Chapter 3 provides a brief introduction to the existing Maple product. If you are a beginning user of Maple, read this chapter over carefully and try some of the examples. A more experienced user may read through it more quickly.

The remainder of this book both illustrates the uses of *The Practical Approach Utilities for Maple*, and familiarizes you with *how* the Utilities were programmed, thereby enabling you to quickly and efficiently create your own personalized commands in the future. With that in mind, each subsequent chapter of *Using Maple Efficiently* is laid out in four sections.[1]

Section 1—*What Maple Has* describes the structure, capabilities, and limitations of the object (e.g., lists, arrays, plotting commands) as currently implemented by the standard Maple product. Knowing what is possible

---

[1] Except the chapter *MiscTools*, which has only one section, *Utility Commands*.

and available lays the foundation for the Utilities to come, and for your own future use of Maple.

Section 2—*Utility Commands* describes the Utilities we have provided for you, and gives precise, helpful examples of their use.

Section 3—*Examples* gives more involved examples, using information from both **Section 1** and **Section 2**.

Section 4—*Programming Tips* describes how the Utilities in this chapter were created, giving you insight into special Maple "tricks" that were used, as well as tips on how to make your future calculations more efficient.

At the end of a chapter, you should be totally equipped to handle *any* situation involving that particular topic of study. If you wish, you can postpone reading the *Programming Tips* section of each chapter until you are more comfortable with Maple as a whole; this will not in any way affect the usefulness of the rest of this book.

Design Issues

In creating these Utilities, we have tried to keep the issue of command design at the forefront. *Consistent, intuitive* design is crucial to the usability of any product, but is especially important in a computer *language* such as Maple.

There are two main areas of command design to which extra special attention has been paid:

1. Naming Conventions—This area covers not only what names are given to the commands themselves but also the names used for optional parameters. Not only must the use of names be consistent within a subset of similar commands, but the general principles adhered to must apply across *all* commands in the Utilities. The following are just a few of the rules we have adopted for the Utilities.
   - Command names are entirely in lowercase characters, unless they are *unevaluated* commands or rely *heavily* upon a proper name.
   - A command name should always reflect the *most common usage* of the command.
   - Underscore characters are not used in command names or in optional parameters, but are used only in *environment variables*. For example, the environment variable _TypeNames is used in conjunction with the command listtypes.
   - If a command performs an action and has a verb in its name, then the verb describing the action should be the first part of the name. For example, deletestring, not stringdelete.

- If an adjective or adverb is used in the name, it should appear before the noun or verb. For example, uniquelist, not listunique.
- If a command, in its simplest form, calls for more than one of a specific object type, make sure that the object type ends in an "s" in the command name. For example, ziplists, not ziplist.
- If two or more commands perform similar actions on different types of Maple objects, they should have related names. For example, deletelist and deletestring.
- Redundant or superfluous information should not be included in a command name. For example, sphere, not sphere3d.
- Alternative or slang spelling and "numbers-for-letters" should not be used. For example, avoid litecolor or list2set.

2. Parameter Conventions—This area covers, among other things, how parameters are ordered and grouped. The following are just a few of the rules we have adopted for the Utilities.

    - If two separate elements of relatively equal importance are being acted upon by a command, the *active* one is listed first. For example, insertlist(list1, list2), where list1 is the list whose elements are being inserted into list2.
    - If parameter x relies upon parameter y for its definition, then parameter y is listed first, and x is listed *directly* after. For example, reverselist(list, a..b), where a..b defines the subsection of list being reversed. Without list, a..b has no intrinsic meaning.
    - If it is admissible to have an unknown number of similar parameters passed to a command, these parameters should be enclosed in a set or a list.
    - When a parameter can be a set or list of values, and one value alone is also valid, that one value should be entered as either a one-element list or set, or just a single expression without the brackets.
    - In matters of satisfying conditions, a *set* of conditions specifies that *any one* of those conditions must be met, and a *list* of conditions specifies that *every one* of those conditions must be met.
    - Optional parameters always appear after non-optional parameters and can be entered in any order.
    - If two or more similar commands have similar types of parameters, the ordering of parameters should be identical across these commands.

Of course, there are always going to be exceptions to these rules. Keep firmly in mind that our best judgement was used to make the commands as consistent and, at the same time, as intuitive as possible.

There are many other areas of design that have been taken into consideration in these Utilities, but we won't go further into them at this time.

How This Book Was Created

Using Maple Efficiently is based on the internal design document for *The Practical Approach Utilities for Maple* and was written using the LaTeX document creation language. The raw LaTeX files were processed with the automatic production tools available from Waterloo Maple Software, inserting the correct output fields into the document. The LaTeX macros used to manipulate the processed files were created by the production staff at Springer-Verlag, New York.

Your Input Is Wanted

Since these Utilities were written for *you*, the everyday users of Maple, we sincerely want your feedback. Any comments are welcome, but the following are a few of the areas in which we are most interested.

1. Are there any additional commands that you would like to see in any of the existing command sections in a future version of this product? Are there any *new* areas that you would like to see covered?

2. Do you have any real-life examples of how these Utilities were used in your work? Any sample code or worksheets that you would like to share with us and other Maple users?

3. Have you found any bugs (heaven forbid!) in our code that we were unable to catch? If so, please include as many details as possible about how the bug was encountered. Any sample worksheets showing the problem would be greatly appreciated.

Any suggestions that we use in future versions of the Utilities will be recognized in future editions of this book. Please send any and all comments to Practical Approach at one of the following addresses:

Ground Mail: Practical Approach Corporation
               115 Randall Drive, Suite 2
               Waterloo, ON
               Canada N2V 1C5

FAX: (519) 747-0702

Email: info@practical.on.ca
            darren@practical.on.ca
            david@practical.on.ca

WWW: http://www.practical.on.ca/practical

Future Editions of These Utilities

Waterloo Maple Software releases a new version of its product every year or two. The current version (Maple V Release 3) is scheduled to eventually be replaced by Maple V Release 4.

For every new version of the Maple product, there will be a new edition of *The Practical Approach Utilities for Maple*. Each new edition will address the following concerns:

- The existing commands in the Utilities will be recoded to take advantage of any changes in the new version of Maple.
- New and improved Utility commands will be added to the package as we respond to user input.
- The book *Using Maple Efficiently* will be reworked to reflect any changes in the product.

Included in this package (on a tearout card at the back of this book) is an easy upgrade offer for existing owners of *The Practical Approach Utilities for Maple*, providing discounts compared to the "over-the-counter" price. This card can be sent in any time after a new release of Maple is announced.

Acknowledgments

No acknowledgments for this project would be complete without mention of my major collaborator and friend of many years, Dave Doherty. Ever since I first approached Dave with the idea of these Utilities, he has proven himself an enthusiastic and capable partner. Dave is responsible for most of the programming, testing, and code organization that went into *The Practical Approach Utilities for Maple*. He has managed to take my often changing design and my frequent flights of fancy in stride over the last two years, and I do not exaggerate when I say I couldn't have done this without him.

A hearty thank you also goes out to those other colleagues who provided their time and expertise to the project. Included in their ranks are Ian McGee, Tom Casselman, Jonathan Borwein, Colin Campbell, Kophu Chiang, and Bruce Barber.

CHAPTER 2

Installing the Utilities

Please read this chapter carefully *before* attempting to install your copy of *The Practical Approach Utilities for Maple*.

System Requirements

The following are the system requirements for installing and using *The Practical Approach Utilities for Maple*. More about each requirement is explained in the following sections.

- A computer system containing a working version of *Maple V Release 3*. The Utilities do *not* work with earlier versions of Maple.[1]
- Approximately 1.2 Meg of available disk storage.
- A method of retrieving information from a 3-1/2" DOS-formatted diskette.

The Contents of the Utility Diskette

This product comes with a single diskette, which contains three directories holding the following files:

- Directory: utility
  - maple.lib
  - maple.ind

---

[1] When subsequent versions of Maple are released, new versions of these Utilities will soon follow.

- Directory: `source`
  - utility.src
- Directory: `other`
  - 12 textual files

The following sections explain what these files are and how to install them on your system so that they work seamlessly with Maple.

32-bit Versus 64-bit Machines

Maple supports both platforms that operate with 32-bit processors and platforms that operate with 64-bit processors. Unfortunately, the files that Maple creates to store information (in this case, including `library` files and `index` files) are different for each class of processor. That is, files saved on 32-bit machines will *not* work on 64-bit machines and vice versa.[2]

There is only one 64-bit platform that Maple supports, the DEC Alpha. All other (and more popular) platforms are 32-bit based. Because of this, we have only provided `maple.lib` and `maple.ind` files for 32-bit machines. If you happen to be installing *The Practical Approach Utilities for Maple* on a DEC Alpha system, please contact us at one of the addresses provided on page 6, and we will provide you with files customized to your situation.

Reading the Files from the Diskette

The *Utility Diskette* is a DOS format diskette. This format was chosen because most non-DOS machines have the capability to read information from a DOS diskette. For example, most Macintoshes have a utility called `AppleFileExchange` which allows such sharing of information.

If your particular machine cannot read the DOS diskette, try to find someone who can perform the transfer for you. If that fails, please contact us at one of the addresses listed on page 6.

Installing the Library Files

The basic steps for installing the Utility library files are identical for every Maple platform. The only differences are in how these actions are

---

[2] I have been told that this difficulty will be addressed in a future version of Maple.

performed on different systems. In the following sections, instructions are given for DOS/Windows, Macintosh, and UNIX-based systems. If your system is of a different type, perform the steps as appropriate to your system.[3]

Creating a Utility Library Directory

When you installed Maple V Release 3 on your computer, it created several levels of directories[4] in which all the files necessary to run Maple were stored. The top-level Maple directory was (unless you specified otherwise) called something like `MapleV3`.

Underneath that directory were created several other directories, including the `lib` directory, which contains the standard Maple library files. The first step in the installation of the Utility library files is to create a `utility` directory at the same level as the `lib` directory. That is, if the standard library directory is named something like:
`C:\MAPLEV3\LIB`
then a new directory
`C:\MAPLEV3\UTILITY`
must be created.

Depending on which type of computer you have, perform the appropriate steps as laid out below.

DOS Computers

1. Determine which existing directory is the top-level Maple directory. If you don't know this already, you should be able to glean this information from either your Maple platform-specific documentation, or by looking at your `autoexec.bat` file.

   Change directories so that the top-level Maple directory is the current directory. For example, if your top-level Maple directory is `C:\MAPLEV3`, then enter the commands:
   `C:`
   `cd \MAPLEV3`

2. Create the Utility library directory with the command:
   `md UTILITY`

---

[3]The *Getting Started* booklet that you received with your copy of Maple V Release 3 should be useful.
[4]If you are using a Macintosh, you are more accustomed to the term *folders*. For most of our purposes here, the two terms are interchangeable.

Macintosh Computers

1. Determine which existing folder is the top-level Maple folder. If you don't know this already, you should be able to glean this information from either your Maple platform-specific documentation, or by performing a `FindFile` search on `Maple`.

    Travel through your folder structure until the top-level Maple folder is the currently selected folder.
2. Create the Utility library folder as follows:
    1. Bring the top-level Maple folder to the front by clicking on it.
    2. Click on the `File` item on the menu bar across the top of the screen, and select `New Folder`.
    3. Edit the folder name, changing it to `utility`.

UNIX Computers

1. Determine which existing directory is the top-level Maple directory. If you don't know this already, you should be able to glean this information from your Maple platform-specific documentation.

    Change directories so that the top-level Maple directory is the current directory. For example, if your top-level Maple directory is /u/maple, then enter the commands:
    `cd /u/maple`
2. Create the Utility library directory with the command:
    `mkdir utility`

Copying the Library Files from Diskette

Now that you have the Utility library directory created, you need to copy the `maple.lib` and `maple.ind` files into it.

> You *must* make sure that you are in the directory created to hold the Utility files, not the directory holding the standard Maple library files, when you perform the following copying commands/actions. The reason for this is that the standard Maple library directory also contains files named `maple.lib` and `maple.ind`. You *do not* want to overwrite these files or affect them in any way whatsoever. Doing so will remove all of the standard Maple functionality that you are used to, and render Maple unusable. (Basically, you would have to re-install these files to be able to use Maple.)

This caution is necessary because Maple only recognizes `library` and `index` files named `maple.lib` and `maple.ind`, respectively. Therefore, you cannot have two separate Maple libraries residing in the same directory.

Once you have verified that you are indeed in the Utility library directory, perform the following steps.

DOS Computers

1. Insert the *Utility Diskette* into your diskette drive.
2. Assuming your diskette drive is the `A:` drive, enter the following:
   `copy A:\UTIL\*.* .`
   Otherwise substitute the proper drive and directory information.
3. Enter the following to make sure that both files were transferred:
   `dir`

Macintosh Computers

1. Transfer the appropriate `MAPLE.LIB` and `MAPLE.IND` files from the *Utility Diskette* onto your computer, using a tool like `AppleFileExchange`.
2. Choose the two files and move them into your previously created utility folder.[5]
3. You will notice that the files `MAPLE.LIB` and `MAPLE.IND` are in uppercase letters. This is because of file names on DOS diskettes are not case-sensitive. These names must be edited to read `maple.lib` and `maple.ind`. You can change the names of these files the same way you would the name of any other Macintosh file or folder.

UNIX Computers

1. Transfer the appropriate `MAPLE.LIB` and `MAPLE.IND` files from the *Utility Diskette* onto your computer using whatever tools you have for such operations.
2. Move into the directory currently containing the two files and move them to the Utility library directory with the commands.
   `mv MAPLE.LIB /u/maple/utility/maple.lib`
   `mv MAPLE.IND /u/maple/utility/maple.ind`
   If your recently created Utility directory is not `/u/maple/utility`, substitute the proper directory information.
   The renaming of the files from using uppercase to lowercase letters performed by the above commands is necessary; do not omit it.
3. Enter the following to make sure that both files were transferred:
   `ls /u/maple/utility`

---

[5]Or, combine steps a) and b) into one step.

Hooking Up the Utility Library to Maple

Now that you have the Utility library files installed in the Utility library directory, you must inform Maple that those files are there. There is a global variable libname that Maple examines every time it tries to load a new command. The basic installation of Maple V Release 3 will assign only one directory to libname. On a DOS-based machine, this variable originally might look like:

> libname;

$$C:\backslash MAPLEV3\backslash LIB$$

This means that Maple will look in that directory every time it encounters a Maple procedure that it doesn't already have in memory.

If you have previously added other directories to the libname search path, it will contain a sequence of directory names separated by commas. Whether you have done this or not, what you must do now is add the recently created Utility library directory to your libname search path. To do that within a Maple session, you could enter the following:

> libname := libname, 'C:\MAPLEV3\UTILITY':

$$libname := C:\backslash MAPLEV3\backslash LIB, C:/MAPLEV3/UTILITY$$

At this point, you should have access to all the commands in *The Practical Approach Utilities for Maple*. But if you hook up the Utilities in this manner, within an active Maple session, then you must enter this command each and every time you start up Maple.

A better idea is to have this addition to libname performed *automatically* every time you start up Maple. In order to do this you must alter the Maple initialization file. Every Maple platform contains such an initialization file, which in most cases already contains a great deal of information. To add the previous Maple command to your initialization file, perform the following steps.

DOS Computers

Your Maple initialization file is called `maple.ini` and should reside in your standard Maple library directory (`lib`). Edit this file with a plain-text editor. If you haven't already added a libname extension to this file, add the following Maple statement as the last line of `maple.ini`:
libname := libname, 'C:\MAPLEV3\UTILITY':
assuming that `C:\MAPLEV3\UTILITY` is your Utility library directory. Make sure that you have reproduced the above syntax *exactly*.

Macintosh Computers

Your Maple initialization file should be named `MapleInit` and, if it exists, should reside in the top-level Maple folder. If no such file exists, create a text file with that name using the `TeachText` utility.

Add the following line to the bottom of this `MapleInit` file:
`libname := libname, ':utility':`
assuming that `utility` is the name of the folder you created. Make sure that you have reproduced the above syntax *exactly*.

UNIX Computers

Your Maple initialization file is called `.mapleinit` and must reside in your home directory. Edit this file with a plain-text editor. If you haven't already added a libname extension to this file, add the following Maple statement as the last line of `.mapleinit`:
`libname := libname, '/u/maple/utility':`
assuming that `/u/maple/utility` is your Utility library directory. Make sure that you have reproduced the above syntax *exactly*.

Testing the Installation

There is a simple way to test if your installation of *The Practical Approach Utilities for Maple* was successful; simply start up Maple[6] and load the pointers to the commands in the utility package using the built-in with command.

```
> with(utility);
```

[*alter, anychars, appendlist, appendstring, arc, banded, bundle, choose, circle, circle3d, comparelists, comparestrings, cone, 'convert/full', 'convert/sparse', cylinder, deletelist, deletestring, density, depth, diagonal, draw, ellipse, exprtree, extend3d, extractlist, extractstring, findexpr, findpat, findtype, flattenlist, fliprows, flipcols, frequency, func2d, func3d, getdiagonal, getitem, insertlist, insertstring, intersectlists, isleaf, line, line3d, listtypes, lowercase, lowertri, makechart, maplists, mapcols, mapexpr, mappat, maprows, markexpr, markpat, nchars, pattern, plane, point, point3d, polygon, polygon3d,*

---

[6] For information on how to start the Maple application, see the *Starting Maple* section on page 19.

polytovec, prependlist, prependstring, printchart, printlist, printplot, printstring, printtable, proddiagonal, prodcols, prodrows, raiselist, readchart, reflect, reflect3d, render, replacelist, replacestring, reverselist, reversestring, rotate, rotatelist, roundtozero, scale, scale3d, selectstring, shape, showexpr, showpat, showtype, sortbycol, sortbyrow, sphere, spheroid, subsexpr, subspat, subsstring, sumdiagonal, sumcols, sumrows, switchcase, transform, transform3d, translate, translate3d, 'type/ds', 'type/loclist', unionlists, uniquelist, unziplist, uppercase, uppertri, vectopoly, wait, whattypes, whichelement, ziplists]

If you get the list of the Utility command names, then the installation was successful. If, on the other hand, you get the error message `Error, (in with) undefined package, utility`, then installation failed. If this happens, reread the installation instructions to see if you made any mistakes. If you still have no luck, then contact us at the address given on page 6.

Installing the Other Directories

There are two other directories on the *Utility Diskette*: `source` and `other`.

- The `source` directory contains a single text file, `utility.src`, which holds a copy of the source code for *all* the commands in the Utilities (but not for the help files). While any of this code can be viewed from within a Maple session,[7] this textual file is easier to access, and also contains the coding comments that we added while developing the Utilities.

- The `other` directory contains textual files pulled from the chapter files for this book. Mostly, code segments used in the *Programming Tips* sections are included here. The names of the individual text files suggest what they contain.

The contents of two directories can be placed anywhere on your system, the location(s) won't affect the operation of Maple or the Utilities. For an idea of how to transfer the files to your system, see the *Copying the Library Files from Diskette* section on page 12.

---

[7]See the section *Viewing a Procedure's Code* of page 77 for details.

Advanced Installation Procedures

Performing the following installation procedures is not strictly necessary to use *The Practical Approach Utilities for Maple* on your system, but you might want to consider them anyway.

Using the Long Form of Utility Command Names

Throughout the rest of this book, the Utility commands are accessed with their *short* names, not the long form, utility[commandname].[8] Using the short names saves excessive typing and doesn't use up any more of your system's memory.

If you *really* want to use the long names, you must add the following line to your Maple initialization file:
```
utility := 'readlib('utility')':
```
For more information on exactly how to add this line, refer to *Hooking Up the Utility Library to Maple* on page 14.

Make sure you duplicate the above syntax exactly. Once this line has been added, long form command names such as utility[draw], utility[findexpr], and utility[roundtozero] will be accessible.

---

[8] For an introduction to the different forms, see the *Functions in Packages* section on page 35.

CHAPTER 3

Getting Started with Maple

This chapter is meant to familiarize you with what Maple does and how it does it. Simple concepts are introduced using simple examples to provide the new Maple user with a gentle introduction to the product.

The information in the following sections lays the groundwork for understanding and making use of the Utilities in the following chapters. Not *all* the basic Maple concepts are introduced here; some are so tightly related to individual areas of the Utilities that they are best explained in the *What Maple Has* sections of the appropriate chapters.

If you have never used Maple before, it is recommended that you also read through a more general introductory text such as *Introduction to Maple* by André Heck. If you are already an experienced Maple user, you may want to skim through this chapter, or skip it altogether.

What Is Maple?

In simplest terms, Maple is a computer environment for doing mathematics.

Symbolical, numerical, and graphical computations can all be done with Maple. While simple problems can be solved with Maple, its real power shows when performing calculations that are extremely cumbersome or tediously repetitive to do by hand. Maple is a procedural language, combining an efficient programming language with a bevy of predefined mathematical commands.

The breadth of Maple's functionality is wide—topics covered range from calculus and linear algebra to differential equations, geometry, and logic. As well, Maple's treatment of these topics is deep—each subject area has a wealth of commands encompassing aspects both fundamental and far-reaching.

Maple's Internal Structure

Internally, Maple consists of three component parts: the *kernel*, the *library*, and the *interface*.

The kernel is the "mathematical engine" behind Maple's calculations. This compact, highly optimized set of routines is written and compiled in the C programming language, and performs the majority of the basic computations done by the system.

Most of Maple's built-in commands reside in the Maple library and are written in its own programming language. Code written in Maple is not compiled, but *interpreted* as it is read or entered, allowing you to create Maple commands interactively within a session. You can also add commands to the Maple library. It is this "openness" which we have taken advantage of to bring you *The Practical Utilities for Maple*.

The interface is Maple's eyes to the world and defines, to a large extent, how you interact with commands and procedures. Depending on the quality of your terminal, and the version of Maple you are running, the interface may range from a TTY terminal version to a sophisticated interface supporting Maple documents which combine input, output, text, and graphics.

Starting Maple

On systems which support command line interfaces (e.g., UNIX, DOS), Maple is typically started by entering the command maple at the prompt.

Systems with more advanced graphical user interfaces (e.g., Macintosh, Windows) have a Maple program icon that activates the application.

Regardless of what system you are using, once Maple is started you are presented with a Maple input prompt, typically:

>

Computations can be started right away. For much of the Maple language, Maple needs no further prompting to load in any code necessary to complete your requests. If the routines are not already in memory, Maple knows where to find them and does so efficiently.[1]

---

[1] readlib-defined commands and commands in packages are covered later in this chapter.

20 • Chapter 3. Getting Started with Maple

When one command or statement is entered and computed, another Maple prompt appears, ready for the next input. All interfaces to Maple have this in common.

This book does not delve further into the details of individual interfaces. For more information on them, refer to your standard Maple manuals or other supporting documentation. *The Practical Approach Utilities for Maple* are designed to work under any platform that Maple supports, if you have a copy of Maple on the computer and the installation instructions have been followed properly.[2]

Basic Maple Syntax

Input to Maple is typed in at the input prompt. A *complete* input statement can consist of Maple commands, expressions, procedures, etc., and *must* be properly terminated. There are two ways to terminate a Maple statement: a semicolon (;) is the most commonly used Maple terminator, and the resulting output is displayed directly below the input; a colon (:) terminator tells Maple to suppress the output, and is particularly useful when the output is an inconsequential intermediate result or is expected to be too large to view conveniently.

When you have typed all the input that you wish to enter on any individual line, the **Enter** key sends it to Maple's mathematical engine to be interpreted. If your input contains a *complete* Maple statement (or completes a previously incomplete one), that complete statement is executed and the result displayed in an output region directly below. If your input consists of an *incomplete* Maple statement, then the system simply holds the incomplete statement in a buffer and gives you another input prompt, patiently waiting for you to complete that statement.

Some common problems can arise when beginners (or even experts) enter input lines.

If the input is an incomplete statement, Maple does not perform any calculations, but merely provides you with another input prompt directly below the line just entered. This behavior can happen naturally, when an input stretches over several lines, but most commonly it is because a semicolon or colon was omitted. Beginning users often mistake lack of activity for inability to perform the calculation. Simply add a terminator on the new line and hit **Enter**.

```
> factor(x^3 - 13*x + 12)
```

---

[2] See the chapter *Installing the Utilities* for more details.

```
> ;
```
$$(x-1)(x-3)(x+4)$$

A common reaction to forgetting a terminator is to retype the entire command on the second line. This only leads to a syntax error, as Maple concatenates the two input lines and tries to execute the resulting expression.

```
> expand((x+1)^4)
> expand((x+1)^4);

syntax error:
expand((x+1)^4);
       ^
```

When there is a syntax error in the input, Maple prints a syntax error message. A caret (^) marks where Maple's interpreter first ran into trouble—it is then up to you to decide how to correct the error.

If your input is syntactically correct but contains another type of error, Maple issues an error message. Be warned that Maple's error messages are occasionally rather obtuse, and fail to indicate exactly what you did wrong or how to go about fixing it.

```
> divide(x^2+1);

Error, wrong number (or type) of parameters in function divide

> assign([1,2,3,4]);

Error, (in assign) invalid arguments
```

Another basic consideration is the addition of blank spaces in Maple input. For the most part, blank spaces can be added at will and are automatically removed by Maple's parser if redundant, but there are a few rules and exceptions. For example, blank spaces cannot be added to the middle of a number or a command name.

```
> 1 234 567 / 89;

syntax error:
1 234 567 / 89;
  ^
```

If you wish, use the continuation character, \, to organize large numbers or expressions. This character is simply ignored by the parser.

```
> 1\234\567 / 89;
```
$$\frac{1234567}{89}$$

Basic Maple Objects

Numbers, constants, strings, and names are the simplest objects in Maple. The following sections give you a basic understanding of how to recognize, create, and use these objects.

Integers and Rationals

There are different ways of specifying explicit values in Maple. Because Maple works in the symbolic realm, numbers need not always be given in decimal representation (although you certainly may do so if you wish). Integers are the simplest exact numbers to specify, while rational numbers use the division operator (/) to separate numerator and denominator.

```
> 23;
```
$$23$$

```
> 4/9;
```
$$\frac{4}{9}$$

```
> -124/48;
```
$$\frac{-31}{12}$$

```
> 16/2;
```
$$8$$

As you can see, rationals are automatically put into their lowest terms.

Floating-point Numbers

Decimal representations of exact values are expressed as you would expect, and appear as the results of many of Maple's numerical procedures. As well, numerical values can be represented in base 10 or scientific notation.

```
> 2.3;
```
$$2.3$$

```
> -123.45678;
```
$$-123.45678$$

```
> .143 * 10^(-44);
```
$$.1430000000 \, 10^{-44}$$

```
> Float(3141, -3);
```
$$3.141$$
```
> -.12345678e3;
```
$$-123.45678$$

Mathematical Constants

While integers, rationals, and floating-point numbers can be thought of as constants of a sort, Maple also supports many other common mathematical constants. The list includes:

Pi	π, 3.1415926535...
exp(1)	e, natural log base
I	$\sqrt{-1}$
infinity	∞
-infinity	$-\infty$
gamma	Euler's constant
Catalan	Catalan's constant
true, false	boolean values

Maple is case sensitive, so be sure to use proper capitalization when stating these constants. The names Pi and pi are not equivalent!

Global Variables

Global variables are set to initial values when Maple is started and they can be updated by either you or the system during operation. Some of the more common global variables include:

Digits	number of digits carried
Order	truncation order for series
constants	the currently defined constants
libname	location of the standard library
printlevel	how much debugging information is displayed
lasterror	last ERROR message encountered
status	status of system variables

Mixing and Matching Different Number Types

The ability to leave values in their exact representation (e.g., Pi not 3.14159...) is part of the beauty of symbolic algebra. Normally, Maple allows you to retain values in their exact form throughout many calculations. One situation when exact values do get converted to approximations is when you mix and match types in an expression. The following examples illustrate this idea. For more information on putting together Maple expressions, see the section *Maple Expressions* on page 25.

> 2/5 + 6;

$$\frac{32}{5}$$

> 2/5 + 6.0;

$$6.400000000$$

Placing even one floating-point value in a large exact expression causes complete conversion to floats.

> 1/2 + 2/3 + 3/4 + 4/5 + 5/6 + 6/7 + .875;

$$5.282142857$$

Strings and Names

A *string* in Maple consists of a number of characters of any sort surrounded by backward quote characters ('). Following are examples of Maple strings.

> 'This is a Maple string';

This is a Maple string

> 'invert.src';

invert.src

Strings are explored in greater depth in the *What Maple Has* section of the *StringTools* chapter on page 247.

A *name* in Maple is a special type of string, which typically contains a letter (a-z, A-Z) followed by zero or more letters, digits (0-9), and underscores (_). Both strings and names are case sensitive. The name MyName is distinct from myname.

One difference between names and strings is that names do not need to be enclosed with backward quotes, *unless* the name contains special characters that you do not wish to be evaluated. The following are examples of valid Maple names,

> MyVariable;

MyVariable

> hello;

hello

```
> `greatest common divisor`;
```

$$\textit{greatest common divisor}$$

while these are examples of invalid Maple names.

```
> /thequotient;
syntax error:
/thequotient;
^

> ...etc;
syntax error:
...etc;
   ^

> `no backquotes `round me!;
syntax error:
`no backquotes `round me!;
                ^
```

Maple Expressions

Expressions are extremely important structures in Maple. All Maple objects are, at one level or another, made up entirely of expressions. At its most basic level, an expression consists of a single value, unknown, or string. Conversely, Maple expressions can consist of thousands upon thousands of values, unknowns, and strings strung together with various arithmetic operators.[3]

Maple's arithmetic operators include:

```
+        addition
-        subtraction
*        multiplication
/        division
^        exponentiation
!        factorial
abs()    absolute value
iqou()   integer quotient
irem()   integer remainder
```

---

[3]For examples of large expressions and how to operate upon them, see the *ExpressionTools* chapter.

When necessary, use blank spaces between terms to keep your expressions readable. Following are examples of simple Maple expressions.

> a+b+c;
$$a + b + c$$

> 3*x^3 - 4*x^2 + x - 7;
$$3x^3 - 4x^2 + x - 7$$

> x^2/25 + y^2/36;
$$\frac{1}{25}x^2 + \frac{1}{36}y^2$$

Maple echoes these expressions in a "pretty" form, the quality of which depends upon the capabilities of your monitor.

Order of Operations

In Maple expressions, the precedence of operators follows the standards found in most other areas of computation. If there are any ambiguities, use parentheses, (), to specify the order of operations.

> 2+3*4-5;
$$9$$

> (2+3)*4-5;
$$15$$

> (2+3)*(4-5);
$$-5$$

It is a good idea to use parentheses whenever there is any chance of ambiguity. If a set of parentheses is redundant, Maple's parser eliminates it during computation.

Expression Sequences

Another often used data structure in Maple is the *expression sequence*. An expression sequence is one or more Maple expressions separated by commas. Most Maple commands require an expression sequence as input, and many return a result that includes an expression sequence.

The most basic way to create an expression sequence is simply to enter it as such.

```
> 1, 2, 3, 4, 5;
```
$$1, 2, 3, 4, 5$$

```
> a+b, b+c, c+d, e+f, f+g;
```
$$a+b, b+c, c+d, e+f, f+g$$

Alternatively, there are two automatic ways to generate a *well-ordered* expression sequence. First, the $ operator can be used alone to create sequences containing multiples of one element or, in conjunction with the ellipsis operator .., to create more ambitious sequences.

```
> a$6;
```
$$a, a, a, a, a, a$$

```
> $1..6;
```
$$1, 2, 3, 4, 5, 6$$

```
> i^2 $ i=1..6;
```
$$1, 4, 9, 16, 25, 36$$

As well, there is a Maple command, seq, that allows even more control in the creation of expression sequences.

```
> seq(i!/i^2, i=1..7);
```
$$1, \frac{1}{2}, \frac{2}{3}, \frac{3}{2}, \frac{24}{5}, 20, \frac{720}{7}$$

```
> seq(k*(k+1)/(k+2), k=-1..4);
```
$$0, 0, \frac{2}{3}, \frac{3}{2}, \frac{12}{5}, \frac{10}{3}$$

It is recommended that you use the seq command whenever possible. It operates quickly and can be used in many situations to increase the speed of your Maple calculations or the efficiency of your Maple programs.[4]

Lists and Sets

Two of the most fundamental and important data structures in Maple are lists and sets. Each consists of an expression sequence surrounded by different characters.

---

[4] See the *Efficiency Concerns* section on 80 for more details about seq.

Lists are enclosed by square brackets:

> [1, 2, 3, 4, 5, 6];

$$[1,2,3,4,5,6]$$

> [x, y^2+3, [3,4], Int(exp(x), x)];

$$\left[x, y^2 + 3, [3,4], \int e^x \, dx\right]$$

Sets are enclosed by curly braces:

> {1, 2, 3, 4, 5, 6};

$$\{1,2,3,4,5,6\}$$

> {M,i,s,s,i,s,s,i,p,p,i};

$$\{i, M, s, p\}$$

These two structures have many different properties, operators, and uses, many of which are described in the *ListTools* chapter.

Calling Maple Commands

Command Names

Maple expressions and other data types are most commonly used as parameters in commands. Maple has a wealth of built-in commands stored in its standard library. Typically, commands are called in the following manner:

   commandname(parameter$_1$, parameter$_2$, ..., parameter$_n$);

Most command names have been chosen to best represent the functionality of a command and, at the same time, to require the least amount of typing possible. For example, the command for integration by parts is called intparts and the command for changing variables is called changevar. Some command names are as short as one character long (e.g., D), while others are over ten characters long (e.g., completesquare).

Unfortunately, some of Maple's command names are less than intuitive. For example, while Int is the unevaluated form of int[5] and Diff is the unevaluated form of diff, the DESol command represents an unevaluated dsolve and the RootOf command an unevaluated solve. The names chosen for the Utilities are consistent within themselves and, as much as possible, follow the standard Maple conventions.[6]

---

[5] Remember that Maple is case sensitive.

[6] See *Design Issues* on page 4 for more details.

While blank spaces can be inserted before a command name or between a command name and its parameters, they cannot appear in the middle of a command name.

Composition of Commands

By using the @ operator, you can compose two or more commands. For example, (cos@sin)(x) is equivalent to cos(sin(x)), and (exp@@4)(x) is equivalent to exp(exp(exp(exp(x)))). Create a few examples yourself to understand better the workings of @.

Parameter Sequences

Each Maple command takes a parameter sequence as input. This sequence may contain several numbers, expressions, sets, or lists, or it may contain no parameters at all. Regardless of how many parameters are specified, always enclose the sequence in parentheses, (). Other types of brackets cause the input to be interpreted not as parameters, but as something very different.

Any type of Maple element can be used as a parameter. Entire command calls can be used as input as well; such commands are evaluated and their results are inserted in the parameter sequence. Some commands have restrictions on what type of elements they accept as input and with most commands the ordering of parameters is also important. As well, all commands have a minimum number of parameters with which they can be called. (For example, int must have at least two parameters, an expression and a variable of integration). Many commands, however, can handle more than their minimum number of parameters. These "extra" parameters can represent many things, including additional data and options controlling the functioning of the command.[7]

The following are examples of calls to Maple commands.

```
> isprime(108893);
```

$$true$$

```
> diff(5*x^2-2*x-16, x);
```

$$10x - 2$$

```
> diff(5*x^2-2*x-16, x, x);
```

$$10$$

---

[7]See *Design Issues* on page 4 for more details on how the Utilities use parameter sequences.

```
> int(int(x^3*y^2, x), y);
```
$$\frac{1}{12} x^4 y^3$$

Where's That Command?

It is not always sufficient simply to know the name of the command that you want to enter—sometimes you must *explicitly* load the command from some part of the Maple library before you can execute it. Because Maple is very forgiving in its nature, it lets you issue a command that has not been loaded or does not yet exist and simply echoes the input back at you as if to say, "OK, I'll let you use that command name, even though it doesn't mean anything to me right now." Following are examples of such behavior.

```
> INT(x^2, x);
```
$$\text{INT}(x^2, x)$$

```
> realroot(x^3+37*x-21,1/100);
```
$$\text{realroot}\left(x^3 + 37x - 21, \frac{1}{100}\right)$$

```
> mean(1, 2, 3, 4, 5, 6);
```
$$\text{mean}(1, 2, 3, 4, 5, 6)$$

When this happens, check if you have spelled the command correctly (including proper lowercase and uppercase letters) and loaded the command into Maple's memory.

Maple's Help Facility

One way to check whether you are using a command correctly is through the use of Maple's on-line help facility. Help pages are available for most built-in commands and for every Utility command. Simply prepend the name (or suspected name) of a command with a question mark, and the system is automatically invoked.

```
> ?ifactor

FUNCTION: ifactor - integer factorization

CALLING SEQUENCE:
   ifactor(n)
   ifactor(n, method)

PARAMETERS:
```

```
    n       - integer or a rational
    method  - (optional) name of base method for factoring
```

SYNOPSIS:
- ifactor returns the complete integer factorization of n.

- The answer is in the form: u * ``(f1)^e1 * ... * ``(fn)^en such that
  n = u * f1^e1 * ... * fn^en where u equals sign(n), f1, ..., fn are the distinct prime factors of n, and e1, ..., en are their multiplicities (negative in the case of the denominator of a rational).

- The expand function may be applied to cause the factors to be multiplied together again.

- If a second parameter is specified, the named method will be used when the front-end code fails to achieve the factorization. By default, the Morrison-Brillhart algorithm is used as the base method. Currently accepted names are:

```
        'squfof'   - D. Shanks' undocumented square-free factorization;
        'pollard'  - J.M. Pollard's rho method;
        'lenstra'  - Lenstra's elliptic curve method; and
        'easy'     - which does no further work.
```

- If the 'easy' option is chosen, the result of the ifactor call will be a product of the factors that were easy to compute, and a name _c.m indicating an m-digit composite number that was not factored.

- The pollard base method accepts an additional optional integer: ifactor(n,pollard,k), which increases the efficiency of the method when one of the factors is of the form k*m+1.

EXAMPLES:
```
> ifactor( 61 );
                                (61)

> ifactor( 60 );
                                  2
                              (2)  (3) (5)

> ifactor( -144 );
                                4    2
                            - (2)  (3)

> expand(");
                                -144
```

```
> ifactor( 60, easy );
                              2
                           (2)  (3) (5)

> ifactor( 4/11 );
                              2
                           (2)
                           ----
                           (11)

> n := 8012940887713968000041:
> ifactor( n, easy );
                        (13) (457) _c19

> ifactor( n );
                  (13) (457) (473638939) (2847639359)

SEE ALSO: ifactors, isprime, factor, type[facint]
```

As you can see, no terminator is required for this statement.

Each help page is made up of the following sections:

- FUNCTION—lists the command name and a brief description of its functionality.
- CALLING SEQUENCE—lists the different types of parameter sequences allowable.
- PARAMETERS—provides more details on what type each of the parameters listed above must be.
- SYNOPSIS—describes the working of the command in more detail, possibly including information on the algorithms used.
- EXAMPLES—shows examples of typical input and output sequences for the command.
- SEE ALSO—lists other related commands about which you can read.

The help pages for *The Practical Approach Utilities for Maple* follow this general approach.

```
> ?flipcols

FUNCTION: flipcols  -  reverse the order of the columns in a matrix

CALLING SEQUENCES:
   flipcols(M)
   flipcols(M, int1..int2)
   flipcols(transpose(V)) or flipcols(transpose(V), int1..int2)
```

PARAMETERS:
  M   - a two-dimensional matrix
  int1..int2   - an integer range
  transpose(V) - a row vector

SYNOPSIS:
- The flipcols command reverses the order the columns appear in matrix M,
  while maintaining the ordering of the elements in each individual
  column. The result is a matrix of the same dimensions as M. This command
  does not affect the original matrix.

- When the integer range int1..int2 is supplied, the specified columns are
  reversed in place. Those columns not included in the range remain where
  they were in the original matrix.

- If a vector is passed to sumcols, it must be a row vector. Row vectors are
  represented by transpose(V), where V is a normally defined vector. A row
  vector with its entries reversed is returned.

- To reverse the order of the rows of a matrix, use the fliprows command.
  To sort the columns according to the values in a row, use the sortbyrow
  command.

EXAMPLES:
> with(utility):
> M := linalg[matrix](6, 4, [$1..24]);

$$M := \begin{bmatrix} 1 & 2 & 3 & 4 \\ 5 & 6 & 7 & 8 \\ 9 & 10 & 11 & 12 \\ 13 & 14 & 15 & 16 \\ 17 & 18 & 19 & 20 \\ 21 & 22 & 23 & 24 \end{bmatrix}$$

> flipcols(M);

$$\begin{bmatrix} 4 & 3 & 2 & 1 \\ 8 & 7 & 6 & 5 \\ 12 & 11 & 10 & 9 \end{bmatrix}$$

```
                                    [ 16  15  14  13 ]
                                    [                ]
                                    [ 20  19  18  17 ]
                                    [                ]
                                    [ 24  23  22  21 ]

> flipcols(M, 2..4);
                                    [  1   4   3   2 ]
                                    [                ]
                                    [  5   8   7   6 ]
                                    [                ]
                                    [  9  12  11  10 ]
                                    [                ]
                                    [ 13  16  15  14 ]
                                    [                ]
                                    [ 17  20  19  18 ]
                                    [                ]
                                    [ 21  24  23  22 ]

> flipcols(transpose(linalg[vector](5, [a, 3, b^2, -2, a*b*4])));
                                              2
                    transpose([ 4 a b, -2, b , 3, a ])

SEE ALSO:  fliprows, sortbyrow, mapcols, sumcols, prodcols, linalg[matrix]
```

If a help command is entered for a help page that does not exist, Maple tries to compensate by listing those pages available for similarly named commands.

```
> ?integ

Try one of the following topics:
```

{*int, integer, intersect, interface, interp, Int, Interp, inter, intro, integrand,*

intercept, internal, interpolation, intbasis, intparts, introduction, intrefs}

There are a few ways to return selected parts of a help page:[8]

- example(name) or ???name—returns the EXAMPLES section.
- info(name)—returns the FUNCTION section.
- usage(name) or ??name—returns the CALLING SEQUENCE section.
- related(name)—returns the SEE ALSO section.

---

[8]These commands *do* work on Utility help pages.

Most window-based interfaces for Maple have a help topic browser for built-in help pages and a rudimentary keyword search facility. In most cases, both are found under the **Help** menu.

Automatically Loaded and readlib Defined Functions

When Maple starts up, it does not have *any* commands entirely loaded into memory. There are, however, many standard commands that have pointers to their locations loaded, so that when you call them for the first time, Maple automatically knows where to go to load them. Some other functions that reside in the library are not automatically loaded, but must be explicitly loaded with the Maple command readlib (*read* from the *lib*rary). If you enter a command that is in the standard library and it does not seem to work, try doing a readlib and calling it again.

The following are examples of one automatically loaded command and one readlib defined function.

```
> expand((x-2)*(x+5));
```
$$x^2 + 3x - 10$$
```
> realroot(x^3+37*x-21, 1/100);
```
$$\text{realroot}\left(x^3 + 37x - 21, \frac{1}{100}\right)$$
```
> readlib(realroot);
```
```
proc(poly,widthgoal) ... end
```
```
> realroot(x^3+37*x-21, 1/100);
```
$$\left[\left[\frac{9}{16}, \frac{73}{128}\right]\right]$$

Once a command has been loaded into memory, it does not need to be reloaded during the current Maple session.

Functions in Packages

Maple contains over a dozen specialized sets of commands called *packages* (e.g., linalg, liesymm, etc.). The routines in these packages are not automatically loaded, nor can they be accessed with the readlib command. The first method to access these commands is to use the with command, which loads in pointers to all the commands in a particular package. Then, when any command in that package is called, it is automatically loaded into memory. Another way is to call the command with its package name prepended to it. A few examples will illustrate these methods.

```
> with(combinat);
```
Warning: new definition for   choose

[Chi, *bell*, binomial, *cartprod*, *character*, *choose*, *composition*, *conjpart*, *decodepart*, *encodepart*, *fibonacci*, *firstpart*, *graycode*, *inttovec*, *lastpart*, *multinomial*, *nextpart*, *numbcomb*, *numbcomp*, *numbpart*, *numbperm*, *partition*, *permute*, *powerset*, *prevpart*, *randcomb*, *randpart*, *randperm*, *stirling1*, *stirling2*, *subsets*, *vectoint*]

```
> numbperm([1,2,3,4]);
```
$$24$$

```
> numtheory[euler](6,x);
```
$$x^6 - 3x^5 + 5x^3 - 3x$$

The commands in four packages of Maple code cannot be accessed with the long form of their names. Before the commands in these packages are used, a with(packagename) or with(packagename, commandname) command must be entered. The packages are:

- geometry
- geom3d
- NPspinor
- projgeom

The Utilities themselves are set up as one large Maple package. In order to access them, first load the package:

```
> with(utility);
```

[*alter*, *anychars*, *appendlist*, *appendstring*, *arc*, *banded*, *bundle*, *choose*, *circle*, *circle3d*, *comparelists*, *comparestrings*, *cone*, 'convert/full', 'convert/sparse', *cylinder*, *deletelist*, *deletestring*, *density*, *depth*, *diagonal*, *draw*, *ellipse*, *exprtree*, *extend3d*, *extractlist*, *extractstring*, *findexpr*, *findpat*, *findtype*, *flattenlist*, *fliprows*, *flipcols*, *frequency*, *func2d*, *func3d*, *getdiagonal*, *getitem*, *insertlist*, *insertstring*, *intersectlists*, *isleaf*, *line*, *line3d*, *listtypes*, *lowercase*, *lowertri*, *makechart*, *maplists*, *mapcols*, *mapexpr*, *mappat*, *maprows*, *markexpr*, *markpat*, *nchars*, *pattern*, *plane*, *point*, *point3d*, *polygon*, *polygon3d*, *polytovec, prependlist, prependstring, printchart, printlist, printplot, printstring, printtable, proddiagonal, prodcols, prodrows, raiselist, readchart, reflect, reflect3d, render, replacelist, replacestring, reverselist, reversestring, rotate, rotatelist, roundtozero, scale, scale3d, selectstrin, shape, showexpr, showpat, showtype, sortbycol, sortbyrow, sphere, spheroid, subsexpr, subspat, subsstring, sumdiagonal, sumcols, sumrows, switchcase, transform, transform3d, translate, translate3d, 'type/ds', 'type/loclist', unionlists, uniquelist, unziplist, uppercase, uppertri, vectopoly, wait, whattypes, whichelement, ziplists*]

```
> uppercase('What was that you said?');
```
WHAT WAS THAT YOU SAID?

It is recommended that you use with to load in the pointers and then access the commands with their short names. When this is done, very little memory is used—the actual code for the commands themselves are not read in until each individual command is called. This short name method is used throughout the rest of this book for accessing Utility commands.

If you really want to use the long forms of the Utility command names, there are some special steps that you must have performed in the installation. See the *Advanced Installation Procedures* section on page 17.

Assignments and Equations

This section explains the difference between the assignment operator, := (the colon character immediately followed by the equal sign), and the equation operator, = . It is important to understand the distinction between the two.

Assignments

You have previously learned how to create expressions, special data types, and Maple command calls, but these objects are transitory until you actually assign their values (or results) to some holder or variable. For example, if you we create a list containing the first ten prime numbers in order and *do not* assign this to a variable name, then each time you wish to use that structure within a Maple command or larger data structure, you must recreate it from scratch. If, instead, you assign the list (with the := operator) to a variable name, say first10primes, then you can easily use it in other calculations or as input to other Maple commands.

> first10primes := [ithprime(i) $ i=1..10];

$$first10primes := [2, 3, 5, 7, 11, 13, 17, 19, 23, 29]$$

> product(first10primes[i], i=1..10);

$$6469693230$$

Bear in mind that when you make an assignment, the expression to the right of := is first evaluated, and then that value is assigned to the name on the left of := until you tell Maple differently. Maple only remembers the most recently assigned value for any variable—if you assign the variable x to 5 and then later assign it to 7.5, only the latter assignment is remembered.

You must also use caution when choosing names for assigned variables. Maple has a protection facility for special names (e.g., sin, set, int, etc.), which does not allow you to overwrite their values. Most of the built-in Maple commands are initially protected in this way, but the Utility commands are not. (See the help pages for **protect** and **unprotect** for more information.) To be sure that you are not using any predefined names, try a Maple help command (i.e., ?<name>) for the variable name before using it. One particular set of names to which Maple *never* allows you to assign values are *keywords*. Keywords are special words used by Maple in its programming language, and are listed in the following table.

and	by	do	done	elif	else
end	fi	for	from	if	in
intersect	local	minus	mod	not	od
option	options	or	proc	quit	read
save	stop	then	to	union	while

Equations

The most important thing to realize about equations is that they are not the same as assignments. Equations are simply mathematical expressions that show relationships between certain variables and values; they do not infer any *explicit* values on the variables they contain. For example:

> x = y + 3;

$$x = y + 3$$

> x;

$$x$$

```
> y;
```

$$y$$

As you can see, the variables x and y are still unassigned.

The = operator is most frequently seen in either input to or output from a Maple command. One common family of built-in commands that makes extensive use of the = operator is the solve family (i.e., solve, rsolve, dsolve, etc.). These commands take equations of various forms and try to find a solution for a given set of variables.

For example, solve takes a set of linear or nonlinear equations and tries to find a closed-form solution.

```
> sols := solve({x + y = 3, x - y = 1}, {x, y});
```

$$sols := \{x = 2, y = 1\}$$

```
> x, y;
```

$$x, y$$

The solution that you get is a set of equations for the specified variables. If there are multiple solutions, all are presented. Be aware that x and y have *not* been assigned to the values 2 and 1, respectively. If you wish to make such an assignment, use the assign command, which takes an equation or set of equations and changes each equation to an assignment.

```
> assign(sols);
> x, y;
```

$$2, 1$$

Another common use of the equation operator is in boolean (true or false) statements. When you want to make a decision on how to proceed which depends on the relationship between the values of two variables, the = operator can be used to construct boolean statements. Other such relational operators include: <, < =, <>, and, or, and not. The Maple command evalb can then be used to evaluate a boolean statement. Some examples follow.

```
> evalb(3! = 4!/2^2);
```

true

```
> evalb(isprime(5) and isprime(541));
```

true

A third reason for using equations is to set values to optional parameters. For example, the built-in plot command can end with a large number of these "option equations."

```
> plot(sin(x), x=-2*Pi..2*Pi, style=POINT, numpoints=100);
```

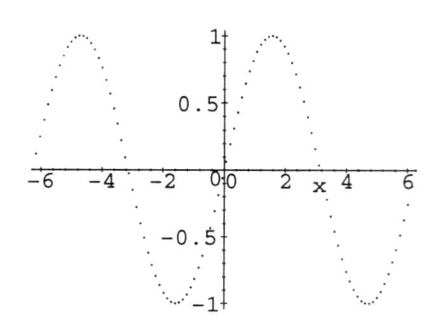

Option equations are the most common use of the = syntax in *The Practical Approach Utilities for Maple*.

The Use of Quotes in Maple

There are three types of quotes used in Maple. Each has a separate meaning, and it is important that you understand how to use each of them correctly.

Double Quote

The double quote operator, ", is perhaps the easiest quote to remember. Double quotes recall previous output in a Maple session. One double quote recalls the most recent output, two ("") recall the second most previous result, and three (""") recall the third most previous output. You cannot go further back than three outputs.

Using double quotes remains straightforward when in command line mode. Even if you use the colon terminator to suppress the display of output from a particular command, the double quote operator can be used to display that previously suppressed output.

Another way of looking at the double quote operator is as a short-term replacement for assignment. In most cases, it is better to immediately assign output to some variable name (which allows you to refer to it *any* time later in that session).

```
> expand((x-2)^3*(x-1));
```
$$x^4 - 7x^3 + 18x^2 - 20x + 8$$
```
> factor(");
```
$$(x-2)^3(x-1)$$

```
> ""/(x^2+3*x-2);
```
$$\frac{x^4 - 7x^3 + 18x^2 - 20x + 8}{x^2 + 3x - 2}$$

Backward Quote

The backward quote operator, `, is used to enclose Maple strings. See the *What Maple Has* section of the *StringTools* chapter on page 247 for more details.

Forward Quote

Perhaps the most difficult quote to use effectively, the forward quote (') can both eliminate ambiguities and cause confusion. Put simply, enclosing an expression in forward quotes delays evaluation of that expression for one trip through Maple's parser. Another way of thinking of this is that each time the parser encounters an expression enclosed by forward quotes, the *evaluation* that is performed consists of stripping away one layer of these quotes. Therefore, if you want to delay evaluation of the expression for two trips through the parser, use two layers of forward quotes.

```
> ''factor(x^2-x-2)'';
```
$$'\text{factor}(x^2 - x - 2)'$$

```
> ";
```
$$\text{factor}(x^2 - x - 2)$$

```
> ";
```
$$(x+1)(x-2)$$

The trick to using forward quotes is understanding when to apply them and what exactly their effect is on an *entire* calculation. Two common examples are illustrated here.

Forward quotes can be used to unassign a variable that was previously assigned to a value.

```
> x := 3;
```
$$x := 3$$

```
> x := 'x';
```
$$x := x$$

As well, forward quotes can be used for clarification within commands that use indices (e.g., sum, product).

```
> i := 3:
> sum(i^2, i=1..6);

Error, (in sum) summation variable previously assigned,
              second argument evaluates to, 3 = 1 .. 6

> sum('i^2', 'i'=1..6);
```
$$91$$

Maple as a Programming Language

Maple can be used as a programming language to add your own functionality to the system. In fact, all of *The Practical Approach Utilties for Maple* as well as most of the built-in commands in Maple were created using this facility.

While this book is not meant to be a complete introduction to Maple programming, the most basic structures involved are briefly discussed here.[9] First, the individual programming structures are investigated, and then the structure used to bind these into complete commands.

Conditional Structures

Maple handles conditional statements with the if/then/else/fi construct. Basically, you provide Maple with conditions (that evaluate to either true or false) and Maple branches accordingly.

```
> if 9/23 < 13/33 then 13/33 else 9/23 fi;
```
$$\frac{13}{33}$$

The above example compares two fractions and prints out the larger. Note the fi (if backwards) at the end—this is the terminator for the structure. Any amount of code can be inserted after each of then and else; you need not restrict yourself to a single expression. Note also that the entire structure ends in a semicolon. This is not a coincidence; the if/then/else/fi structure is a Maple expression as much as any command or polynomial, and so must end with a valid terminator.

An extra element, elif, can be added to make it if/then/elif/then ... /else/fi. Any number of these secondary conditions can be provided.

---

[9]The *Programming Tips* sections in the following chapters provide even more insight into expanding Maple's functionality. Read a more complete introduction to Maple programming before you delve into these *Programming Tips* sections.

```
> if isprime(221) then p
> elif numtheory[issqrfree](221) then s
> else neither
> fi;
```

$$s$$

Looping Constructs

Maple handles repetition with three different constructs. The first, for/from/by/to/do/od, takes an upper and lower bound on a repetition variable and a step value, then performs the statements between do and od the appropriate number of times. The repetition variable can be included in the calculations, but does not strictly have to be. Again, as with if/then/else/fi, any number of statements can be included between do and od.

```
> for i from 1 to 11 by 2 do print(i!) od;
```

$$1$$
$$6$$
$$120$$
$$5040$$
$$362880$$
$$39916800$$

Repetition can also be done with the for/from/by/while/do/od structure. Maple loops through the statement(s) between do and od as long as the condition stated after while is true.

```
> for x from 1 by 4 while ithprime(x) < 100 do
> print(x, ithprime(x));
> od;
```

$$1, 2$$
$$5, 11$$
$$9, 23$$
$$13, 41$$
$$17, 59$$
$$21, 73$$
$$25, 97$$

The third method is the for/in/do/od structure. Maple loops through the statement(s) between do and od once for each operand of the expression following in.

```
> i := 'i':
> x := 'x':
```

```
> for i in 4*x-3*y-6 do i/2 od;
```

$$2x$$
$$-\frac{3}{2}y$$
$$-3$$

Creating Procedures

You have now seen the basic constructs of Maple's programming language, but the above examples only work when they are typed in fully each time. The major advantage in programming is that you can set up procedures that *automate* these calculations for you. To create a procedure that you can use over and over again with different input, you must use the proc/local/global/options/end structure.

When you define a procedure with the proc/end structure, you extend Maple's functionality. And if you save the procedure appropriately, this extension can be carried over to other Maple sessions. In the following example, a very simple procedure, largestfactor, takes integer n and finds its largest prime factor (and its multiplicity).

```
> largestfactor := proc(n:integer)
>    op(nops(ifactor(n)), ifactor(n));
> end;
```

```
largestfactor := proc(n:integer) op(nops(ifactor(n)),ifactor(n)) end
```

Basically, we have pulled off the last operand (the placement of which is equal to the number of operands) of the integer factorization of n. Let's try using it a few times.

```
> largestfactor(2387);
```

$$(31)$$

```
> largestfactor(118277523);
```

$$(23)^2$$

Of course, this is a extremely simplified example of a Maple procedure. Many procedures in the Maple library are hundreds of lines long and contain extensive type testing, error checking, and alternative algorithms.

Special Built-in Commands and Operators

There are some built-in commands that are used throughout the remaining chapters of this book that need to be examined in depth.

Creating Functions with >

The notion of a *function* in Maple is similar to that of a command, but has subtle differences. As an example, say you want to create a Maple representation of the mathematical function $f(x) \to x^2 - 2$.

First, you could use the proc command to build a simple procedure (command) that returns the desired value.

```
> f := proc(x) x^2-2 end;
```

$$f := \mathrm{proc}(x)\ x\texttt{\^{}}2\text{-}2\ \mathrm{end}$$

```
> f(2);
```

$$2$$

```
> f(fred);
```

$$fred^2 - 2$$

Alternatively, the arrow operator provides a syntax for function definition that is much closer to the actual mathematical representation.

```
> f := x -> x^2-2;
```

$$f := x \to x^2 - 2$$

```
> f(2);
```

$$2$$

```
> f(fred);
```

$$fred^2 - 2$$

Functions of more than one variable can be created in a similar way.

```
> g := (x,y,z) -> x^2-y*z;
```

$$g := (x, y, z) \to x^2 - yz$$

```
> g(2, 1, 5);
```

$$-1$$

```
> g(x, y, z);
```

$$x^2 - yz$$

Of course, these functions can be combined and composed just as more traditional commands can be.

> f(g(1, 2, -3));

$$47$$

> (f@g)(1, 2, -3);

$$47$$

You must not confuse functions with expressions. For example, the plot command takes an expression as its first parameter.[10] If you pass the function name f to plot, it will not be able to handle it properly. To turn the function into an expression, you must provide it with the variable that matches the one in the second parameter (in this case, x).

> plot(f(x), x=-2..2);

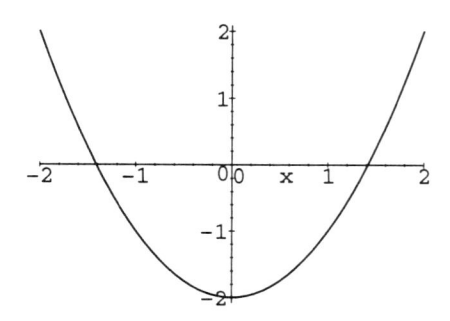

For more information on -> and other functional operators, see the help page for ?->.

map

map is an extremely useful command, yet it is unfortunately limited in its functionality. Basically, map applies a function or command to the elements of a Maple expression. *Any* type of expression (with the exception of an expression sequence) can be used; and, for most types, Maple simply applies the function or command to each first-level element of the expression. A few examples are worth a thousand words.

> map(sqrt, 2*z - y + 4);

$$\sqrt{2}\sqrt{z} + \sqrt{-y} + 2$$

---

[10] See the *What Maple Has* section of the *DrawTools* chapter on page 189 for more information on existing plotting commands.

```
> map(x -> x^2, ");
```
$$2z - y + 4$$
```
> Int(x^2, z*x);
```
$$\int x^2 \, dz \, x$$
```
> map(y -> y/z, ");
```
$$\int \frac{x^2}{z} \, dx$$
```
> map(isprime, [1, 3, 5, 7, 9, 11, 13]);
```
$$[\,false, true, true, true, false, true, true\,]$$

As you can see, the new expression created combines the values of the resulting applications, returning an expression of the same form as the original.

In more detailed language, map takes the first level *operands* of the expression (as found by the op command)[11] and passes each of those, in turn, as the only parameter to the given function or command. The *commands* used in the previous examples (i.e., sqrt and isprime) accept a single parameter as input. What if the function you want to apply takes more than one parameter?

map allows you to specify additional parameters to be sent to the applied command, *as long as they are the second, third, fourth, etc. parameters*. In other words, map always uses the elements from the given expression as the *first* parameter in its calls to the given command.

```
> map(diff, [x, y^2, z*x, y/x, z*(y+x)], x);
```
$$\left[1, 0, z, -\frac{y}{x^2}, z\right]$$

The derivative of the expressions in the list are all computed with respect to x, in the same way as if you had entered

```
> [diff(x, x), diff(y^2, x), diff(z*x, x), diff(y/x, x), diff(z*(y+x), x)];
```
$$\left[1, 0, z, -\frac{y}{x^2}, z\right]$$

Taking the second derivative with respect to x is just as easy.

```
> map(diff, [x, y^2, z*x, y/x, z*(y+x)], x, x);
```
$$\left[0, 0, 0, 2\frac{y}{x^3}, 0\right]$$

---

[11] See the chapter *ExpressionTools* for more information on the internal structure of Maple expressions.

What if you want instead to take several derivatives of a single expression with respect to various variables; that is, map for the *second* parameter of diff? There is no *simple* way to do this with map.[12]

What if you want to map more than one parameter into each invocation of the supplied command? There is no way to do this in map.

There are several map-like commands in *The Practical Approach Utilities for Maple*, designed to take care of both the above limitations. They are:

- maplists
- mapexpr
- mappat
- maprows
- mapcols

Each of these commands is designed in a very similar way, so that once you learn to use one of them, the rest fall into place. The only differences between them is that they each treat the elements of the structures passed to them (i.e., lists, expressions, patterns, rows of a matrix, and columns of a matrix, respectively) in unique and useful ways.

The introduction to maplists, found in *Mapping Lists* on page 70, contains the most detailed description of the working of all these mapping commands. Further information specific to each command can be found in the appropriate chapters throughout this book.

---

[12] There is a method using map and the -> operator, but we don't go into it here.

CHAPTER 4

ListTools

Lists are among the most commonly used types of Maple data structures. While simple in themselves, lists can be used to create extremely complex types of objects. Because of this, they frequently appear as both required input to and as standard output from Maple commands.

We have chosen to place *ListTools* first, not because they are the most important or powerful tools in the Utilities, but because they are extremely simple to illustrate, understand, and use.

What Maple Has

A list is simply a collection of any number of objects or elements. These objects can be of any type, such as integers, expressions, or unevaluated functions. Other lists are valid elements within a list. The syntax for a list is straightforward—simply separate the elements with commas and enclose them all within a set of brackets, [ ]. The following are all valid Maple lists.

```
> [1, 3, 5, 6, 2, 3, 3, 2];
```
$$[1,3,5,6,2,3,3,2]$$

```
> [x+2, b, 36/7, exp(y^2)];
```
$$\left[x+2, b, \frac{36}{7}, e^{(y^2)}\right]$$

```
> [[1,2,3], [4,5,6], [7,8,9]];
```
$$[[1,2,3],[4,5,6],[7,8,9]]$$

```
> [];
```
$$[\,]$$

The last of these lists is the *empty list*, and contains zero elements.

Lists Versus Sets

Another data structure which is similar to a list is a *set*. Sets are also commonly seen as input to and output from Maple commands. They are discussed here to define the differences between them and lists, casting light upon some basic, yet sometimes overlooked, features of both. Sets are also collections of objects or elements of any type, but are enclosed with braces, { }, instead of brackets. Other than this syntactical distinction, the two major differences between sets and lists are:

1. The order in which you define elements in a list is always preserved; the order in which you define elements in a set is *not* always preserved.

    ```
    > [3, 2, 4, 1, 5, 6];
    ```
    $$[\,3,2,4,1,5,6\,]$$
    ```
    > {3, 2, 4, 1, 5, 6};
    ```
    $$\{\,1,2,3,4,5,6\,\}$$

    The reason for this has to do with how Maple stores the structures internally, and is not explained further at this time.

2. Duplicate elements are preserved in a list. Duplicate elements are removed from a set.

    ```
    > [a, b, a, b, b, c, a];
    ```
    $$[\,a,b,a,b,b,c,a\,]$$
    ```
    > {a, b, a, b, b, c, a};
    ```
    $$\{\,a,b,c\,\}$$

    This is consistent with the algebraic notion of a set.

These qualities of *ordering* and *conservation* are what make lists such useful and versatile data structures: you know that what you put in is what you get out.

Accessing Elements of Lists

Of course, when dealing with actual lists of data, you will assign them to meaningful variable names. For example, the following is a list of the first ten prime numbers.

```
> first10primes := [2, 3, 5, 7, 11, 13, 17, 19, 23, 29];
```
$$first10primes := [\,2, 3, 5, 7, 11, 13, 17, 19, 23, 29\,]$$

Brackets are once again used to *access* the individual elements of first10primes, denoting the position of the desired element.

```
> first10primes[1];
```
$$2$$

```
> first10primes[4];
```
$$7$$

While it may be confusing at first, it is important that you distinguish clearly between brackets used as position indicators, and brackets used as list delimiters. As well, keep in mind that using position brackets with an unassigned list is invalid Maple syntax. For example:

```
> [2, 3, 5, 7, 11, 13, 17, 19, 23, 29][1];

syntax error:
[2, 3, 5, 7, 11, 13, 17, 19, 23, 29][1];
```

A consecutive sequence of elements can be accessed from a list by using the range operator, (..).

```
> first10primes[3..7];
```
$$5, 7, 11, 13, 17$$

The endpoints of the range must be positive integer values, both less than or equal to the number of elements in the list and with the first endpoint no greater than the second endpoint.

The op command may also be used to extract the elements of a list, but is no more powerful than using position brackets. For more information on the internal structure of lists, see the *ExpressionTools* chapter.

While the individual elements of a list can be *accessed* with the bracket syntax, you cannot *assign* new values to elements in a similar way.

```
> first10primes[3] := 6;

Error, cannot assign to a list
```

Nor can you add new elements to a list by supplying a position out of the current range of the list.

```
> first10primes[11] := 31;

Error, cannot assign to a list
```

If you really want to change the values of individual elements of a list, you must reconstruct the entire list, as follows.

> `[first10primes[1..2], 6, first10primes[4..10]];`

$$[\,2, 3, 6, 7, 11, 13, 17, 19, 23, 29\,]$$

This is tedious and unwieldy. When you know that you will want to *frequently* change individual elements (such as when keeping tallies), it is recommended that you use a *table* instead of a *list*. You can use the above method for lists, or the Utility command replacelist, but both use memory inefficiently when employed repeatedly.

Creating Well-Ordered Lists

A list can also be described exactly as an *expression sequence* enclosed with brackets. As seen in the *Getting Started With Maple* chapter, expression sequences can be written explicitly, or created with the seq command or $ operator. Combining these two facts, you can quickly and efficiently define well-sequenced lists.

> `[$1..100];`

$$[1, 2, 3, 4, 5, 6, 7, 8, 9, 10, 11, 12, 13, 14, 15, 16, 17, 18, 19, 20, 21, 22, 23, 24, 25,$$
$$26, 27, 28, 29, 30, 31, 32, 33, 34, 35, 36, 37, 38, 39, 40, 41, 42, 43, 44, 45,$$
$$46, 47, 48, 49, 50, 51, 52, 53, 54, 55, 56, 57, 58, 59, 60, 61, 62, 63, 64, 65,$$
$$66, 67, 68, 69, 70, 71, 72, 73, 74, 75, 76, 77, 78, 79, 80, 81, 82, 83, 84, 85,$$
$$86, 87, 88, 89, 90, 91, 92, 93, 94, 95, 96, 97, 98, 99, 100]$$

> `[seq(i^2, i=1..15)];`

$$[\,1, 4, 9, 16, 25, 36, 49, 64, 81, 100, 121, 144, 169, 196, 225\,]$$

In the latter example, the seq command gets evaluated before the list is created, filling in the 15 values as expected. Using the seq command and the ithprime command (which determines the ith prime number), you can recreate first10primes in a more concise way.

> `first10primes := [seq(ithprime(i), i=1..10)];`

$$\mathit{first10primes} := [\,2, 3, 5, 7, 11, 13, 17, 19, 23, 29\,]$$

For more information on the use of seq with lists, see the *Efficiency Concerns* section on page 80.

Built-In List Commands

There are a few special built-in commands that are useful for processing lists. member determines whether a specific expression is a member of a given list.

> `member(x^2, [1, 2, y+3, x^2, 5/7]);`

$$true$$

> `member(x^2, [1, 2, y+3, x^2+4, 5/7]);`

$$false$$

As you can see, member only compares the expression to determine if it is identical to a *complete* element from the list; it does not look at subexpressions of elements. To determine if an expression occurs as a subexpression (at any level) within a list, use the Utility command whichelement. member can be used on *any* Maple structure, not just lists—it always searches the first-level operands.

Another useful command is select, which allows you to test elements of a list for certain attributes. The first parameter to select must be a procedure name that returns either true or false when given a parameter.

> `list1 := [seq(2^i+1, i=1..10)];`

$$list1 := [\,3, 5, 9, 17, 33, 65, 129, 257, 513, 1025\,]$$

> `select(isprime, list1);`

$$[\,3, 5, 17, 257\,]$$

The elements that returned false when passed to isprime have been removed from the list. If the procedure you are passing takes more than one parameter, select allows you to add the extra parameters within itself, provided that the *first* parameter is the one being replaced by the elements of the given list. In the following example, iscont takes two parameters, an expression and a range, and determines if the expression is continuous over the range.

> `readlib(iscont):`
> `select(iscont, [x, 1/x, ln(x), tan(x)], x=-1..1);`

$$[\,x, \tan(x)\,]$$

What if you want to keep the expression fixed but vary the range? At first, it appears that select cannot handle this; but if you define a "test" function with the -> operator notation, you can get around this difficulty.

> `test := y -> iscont(tan(x), x=y);`

$$test := y \rightarrow iscont(\tan(x), x = y)$$

```
> select(test, [-5..-3, -3..-1, -1..1, 1..3, 3..5]);
```

$$[-1..1]$$

Also, by using the and, or, and not operators, you can extend the above method to include several testing requirements.

This arrow operator technique is not very intuitive to the beginning user, but it is worth learning. It can also be used to overcome shortcomings of the built-in map command, which was introduced in the *Getting Started With Maple* chapter. We have programmed several map-like commands in the Utilities, and these all contain a more intuitive technique for getting around this particular problem.

Utility Commands

Lists are useful in creating complicated data structures. Because these structures can contain individual elements of any length and complexity, it is particularly wasteful to re-enter any elements when manipulating lists. Also, because real-life lists often contain hundreds and hundreds of elements, it is equally as prodigal to manually repeat operations for even a small subset of those elements. The following compact, easy-to-understand Utility commands address these issues among others. For more information on what makes these Utility commands efficient, see the *Programming Tips* section later in this chapter.

Adding and Removing Elements

deletelist(list, a..b)	delete elements from a list
extractlist(list, a..b)	extract elements into a new list
insertlist($list_1$, $list_2$, n)	insert elements into an existing list
replacelist($list_1$, $list_2$, a..b)	replace elements of an existing list
prependlist(expr, list)	add an element to the beginning of a list
appendlist(expr, list)	add an element to the end of a list

```
> with(utility):
```

All of these commands take an existing list and either update it with new elements or remove selected elements from it.

The first two commands, deletelist and extractlist, take a list as their first parameter and a range, a..b, as their second parameter. The difference between them is that deletelist removes the elements of list at positions a through b to produce the resulting list, while the resulting list from extractlist retains only those b - a + 1 elements that were deleted in deletelist.

```
> list20 := [$1..20];
```
$$list20 := [\,1, 2, 3, 4, 5, 6, 7, 8, 9, 10, 11, 12, 13, 14, 15, 16, 17, 18, 19, 20\,]$$

```
> deletelist(list20, 4..11);
```
$$[\,1, 2, 3, 12, 13, 14, 15, 16, 17, 18, 19, 20\,]$$

```
> extractlist(list20, 4..11);
```
$$[\,4, 5, 6, 7, 8, 9, 10, 11\,]$$

Neither of these commands has any effect on list20. This is standard Maple behaviour; a command does not directly affect the value of the parameters passed to it.

```
> list20;
```
$$[\,1, 2, 3, 4, 5, 6, 7, 8, 9, 10, 11, 12, 13, 14, 15, 16, 17, 18, 19, 20\,]$$

If you want list20 to be affected by the deletion, simply assign the result of the command to list20.

By supplying a single positive integer value as the second parameter, you can work on just one element.

```
> deletelist(list20, 18);
```
$$[\,1, 2, 3, 4, 5, 6, 7, 8, 9, 10, 11, 12, 13, 14, 15, 16, 17, 19, 20\,]$$

```
> extractlist(list20, 18);
```
$$[\,18\,]$$

By supplying a list of integer values and ranges as the second parameter, you can work on several groups of elements.

```
> deletelist(list20, [13..15, 1..3, 6, 14..19]);
```
$$[\,4, 5, 7, 8, 9, 10, 11, 12, 20\,]$$

```
> extractlist(list20, [13..15, 1..3, 6, 14..19]);
```
$$[\,13, 14, 15, 1, 2, 3, 6, 14, 15, 16, 17, 18, 19\,]$$

Notice that the integer values and ranges do not have to be provided in ascending numeric order. Also, deletelist ignores any repeated values (such as 14 and 15 in 13..15 and 14..19), while in the same situation extractlist creates multiple copies.

The next two commands, insertlist and replacelist, take lists as their first two parameters. In both commands, the elements in $list_1$ are placed into $list_2$; the only difference is the method of insertion.

In insertlist, the elements of list$_1$ are inserted into list$_2$ starting after the nth element of list$_2$. (n is provided as the third parameter.)

> newlist := [a, b, c];

$$newlist := [\,a, b, c\,]$$

> insertlist(newlist, list20, 8);

$$[\,1, 2, 3, 4, 5, 6, 7, 8, a, b, c, 9, 10, 11, 12, 13, 14, 15, 16, 17, 18, 19, 20\,]$$

In replacelist, the elements of list$_1$ replace the elements of list$_2$ at positions a through b inclusive. (The range a..b is provided as the third parameter.)

> replacelist(newlist, list20, 4..12);

$$[\,1, 2, 3, a, b, c, 13, 14, 15, 16, 17, 18, 19, 20\,]$$

Notice that in replacelist, the number of elements in list$_1$ does not have to equal the number of elements being removed from list$_2$. Also, in both commands it is the *elements* of list$_1$, not the list itself, that is being inserted into list$_2$. If you want to insert a complete list into list$_2$, include the complete list as an *element* of list$_1$.

> insertlist([a, [b,c,d], e], list20, 8);

$$[\,1, 2, 3, 4, 5, 6, 7, 8, a, [\,b, c, d\,], e, 9, 10, 11, 12, 13, 14, 15, 16, 17, 18, 19, 20\,]$$

In both commands, if list$_1$ is not a list, it is treated as a single element and inserted as such.

The last two commands in this section, prependlist and appendlist, are really special versions of insertlist which add elements either to the beginning or the end of an existing list.

> prependlist(7/3, newlist);

$$\left[\frac{7}{3}, a, b, c\right]$$

> appendlist(7/3, newlist);

$$\left[a, b, c, \frac{7}{3}\right]$$

As before, newlist is *not* affected by these commands. If you wish to actually update newlist with the new values, assign to newlist as in the following example.

If the first parameter to either command is a list, all the elements of that list are added to the other list.

```
> newlist := prependlist([2,3,5], newlist);
```
$$newlist := [2, 3, 5, a, b, c]$$
```
> newlist := appendlist([[2,3,5]], newlist);
```
$$newlist := [2, 3, 5, a, b, c, [2, 3, 5]]$$

Notice the second set of brackets used to create a list within a list in the last example, and examine the result.

Merging and Separating Lists

ziplists($list_1$, $list_2$, firstskip, thenskip)	zip two lists together
unziplist(list, name, firstskip, thenskip)	separate a list into two lists

The commands ziplists and unziplist are used for merging and separating lists, respectively. It is a little challenging to understand their workings at first, but it is helpful to compare their mechanics to those of a zipper. Both commands take third and fourth parameters firstskip and thenskip.

In ziplists, as the pluralized name infers, you are taking *two* lists and zipping them together to create one unified list. Picture the unconnected zipper of a jacket. $list_1$ represents the side of the zipper without the slide-fastener, and $list_2$ represents the side with the slide-fastener. In other words, $list_2$ is being zipped into $list_1$. firstskip represents how many elements of $list_1$ are skipped before the first element of $list_2$ is inserted. thenskip represents how many subsequent elements of $list_1$ are skipped before the next element of $list_2$ is inserted, and so on. Both variables have a default value of 1.

Given two lists, a and b, and the default values for firstskip and thenskip, the following picture illustrates the act of zipping them together to create list c.

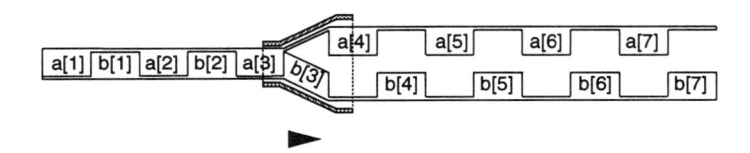

The following examples illustrate this concept in Maple. Use lists list1, with all 1s, and list2, with all 2s, for clarity and simplicity. Odds are that you will not have such straightforward lists in your work; but this way you can get the feel for how ziplists works.

```
> list1 := [1, 1, 1, 1, 1, 1, 1];
```
$$list1 := [1, 1, 1, 1, 1, 1, 1]$$

> list2 := [2, 2, 2, 2, 2, 2, 2];
$$list2 := [2,2,2,2,2,2,2]$$
> ziplists(list1, list2, 1, 1);
$$[1,2,1,2,1,2,1,2,1,2,1,2,1,2]$$

The above example represents, in the physical example, a perfectly matched zipper, and is easy enough to understand. It should be noted that there are also built-in commands for accomplishing this zipping when both firstskip and thenskip are 1. The built-in command zip can be used (though the syntax can be difficult to comprehend).

> zip((x,y)->op([x,y]), list1, list2);
$$[1,2,1,2,1,2,1,2,1,2,1,2,1,2]$$

To see more practical uses of zip, read the on-line help page accessed with ?zip.

The zip command is not as useful when the two lists are the slightest bit non-standard. For example, what happens if the two lists are of different lengths? ziplists is designed to append the "extra" elements from the longer list at the end of the result.

> list2 := [2, 2, 2, 2];
$$list2 := [2,2,2,2]$$
> ziplists(list1, list2, 1, 1);
$$[1,2,1,2,1,2,1,2,1,1,1]$$
> list2 := [2, 2, 2, 2, 2, 2, 2, 2, 2, 2];
$$list2 := [2,2,2,2,2,2,2,2,2,2]$$
> ziplists(list1, list2, 1, 1);
$$[1,2,1,2,1,2,1,2,1,2,1,2,2,2,2]$$

zip, on the other hand, simply ignores any "extra" elements in the longer list.

> zip((x,y)->op([x,y]), list1, list2);
$$[1,2,1,2,1,2,1,2,1,2,1,2,1,2]$$

What if you want to skip more than one initial element of $list_1$ or want to skip multiple elements of $list_1$ before each subsequent insertion? ziplists takes care of this easily. In this case, a few examples are worth thousands of words.

```
> list1 := [1, 1, 1, 1, 1, 1, 1, 1, 1, 1, 1, 1, 1]:
> list2 := [2, 2, 2, 2, 2, 2]:
> ziplists(list1, list2, 3, 1);
```

$$[\,1,1,1,2,1,2,1,2,1,2,1,2,1,2,1,1,1,1,1\,]$$

```
> ziplists(list1, list2, 1, 2);
```

$$[\,1,2,1,1,2,1,1,2,1,1,2,1,1,2,1,1,2,1,1\,]$$

```
> ziplists(list1, list2, 2, 3);
```

$$[\,1,1,2,1,1,1,2,1,1,1,2,1,1,1,2,1,1,2,2\,]$$

As you can see, extra elements are handled in the same, intuitive manner. The built-in zip cannot do this at all.[1]

unziplist is the intuitive counterpart to ziplists. Where ziplists takes two lists and merges them together into one list, unziplist takes a single list and separates it into two lists. This raises the question: How are *two* lists returned from a single command? One list (we'll call it the *resulting* list) can be returned as the result of the command. The second list is returned in an unevaluated variable name passed as the second parameter to the unziplist command. If this is confusing, the following description and examples should help.

Picture unzipping that same jacket you zipped up above. The resulting list is represented by the side of the zipper with the slide-fastener, and name is the side without the slide-fastener. In other words, the resulting list is being separated from list, leaving name. firstskip represents how many elements of list are skipped before the first element is removed to the resulting list. thenskip represents how many subsequent elements of list are skipped before the next element is removed to the resulting list, and so on. Both variable have a default value of 1.

Given a single list, list, and the default values for firstskip and thenskip, the following picture illustrates the act of unzipping it into the resulting list b and the named list a.

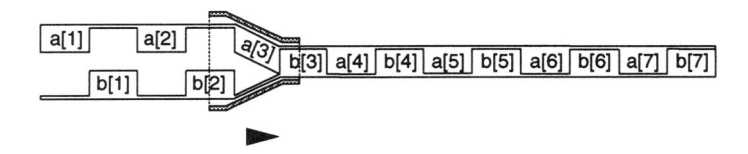

---

[1]To be perfectly fair, there might be some super-elaborate way to finesse zip into recreating such functionality, but just imagining how complex the syntax of such a command would be gives me hives. Use ziplists; it is designed to be straightforward.

The following commands illustrate this concept in Maple. Use list20, a list containing the integers from 1 to 20, for clarity and simplicity.

> list20 := [$1..20];

$list20 := [\,1,2,3,4,5,6,7,8,9,10,11,12,13,14,15,16,17,18,19,20\,]$

> unziplist(list20, 'noslidefast', 1, 1);

$[\,2,4,6,8,10,12,14,16,18,20\,]$

> noslidefast;

$[\,1,3,5,7,9,11,13,15,17,19\,]$

The forward quotes around noslidefast are to ensure that it is passed as an *unevaluated* name. Even if you think that noslidefast has never been assigned a value, it is still good practice to include the forward quotes.

Of course, unziplist works in an intuitive way when the values firstskip and thenskip are different than the default values (1 and 1).

> unziplist(list20, 'noslidefast', 3, 1);

$[\,4,6,8,10,12,14,16,18,20\,]$

> noslidefast;

$[\,1,2,3,5,7,9,11,13,15,17,19\,]$

> unziplist(list20, 'noslidefast', 1, 4);

$[\,2,7,12,17\,]$

> noslidefast;

$[\,1,3,4,5,6,8,9,10,11,13,14,15,16,18,19,20\,]$

> unziplist(list20, 'noslidefast', 2, 5);

$[\,3,9,15\,]$

> noslidefast;

$[\,1,2,4,5,6,7,8,10,11,12,13,14,16,17,18,19,20\,]$

For either ziplists or unziplist, either (or both) of firstskip or thenskip can be equal to 0. When firstskip is 0, the result is easily understandable.

> ziplists(list1, list2, 0, 1);

$[\,2,1,2,1,2,1,2,1,2,1,2,1,1,1,1,1,1,1,1\,]$

When thenskip is 0, ziplists mimics the action of insertlist and unziplist mimics the actions of both deletelist and extractlist.

```
> ziplists(list1, list2, 1, 0);
```
$$[\,1,2,2,2,2,2,2,1,1,1,1,1,1,1,1,1,1,1,1\,]$$
```
> insertlist(list2, list1, 1);
```
$$[\,1,2,2,2,2,2,2,1,1,1,1,1,1,1,1,1,1,1,1\,]$$
```
> unziplist(list20, 'noslidefast', 10, 0);
```
$$[\,11,12,13,14,15,16,17,18,19,20\,]$$
```
> deletelist(list20, 1..10);
```
$$[\,11,12,13,14,15,16,17,18,19,20\,]$$
```
> noslidefast;
```
$$[\,1,2,3,4,5,6,7,8,9,10\,]$$
```
> extractlist(list20, 1..10);
```
$$[\,1,2,3,4,5,6,7,8,9,10\,]$$

What do you think happens when *both* firstskip and thenskip are equal to 0?

When the lists list$_1$ and list$_2$ are "well-numbered" (i.e., they zip together evenly, without any "extra" elements appended to the end), the commands ziplists and unziplist can be used as inverse operations.

```
> lista := [a, a, a, a, a, a, a, a, a, a];
```
$$lista := [\,a,a,a,a,a,a,a,a,a,a\,]$$
```
> listb := [b, b, b, b, b, b];
```
$$listb := [\,b,b,b,b,b,b\,]$$
```
> listba := ziplists(lista, listb, 0, 2);
```
$$listba := [\,b,a,a,b,a,a,b,a,a,b,a,a,b,a,a,b\,]$$
```
> unziplist(listba, 'noslidefast', 0, 2);
```
$$[\,b,b,b,b,b,b\,]$$
```
> noslidefast;
```
$$[\,a,a,a,a,a,a,a,a,a,a\,]$$

When the lists are not "well-numbered", the two commands are not quite mutually inverse. Most of the uses you will have for these lists will be with "well-numbered" lists, so this should not present a problem.

Reordering and Restructuring Lists

reverselist(list)	reverse the elements of a list
rotatelist(list, n)	rotate the elements of a list
flattenlist(list)	flatten all internal lists
raiselist(list, [int_1, ..., int_n])	convert a list into a list of lists of lists of ...

The two simplest of these four commands, reverselist and rotatelist, change the inherent ordering in a list. As its name suggests, reverselist reverses the ordering of the elements of list.

> list10 := [$1..10];

$$list10 := [1, 2, 3, 4, 5, 6, 7, 8, 9, 10]$$

> reverselist(list10);

$$[10, 9, 8, 7, 6, 5, 4, 3, 2, 1]$$

A range can be provided as an optional second parameter, allowing you to specify a subrange of the elements to reverse in place.

> reverselist(list10, 4..7);

$$[1, 2, 3, 7, 6, 5, 4, 8, 9, 10]$$

rotatelist performs a shift upon the elements of list. If the second parameter, n, is a positive number, each element in list is shifted n places to the right. Elements that reach the rightmost "boundary" of the list are cycled to the beginning of the list.

> rotatelist(list10, 3);

$$[8, 9, 10, 1, 2, 3, 4, 5, 6, 7]$$

If n is negative, then the elements are shifted to the left.

> rotatelist(list10, -3);

$$[4, 5, 6, 7, 8, 9, 10, 1, 2, 3]$$

If no second parameter is provided, a default of 1 is used.

The commands flattenlist and raiselist preserve the inherent ordering of the elements, but change the number and types of *internal* lists present in list. flattenlist checks to see if any of the elements of list are lists themselves. If so, then the internal elements of these lists are added at the first level of list. This process is recursive, so lists within lists within list are flattened as well. This is best illustrated by examples.

> list1 := [[1,2,3], [4,5,6], [7,8,9]];

$$list1 := [[1, 2, 3], [4, 5, 6], [7, 8, 9]]$$

```
> flat1 := flattenlist(list1);
```
$$flat1 := [\,1,2,3,4,5,6,7,8,9\,]$$
```
> list2 := [1, [2,3,[4,5,6],7], 8, 9, [10, [[11]], 12]];
```
$$list2 := [\,1,[\,2,3,[\,4,5,6\,],7\,],8,9,[\,10,[\,[\,11\,]\,],12\,]\,]$$
```
> flat2 := flattenlist(list2);
```
$$flat2 := [\,1,2,3,4,5,6,7,8,9,10,11,12\,]$$

raiselist takes a list (which may or may not be "flat") and rebuilds it into a structure of nested lists. The second parameter to raiselist must be a list of integers such that $int_1 * \ldots * int_n$ either exactly equals the number of elements of list or equally divides it (in which case the quotient of that division is automatically appended to the second parameter).

```
> raiselist(flat1, [3, 3]);
```
$$[\,[\,1,2,3\,],[\,4,5,6\,],[\,7,8,9\,]\,]$$
```
> raiselist(flat2, [2, 2, 3]);
```
$$[\,[\,[\,1,2,3\,],[\,4,5,6\,]\,],[\,[\,7,8,9\,],[\,10,11,12\,]\,]\,]$$

The last element of the second parameter to raiselist, int_n, is the number of elements in the deepest level of internal lists created. The second last element of the second parameter is the number of elements in the second deepest level of internal lists created, and so on.

```
> raiselist([seq(i, i=1..120)], [5,3,4,2]);
```
$$[[[[\,1,2\,],[\,3,4\,],[\,5,6\,],[\,7,8\,]\,],[\,[\,9,10\,],[\,11,12\,],[\,13,14\,],[\,15,16\,]\,],$$
$$[\,[\,17,18\,],[\,19,20\,],[\,21,22\,],[\,23,24\,]\,]\,],[$$
$$[\,[\,25,26\,],[\,27,28\,],[\,29,30\,],[\,31,32\,]\,],$$
$$[\,[\,33,34\,],[\,35,36\,],[\,37,38\,],[\,39,40\,]\,],$$
$$[\,[\,41,42\,],[\,43,44\,],[\,45,46\,],[\,47,48\,]\,]\,],[$$
$$[\,[\,49,50\,],[\,51,52\,],[\,53,54\,],[\,55,56\,]\,],$$
$$[\,[\,57,58\,],[\,59,60\,],[\,61,62\,],[\,63,64\,]\,],$$
$$[\,[\,65,66\,],[\,67,68\,],[\,69,70\,],[\,71,72\,]\,]\,],[$$
$$[\,[\,73,74\,],[\,75,76\,],[\,77,78\,],[\,79,80\,]\,],$$
$$[\,[\,81,82\,],[\,83,84\,],[\,85,86\,],[\,87,88\,]\,],$$
$$[\,[\,89,90\,],[\,91,92\,],[\,93,94\,],[\,95,96\,]\,]\,],[$$

[[97, 98], [99, 100], [101, 102], [103, 104]],

[[105, 106], [107, 108], [109, 110], [111, 112]],

[[113, 114], [115, 116], [117, 118], [119, 120]]]]

While in most respects raiselist is the inverse of flattenlist, it cannot produce oddly structured lists such as [1, [2,3,[4,5,6],7], 8, 9, [10, [[11]], 12]].

Comparing Lists

comparelists($list_1$, $list_2$)	compare elements in corresponding positions
intersectlists($list_1$, $list_2$)	find the elements common to both lists
unionlists($list_1$, $list_2$)	find the elements that are in either list

As you can see, all the commands in this section have names ending in *lists*, indicating that they work with multiple (in this case two) lists. Entering any more or less than two lists causes an error message to be generated.

The first command, comparelists, examines corresponding elements from two lists to determine if they are identical. If the elements differ, their position is recorded. The result is a list containing integers and/or integer ranges representing those elements that do *not* match.

```
> list1 := [1, 2, 3, 4, 5, 6, 7, 8, 9, 10]:
> list2 := [1, 2, 4, 3, 5, 6, 6, 6, 9, 11]:
> comparelists(list1, list2);
```

$$[3..4, 7..8, 10]$$

The resulting list from comparelists can be used directly in any other command that accepts lists of position indicators, such as deletelist.

```
> deletelist(list1, ");
```

$$[1, 2, 5, 6, 9]$$

```
> deletelist(list2, "");
```

$$[1, 2, 5, 6, 9]$$

If one of the lists passed to comparelists contains more elements than the other, then the comparison is only performed for the number of elements in the shorter list.

```
> comparelists([1, 3, 7, 15, 31], [2, 3, 7, 13]);
```
$$[1,4]$$

Another optional parameter sequence allows you to compare only a range of elements from the two lists.

```
> comparelists(list1, list2, 4..8);
```
$$[4, 7..8]$$

The remaining two commands in this section are meant to provide you with similar capabilities that are available for sets. The binary operators intersect, union, and minus allow you to compare the elements of two sets and return the appropriate results.

```
> {W,e,d,n,e,s,d,a,y} intersect {T,h,u,r,s,d,a,y};
```
$$\{a, d, s, y\}$$

```
> {S,a,t,u,r,d,a,y} union {S,u,n,d,a,y};
```
$$\{r, S, a, t, d, n, y, u\}$$

The Utility commands intersectlists and unionlists mimic these abilities, while still preserving those qualities which make lists different from sets. See the *What Maple Has* section for more details.

intersectlists compares the elements of two lists and retains only those that are contained in both.

```
> list1 := [1, 3, 5, 7, 9, 11, 13, 15, 17, 19]:
> list2 := first10primes;
```
$$list2 := [2, 3, 5, 7, 11, 13, 17, 19, 23, 29]$$

```
> intersectlists(list1, list2);
```
$$[3, 5, 7, 11, 13, 17, 19]$$

The elements in the resulting list are in the same order they appeared in *both* the initial lists. But what would happen if the two lists were not ordered so predictably?

```
> list1 := [1, 3, 6, 2, 4, 5, 8, 7]:
> list2 := [2, 4, 8, 9, 1]:
> intersectlists(list1, list2);
```
$$[1, 2, 4, 8]$$

```
> intersectlists(list2, list1);
```
$$[2, 4, 8, 1]$$

A different ordering of the parameters causes a different ordering of the result. intersectlists works by looking at each element of the first list in turn, checking to see whether an identical element exists *anywhere* in the second list, and if so adding that element to the end of the resulting list. By these methods, intersectlists retains the list quality of preservation of order.

What about the handling of duplicate elements?

```
> list1 := [1, 2, 3, 4, 3, 5, 7, 4, 2, 6, 2, 4, 2, 1, 1, 6]:
> list2 := [6, 2, 3, 4, 1, 1, 7, 8, 9, 4, 3, 4, 5]:
> intersectlists(list1, list2);
```

$$[1, 2, 3, 4, 3, 5, 7, 4, 6, 4, 1]$$

Take a close look at the result. There are three 1s in the first list, two 1s in the second, and two 1s in the result. There are four 2s in the first list, one 2 in the second, and one 2 in the result. Examining further, you can see that the number of any particular element in the result is equal to the *minimum frequency* of that element in the two lists.[2]

The unionlists command works similarly. The frequency of any particular element in the result is equal to the *maximum frequency* of that element in the two lists. Have a look at how unionlists handles some of the same lists from above.

```
> list1 := [1, 3, 6, 2, 4, 5, 8, 7]:
> list2 := [2, 4, 8, 9, 1]:
> unionlists(list1, list2);
```

$$[1, 3, 6, 2, 4, 5, 8, 7, 9]$$

```
> unionlists(list2, list1);
```

$$[2, 4, 8, 9, 1, 3, 6, 5, 7]$$

```
> list1 := [1, 2, 3, 4, 3, 5, 7, 4, 2, 6, 2, 4, 2, 1, 1, 6]:
> list2 := [6, 2, 3, 4, 1, 1, 7, 8, 9, 4, 3, 4, 5]:
> unionlists(list1, list2);
```

$$[1, 2, 3, 4, 3, 5, 7, 4, 2, 6, 2, 4, 2, 1, 1, 6, 8, 9]$$

```
> unionlists(list2, list1);
```

$$[6, 2, 3, 4, 1, 1, 7, 8, 9, 4, 3, 4, 5, 2, 2, 2, 1, 6]$$

Following the ordering rule for intersectlists means that the first parameter is always contained (intact) at the beginning of the result. The result is not simply a joining of *all* the elements from both lists, but instead the

---

[2] A Utility command frequency, which can determine these values, is found in the next section.

smallest list containing all the elements (with their respective multiplicities) from each of the lists.

Processing Lists

uniquelist(list)	remove multiple elements from a list
frequency(expr, list)	compute the frequency of elements
whichelement(expr, list)	find a subexpression within a list

uniquelist removes all repetitive elements from a list, leaving just the first example of each unique element. Knowing the differences between lists and sets, you might think that this could be accomplished by simply converting the list to a set (which eliminates repetitive elements) and then converting the result back to a list. But there is a special danger there.

> oldlist := [1, 3, 5, 2, 3, 2, 4, 5, 5, 1, 1, 2, 4, 6];

$$oldlist := [1, 3, 5, 2, 3, 2, 4, 5, 5, 1, 1, 2, 4, 6]$$

> newset := {op(oldlist)};

$$newset := \{1, 2, 3, 4, 5, 6\}$$

> newlist := [op(newset)];

$$newlist := [1, 2, 3, 4, 5, 6]$$

The order of elements specified in oldlist has *not* been preserved in newlist. If there were no reason for a specific ordering, then you might as well use a set to contain your data, stopping after the creation of newset. If ordering is important to you, use uniquelist.

> newlist := uniquelist(oldlist);

$$newlist := [1, 3, 5, 2, 4, 6]$$

An optional second parameter can be supplied to allow the first n occurrences of each unique element to remain in the list.

> uniquelist(oldlist, 2);

$$[1, 3, 5, 2, 3, 2, 4, 5, 1, 4, 6]$$

To determine how many times a unique element appears in a particular list, without affecting the elements themselves, use the frequency command. Only the first-level elements are compared to the given expression.

```
> list1 := [x, y, z, x+1/x, w, w, x, 3*x, y, x];
```

$$list1 := \left[x, y, z, x + \frac{1}{x}, w, w, x, 3x, y, x\right]$$

```
> frequency(x, list1);
```

$$3$$

```
> frequency(1/x, list1);
```

$$0$$

If only one parameter is given, it must be a list. In this case, a list of lists is returned representing the frequency of *each* unique element in the list.

```
> frequency(list1);
```

$$\left[[3, \{x\}], [2, \{y, w\}], \left[1, \left\{z, 3x, x + \frac{1}{x}\right\}\right]\right]$$

Each internal list in the result contains two elements: a frequency and a set of elements that have that frequency, in that order.

The last command in this section, whichelement, is principally to be used when you have a list with many, many elements, or a list with several huge expressions. In either of these cases, when you are interested in one particular element, it can be difficult to determine which element that is in the ordering of the list. Examining the list on your screen, however, you should be able to discern a subexpression contained within the desired expression. When passed to whichelement, this subexpression returns the location of the *first* element containing this subexpression.

```
> intlist := [seq(int(1/(1+x^i), x), i=1..10)];
```

$$intlist := \Bigg[\ln(1+x), \arctan(x),$$

$$\frac{1}{3}\ln(1+x) - \frac{1}{6}\ln(x^2 - x + 1) + \frac{1}{3}\sqrt{3}\arctan\left(\frac{1}{3}(2x-1)\sqrt{3}\right),$$

$$\frac{1}{8}\sqrt{2}\ln\left(\frac{x^2 + x\sqrt{2} + 1}{x^2 - x\sqrt{2} + 1}\right) + \frac{1}{4}\sqrt{2}\arctan\left(x\sqrt{2} + 1\right) + \frac{1}{4}\sqrt{2}\arctan\left(x\sqrt{2} - 1\right),$$

$$\frac{1}{5}\ln(1+x) - \frac{1}{20}\ln\left(2x^2 - x - \sqrt{5}x + 2\right)\sqrt{5} - \frac{1}{20}\ln\left(2x^2 - x - \sqrt{5}x + 2\right)$$

Utility Commands

$$+ \frac{\arctan\left(\frac{4x-1-\sqrt{5}}{\sqrt{10-2\sqrt{5}}}\right)}{\sqrt{10-2\sqrt{5}}} - \frac{1}{5}\frac{\arctan\left(\frac{4x-1-\sqrt{5}}{\sqrt{10-2\sqrt{5}}}\right)\sqrt{5}}{\sqrt{10-2\sqrt{5}}}$$

$$+ \frac{1}{20}\ln\left(2x^2 - x + \sqrt{5}x + 2\right)\sqrt{5} - \frac{1}{20}\ln\left(2x^2 - x + \sqrt{5}x + 2\right)$$

$$+ \frac{\arctan\left(\frac{4x-1+\sqrt{5}}{\sqrt{10+2\sqrt{5}}}\right)}{\sqrt{10+2\sqrt{5}}} + \frac{1}{5}\frac{\arctan\left(\frac{4x-1+\sqrt{5}}{\sqrt{10+2\sqrt{5}}}\right)\sqrt{5}}{\sqrt{10+2\sqrt{5}}}, \frac{1}{3}\arctan(x)$$

$$- \frac{1}{12}\sqrt{3}\ln\left(x^2 - \sqrt{3}x + 1\right) + \frac{1}{6}\arctan\left(2x - \sqrt{3}\right) + \frac{1}{12}\sqrt{3}\ln\left(x^2 + \sqrt{3}x + 1\right)$$

$$+ \frac{1}{6}\arctan\left(2x + \sqrt{3}\right), \left(\sum_{\_R=\%4}\_R\ln(x + 7\_R)\right) + \frac{1}{7}\ln(1+x),$$

$$\sum_{\_R=\%3}\_R\ln(x + 8\_R), -\frac{1}{18}\ln(x^2 - x + 1) + \frac{1}{9}\sqrt{3}\arctan\left(\frac{2}{3}\left(x - \frac{1}{2}\right)\sqrt{3}\right)$$

$$+ \left(\sum_{\_R=\%2}\_R\ln(x + 9\_R)\right) + \frac{1}{9}\ln(1+x),$$

$$\left(\sum_{\_R=\%1}\_R\ln(x + 10\_R)\right) + \frac{1}{5}\arctan(x)\Bigg]$$

$\%1 := \text{RootOf}(100000000\_Z^8 - 1000000\_Z^6 + 10000\_Z^4 - 100\_Z^2 + 1)$

$\%2 := \text{RootOf}(531441\_Z^6 + 729\_Z^3 + 1)$

$\%3 := \text{RootOf}(16777216\_Z^8 + 1)$

$\%4 := \text{RootOf}(117649\_Z^6 + 16807\_Z^5 + 2401\_Z^4 + 343\_Z^3 + 49\_Z^2 + 7\_Z + 1)$

> whichelement(arctan(2*x-sqrt(3)), intlist);

$$6$$

> intlist["];

$$\frac{1}{3}\arctan(x) - \frac{1}{12}\sqrt{3}\ln\left(x^2 - \sqrt{3}x + 1\right) + \frac{1}{6}\arctan\left(2x - \sqrt{3}\right)$$

$$+ \frac{1}{12}\sqrt{3}\ln\left(x^2 + \sqrt{3}x + 1\right) + \frac{1}{6}\arctan\left(2x + \sqrt{3}\right)$$

The expressions starting with % contain common subexpressions pulled out from the list.

If you do not want to type in as large a subexpression, you can type in several smaller subexpressions contained in a particular element by enclosing them in a list.

> whichelement([3,6,12], intlist);

$$6$$

Or, alternatively, to locate the first element with *any one* of a given number of subexpressions, enclose them in set braces.

> whichelement({8,9,10}, intlist);

$$4$$

> intlist["];

$$\frac{1}{8}\sqrt{2}\ln\left(\frac{x^2 + x\sqrt{2} + 1}{x^2 - x\sqrt{2} + 1}\right) + \frac{1}{4}\sqrt{2}\arctan\left(x\sqrt{2} + 1\right) + \frac{1}{4}\sqrt{2}\arctan\left(x\sqrt{2} - 1\right)$$

Mapping Lists

maplists(fnc, [list$_1$, ..., list$_n$])	apply a function to the elements of n lists

So far, none of the commands in *ListTools* has performed calculations with the value of the elements of the input lists. Elements have simply been shuffled around, pulled out, and stuck in without performing any operations on their individual values.

The maplists command is the first of a series of mapping commands provided in *The Practical Approach Utilities for Maple* (i.e., mapexpr, maprows, mapcols, etc.). Although these commands all deal with data from different types of Maple structures which is pointed to in several different ways, the overall structure of these commands is the same; understanding one greatly helps in understanding them all. maplists is perhaps the simplest.

All of these mapping commands have one important advantage over Maple's built-in map command:[3] they allow you to easily substitute values for *any* or all of the parameters of the mapped to function.

In its simplest form, maplists calls the given function n times, once for each internal list present in the second parameter. In each invocation of

---
[3] See the *Getting Started With Maple* chapter for an overview of map.

the function, the elements of the appropriate internal list are passed (with ordering preserved) as the sole parameters to that function. The result is a list with n values[4] representing the result of those invocations. The following example should illustrate this most common usage.

```
> mylists := [1, 3, 5, 5, 8], [5, 9, -12], [0, 1, 5, -1234, 67];
```
$$mylists := [1,3,5,5,8],[5,9,-12],[0,1,5,-1234,67]$$
```
> maplists(max, [mylists]);
```
$$[8,9,67]$$

The number of elements in each internal list need not be the same; it all depends on what type and number of parameters the given function can handle. If any of the internal lists causes an error message to be generated, its corresponding position in the result is filled with the value FAIL.

```
> newlists := [21, 45, 333], [12, 6.2],   [1234, 4321, 1324, 3241]:
> maplists(igcd, [newlists]);
```
$$[3, FAIL, 1]$$

In order to determine the actual error associated with the FAIL value, you must pass those parameters alone through igcd.[5]

```
> igcd(op(newlists[2]));
Error, wrong number (or type) of parameters in function igcd
```

If you want to send *single* elements as parameters to a function, maplists can be used with one-element internal lists. Alternatively, if you supply a one-level list as the second parameter it is interpreted in the same way.

```
> maplists(ifactor, [[24], [46], [345], [123], [99], [1003]]);
```
$$\left[(2)^3(3),(2)(23),(3)(5)(23),(3)(41),(3)^2(11),(17)(59)\right]$$
```
> maplists(ifactor, [24, 46, 345, 123, 99, 1003]);
```
$$\left[(2)^3(3),(2)(23),(3)(5)(23),(3)(41),(3)^2(11),(17)(59)\right]$$

This is identical to the operation of the built-in map command; the single element is processed as the first (and, in this case, only) parameter to ifactor. Where maplists and map differ is that with maplists you can assign the single

---
[4]This is assuming that each invocation results in a single expression.
[5]In more complex results from maplists, the whichelement command can be used to determine the position of FAIL.

value to be *any* of the parameters passed to the given function, not just the first one. Remaining parameters can be set at constant values.

The following example of differentiating one expression with respect to different variables demonstrates this principle much better than words ever could.

> `varlist := [u, v, w, x, y, z];`

$$varlist := [u, v, w, x, y, z]$$

> `myexpr := (x^(u+2)+3*y)/exp(z*w);`

$$myexpr := \frac{x^{(u+2)} + 3y}{e^{(zw)}}$$

> `maplists(diff, varlist, [2], {1=myexpr});`

$$\left[\frac{x^{(u+2)} \ln(x)}{e^{(zw)}}, 0, -\frac{(x^{(u+2)} + 3y)z}{e^{(zw)}}, \frac{x^{(u+2)}(u+2)}{x\, e^{(zw)}}, 3\frac{1}{e^{(zw)}}, -\frac{(x^{(u+2)} + 3y)w}{e^{(zw)}} \right]$$

Examining the last call to maplists, the third parameter [2] contains the position(s) that the mapped elements of varlist are to take in the parameter sequence of diff. The fourth parameter, {1=myexpr}, contains equations whose lefthand sides must be positive integers. These integers represent parameter positions for diff, and the corresponding righthand sides represent the constant expressions to be substituted for the corresponding parameters. In plain English, the above call to maplists says, "Differentiate the expression myexpr with respect to each of the six variables in varlist and concatenate the results in a list."

But what if the elements being mapped occur in lists of length greater than one? And what if these lists are not of consistent length? In these cases, you must supply as the third parameter a list of unique integers at least as long as the longest of the lists being mapped.

The following example uses a nonexistent function DIFF so that you may see the command calls created.

> `varlist := [[u, v], [v], [w, x], [x], [y, z], [z, z, z]];`

$$varlist := [[u, v], [v], [w, x], [x], [y, z], [z, z, z]]$$

> `maplists(DIFF, varlist, [2, 3, 4], {1=myexpr});`

$$\left[\text{DIFF}\left(\frac{x^{(u+2)} + 3y}{e^{(zw)}}, u, v\right), \text{DIFF}\left(\frac{x^{(u+2)} + 3y}{e^{(zw)}}, v\right), \text{DIFF}\left(\frac{x^{(u+2)} + 3y}{e^{(zw)}}, w, x\right), \right.$$
$$\left. \text{DIFF}\left(\frac{x^{(u+2)} + 3y}{e^{(zw)}}, x\right), \text{DIFF}\left(\frac{x^{(u+2)} + 3y}{e^{(zw)}}, y, z\right), \text{DIFF}\left(\frac{x^{(u+2)} + 3y}{e^{(zw)}}, z, z, z\right) \right]$$

If there is any conflict between the parameter positions supplied by the third and (lefthand side of the) fourth arguments to maplists, then those cases are dealt with individually and the values specified by the third parameter take precedence.

```
> maplists(DIFF, varlist, [2, 3, 4], {1=myexpr, 3=w});
```

$$\left[\text{DIFF}\left(\frac{x^{(u+2)} + 3y}{e^{(zw)}}, u, v \right), \text{DIFF}\left(\frac{x^{(u+2)} + 3y}{e^{(zw)}}, v, w \right), \text{DIFF}\left(\frac{x^{(u+2)} + 3y}{e^{(zw)}}, w, x \right), \right.$$

$$\text{DIFF}\left(\frac{x^{(u+2)} + 3y}{e^{(zw)}}, x, w \right), \text{DIFF}\left(\frac{x^{(u+2)} + 3y}{e^{(zw)}}, y, z \right),$$

$$\left. \text{DIFF}\left(\frac{x^{(u+2)} + 3y}{e^{(zw)}}, z, z, z \right) \right]$$

When you are using the four-parameter version of maplists, make sure that every invocation of the given function has m parameters in positions 1 through m; that is, that there are no "missing" parameters in the middle.

```
> maplists(DIFF, varlist, [3, 5, 2], {1=myexpr});
Error, (in maplists) argument # , 2,  is missing
```

All the other map-like commands use a similar logic and structure.

Examples

Plotting Points in Three Dimensions

Another (numerical) package has created three files each containing a list (in Maple syntax) with 100 floating-point numbers. The first two files represent corresponding x and y values that together define 100 points in the xy-plane. The third file contains values that some process has produced from those x- and y-inputs. Using Maple, read in the values, plot the xyz-points, and estimate a symbolic expression for z that approximates the data.

First, you need to read in the files with the read command.

```
> read 'X.DAT':
> listx := ":
> read 'Y.DAT':
> listy := ":
> read 'Z.DAT':
> listz := ":
```

Let's have a look at the first ten elements in each list.

> listx[1..10];

$-2.06, -1.55, -4.57, -4.91, -.290, .380, 3.76, 1.53, 3.30, -1.48$

> listy[1..10];

$-.900, -3.39, -.110, .750, .550, 1.29, -3.76, 4.73, .710, 3.92$

> listz[1..10];

$.649, -.610, .970, .990, -.591, -.845, -.04460, -.769, .930, -.748$

To plot the points in three-dimensional space, you need to rearrange the data into a list of lists of the form

---

[[listx$_1$, listy$_1$, listz$_1$], [listx$_2$, listy$_2$, listz$_2$], ...,

[listx$_n$, listy$_n$, listz$_n$]]

---

in order to pass it to the appropriate plotting command. First, zip the *x*- and *y*-points together into a list called listxy.

> listxy := ziplists(listx, listy, 1, 1):

Then zip in the *z*-points where they belong, creating a new list, listxyz.

> listxyz := ziplists(listxy, listz, 2, 2):

To verify that the lists have indeed been properly merged, display the first thirty elements and compare them to the earlier, individual lists.

> listxyz[1..30];

$-2.06, -.900, .649, -1.55, -3.39, -.610, -4.57, -.110, .970, -4.91, .750, .990, -.290,$

$.550, -.591, .380, 1.29, -.845, 3.76, -3.76, -.04460, 1.53, 4.73, -.769, 3.30,$

$.710, .930, -1.48, 3.92, -.748$

Fine, but the resulting list is still "flat." A list of three-element lists is needed; use raiselist to create it.

> listxyz := raiselist(listxyz, [100,3]):

> listxyz[1..10];

$[-2.06, -.900, .649], [-1.55, -3.39, -.610], [-4.57, -.110, .970], [-4.91, .750, .990],$

$[-.290, .550, -.591], [.380, 1.29, -.845], [3.76, -3.76, -.04460],$

$[1.53, 4.73, -.769], [3.30, .710, .930], [-1.48, 3.92, -.748]$

listxyz can now be passed to pointplot in the plots package to render the points in three-dimensional space.

```
> plots[pointplot](listxyz, axes=BOXED);
```

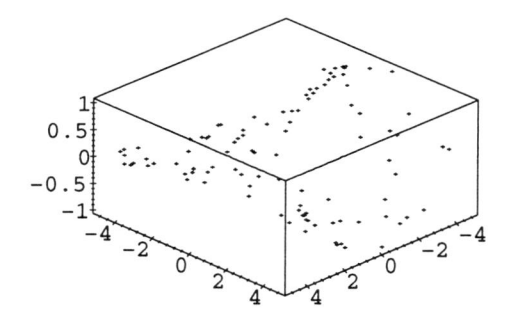

What does this surface appear to be? It bears a close resemblance to a "saddle plot" of some description. Now look at the plot for $z = \frac{x^2-y^2}{x^2+y^2}$ over the same ranges for x and y.

```
> plot3d((x^2-y^2)/(x^2+y^2), x=-3..3, y=-3..3);
```

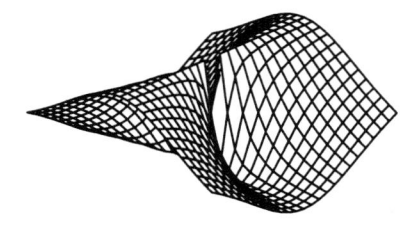

Relatively Prime Numbers

(The following example may or may not have any practical or theoretical use, but it does show an involved example of the replacelist command.)

Suppose that you are given a list (of finite length) of natural numbers, *nlist*. Write a procedure that examines *nlist* from left to right, checking to see if each adjacent pair of values is relatively prime. If a pair (say nlist[m] and nlist[m+1]) is *not* relatively prime, compute its greatest common divisor, *mygcd*, and replace the pair with the *three* elements:

nlist[m]/mygcd, mygcd, nlist[m+1]/mygcd.

This procedure can be written as follows. If the code as a whole is confusing to you, concentrate on the single invocation of replacelist that occurs in the while looping structure.

```
> relprime := proc(l:list)
>    local i, mygcd, nl;
>
>    nl := l;
>    i := 1;
>    while i < nops(nl) do
>       mygcd := igcd(nl[i], nl[i+1]);
>       if mygcd <> 1 then
>          nl := replacelist([nl[i]/mygcd, mygcd, nl[i+1]/mygcd], nl, i..i+1);
>          next;
>       fi;
>       i := i+1;
>    od;
>    RETURN(nl);
> end:
```

As you can see, the list of natural numbers, nl, is reassigned to the result of replacelist each time an offending pair is found. While it is an inefficient use of memory to employ list structures for such manipulation, you cannot use an array; arrays must have a *predefined* number of elements, and in this example the number of elements is constantly growing.

Let's try an example of relprime.

```
> nlist := [6, 56, 456, 3456, 23456];
```
$$nlist := [6, 56, 456, 3456, 23456]$$

```
> relprime(nlist);
```
$$[3, 1, 1, 2, 7, 19, 1, 1, 2, 1, 3, 1, 23456]$$

There are many interesting questions that can be posed about the results of relprime. For example, do you think that the results of passing the list nlist in reverse order will be the same?

```
> relprime(reverselist(nlist));
```
$$[733, 1, 1, 2, 1, 1, 1, 3, 1, 1, 19, 8, 7, 6]$$

Here are some other interesting ideas to investigate:

- What do you notice about the pattern of 1s and non-1s in the result of

```
> relprime([seq(2^i, i=1..10)]);
```
$$[1, 1, 2, 1, 1, 1, 2, 1, 1, 1, 1, 1, 2, 1, 1, 1, 1, 1, 1, 1, 2, 1, 1, 1, 1, 1, 1, 1, 1, 2, 1, 1,$$
$$1, 1, 1, 1, 1, 1, 1]$$

Try the same sequence but with 3^i. What do you notice? What about for 4^i, 5^i, etc.?

- What is the result of relprime on a list of 20 identical numbers? Try adding different numbers as the first element of the input list and see what the result is.

Programming Tips

The *Programming Tips* sections of this book are not meant to be used as an introductory course on Maple programming. For such information, see one of the entry-level Maple books, such as *First Leaves: A Tutorial Introduction to Maple V*. While there is a very basic introduction to creating Maple procedures in the *Getting Started With Maple* chapter, it is assumed from here on in that you are already familiar with the basic constructs and techniques of the Maple programming language.

Viewing a Procedure's Code

One of the great things about Maple is that most of its functionality is written in Maple's own programming language. The upshot of this is that the code for all these procedures is available for you to examine at any time. *The Practical Approach Utilities to Maple* are no exception—once the commands are loaded into memory, they can be viewed in the same way as the rest of Maple's code.

To view the code for a procedure, you must first set the option verboseproc=2 in Maple's interface command.

```
> interface(verboseproc=2):
```

Then, by using eval, you can print out the code for any procedure loaded into Maple.

```
> eval(factor);

proc(x,K)
local f,z;
options system,remember,'Copyright 1993 by Waterloo Maple Software';
    if type(x,{series,list,set,range,relation}) then RETURN(map(factor,args))
    fi;
    if not type(x,algebraic) then ERROR('invalid arguments') fi;
    if nargs = 2 then
        if K = [] or K = {} then
            if type(x,ratpoly(rational)) then factor(x)
            elif type(x,algfun(rational)) then
                factor(x,readlib('evala/GetAlgExt')(x))
            elif type(x,radfun(rational)) then
```

```
                    convert(factor(convert(x,RootOf),K),radical)
                else
                    ERROR('expecting a polynomial over an algebraic number field')
                fi
            elif type(K,{algnum,set(algnum),list(algnum)}) then
                if type(x,polynom(algnum)) then normal(evala(Factor(x,K)))
                elif type(x,algfun(rational)) then normal('factor/algext'(x,K))
                else
                    ERROR('expecting a polynomial over an algebraic number field')
                fi
            elif type(K,{radnum,set(radnum),list(radnum)}) then
                if type(x,polynom(radnum)) or type(x,radfun(rational)) then
                    f := factor(convert(subs(_Z = z,x),RootOf),convert(K,RootOf));
                    subs(z = _Z,convert(f,radical))
                else ERROR('expecting a polynomial over a radical number field')
                fi
            elif
            type(K,{algfun(rational),list(algfun(rational)),set(algfun(rational))})
             then
                if type(x,algfun(rational)) then normal('factor/algext'(x,K))
                else
                    ERROR('expecting a polynomial over an algebraic function field'
                        )
                fi
            elif
            type(K,{radfun(rational),list(radfun(rational)),set(radfun(rational))})
             then
                if type(x,radfun(rational)) then
                    f := factor(convert(subs(_Z = z,x),RootOf),convert(K,RootOf));
                    subs(z = _Z,convert(f,radical))
                else
                    ERROR('expecting a polynomial over an algebraic function field'
                        )
                fi
            else ERROR('2nd argument is not a valid algebraic extension')
            fi
        elif nargs <> 1 then ERROR('wrong number of arguments')
        elif not hastype(x,'+') then x
        elif type(x,polynom(numeric)) then 'factor/factor'(x)
        elif type(x,ratpoly(numeric)) then
            f := normal(x); normal(factor(numer(f))/factor(denom(f)))
        elif type(x,'^') and not type(op(2,x),integer) then map(factor,x)
        elif type(x,polynom(algnum)) then normal(evala(Factor(x)))
        elif type(x,ratpoly(algnum)) then factor(x,readlib('evala/GetAlgExt')(x))
        elif type(x,polynom(radnum)) or type(x,ratpoly(radnum)) then
            f := factor(convert(subs(_Z = z,x),RootOf));
```

```
            subs(z = _Z,convert(f,radical))
        elif type(x,function) then f := op(0,x); f(op(map(factor,args)))
        elif normal(x) <> x then factor(normal(x))
        elif type(x,{'+','*','^'}) then
            f := map(<x = factor(x)|x>,indets(x),args[2 .. nargs]);
            frontend('factor/factor',[subs(f,x),args[2 .. nargs]])
        else x
        fi
    end
```

While the above code seems to be complicated enough on its own, it is not *all* the code for factoring. If you look closely, you will see that factor calls several other second-level procedures, such as 'factor/algext' and 'factor/factor'. Those procedures may themselves call other procedures, and so on.

The code for *The Practical Approach Utilities to Maple* tends to be a lot less complicated. For example, the code for insertlist looks comparatively straightforward.

```
> eval(insertlist);

proc(l1,l2:list,n:realcons)
local a,cnt,l3;
    cnt := nops(l2);
    if type(l1,list) then l3 := l1 else l3 := [l1] fi;
    a := trunc(n);
    if a < 1 then RETURN([op(l3),op(l2)])
    elif cnt < a then RETURN([op(l2),op(l3)])
    fi;
    if a = cnt then RETURN([op(1 .. a,l2),op(l3)])
    else RETURN([op(1 .. a,l2),op(l3),op(a+1 .. cnt,l2)])
    fi
end
```

Most of the code is devoted to checking for errors and verifying the types of parameters passed; very few lines perform any actual *computation*. The same can be said of the top-level code for factor and, for that matter, for all well-programmed Maple procedures.

Recursion

While it is not the most efficient method in some cases (such as computing Fibonacci sequences), recursion can be very effective in simpler, more non-mathematical cases. Recursion is the technique of having a procedure call itself with a slightly altered parameter sequence. This invocation of the procedure then calls itself again, and again, etc., until a previously determined endpoint is reached.

In order to use the recursion method for programming a procedure, the following must be true.

1. The procedure must have a well-defined algorithm that takes a number of parameters, alters those values, and passes the new values as parameters to itself.

2. The algorithm must act upon all valid parameter sequences in such a way that, after a suitable number of passes, they are transformed into a state where the recursion is known to *stop*. At that point, there must be a specific value returned.

3. The algorithm cannot alter the parameters so that they *skip over* the stopping point, thereby recursing infinitely out of control.

One Utility command that is programmed with recursion is flattenlist, which takes a list containing internal lists (which may themselves contain internal lists, etc.) and "flattens" it into a list with no internal lists.

In order to do that, flattenlist calls itself for each element of the list passed as a parameter. If that element itself is a list, then flattenlist is called once again. The following is a simplified version of the Maple code for flattenlist.

```
> flattenlist := proc(lst)
>    local temp,i;
>    temp := [];
>    for i from 1 to nops(lst) do
>       if type(op(i,lst), list) then
>          temp := [op(temp), op(flattenlist(op(i,lst)))];
>       else
>          temp := [op(temp), op(i, lst)];
>       fi;
>    od;
>    RETURN(temp);
> end:
```

If an individual element of the list lst is a list itself, then flattenlist is called recursively. Otherwise, the element is appended to the resulting list. This procedure has a guaranteed stopping point, because after a finite number of passes through flattenlist, a list, no matter how complicated, must have all *nonlist* elements.

Efficiency Concerns

While lists are easy to understand, using them efficiently is not quite as simple. There are many subtle ways to speed up list computations.

The Power of seq

Using the seq command when constructing lists is essential to the efficiency of your code. The best way to show the power of seq is to make a simple comparison of the time required to complete a task with and without using this command.

Task: Create a list of the first n numbers in the sequence $1, 4, 7, 10, \ldots,$ for $n = 1000, 2500,$ and 5000.

To time a segment of Maple code, use the built-in time function, which returns the amount of CPU time (in seconds) used up to that point. That is, before the list is created, call

```
t := time():
```

and afterwards call

```
t - time();
```

to get the elapsed time.

This technique will be *very important* whenever you try to optimize the performance of your Maple code.

Let's examine three methods for completing the above task:

1. Create an empty list and then, using the for/from/to/do/od programming structure, append each new element in the list to the end of the existing list.

    ```
    newlist := []:
    for i from 1 to n do
       newlist := [op(newlist), 1+3*(i-1)]:
    od:
    ```

2. Use the seq command to create the list.

    ```
    newlist := [seq(1+3*(i-1), i=1..n)]:
    ```

3. Use the $ operator to create the list.

    ```
    newlist := [1+3*(k-1)$k=1..n]:
    ```

Notice that in each of the above methods, the colon terminator was used. If the semicolon were used, the extremely lengthy lists would be printed out, both clogging up the terminal and severely affecting the total time needed to complete the operation. The time it takes to display the final list is identical, regardless of which method was used to create it.

The following table shows the amount of time (in seconds) the computation took for each of $n = 1000$, $n = 2500$, and $n = 5000$.

n	for loop	seq	$
1000	4.333	0.084	0.100
2500	24.417	0.200	0.233
5000	96.350	0.417	0.550

Both the seq and $ operator took substantially less time than the for loop. If you examine the numbers more closely, you notice that the time required for the for loop method rises *exponentially* with the size of *n*, while the time required for the other two methods rises *linearly*. This means that for larger values of *n* the difference between the methods is even more pronounced.

The major reason for the above difference in efficiency is that each time you go through an iteration of the for loop, you use the op command to reconstruct the entire list plus one new element. Each time this is done, Maple creates the new list *one element at at time*—this is *extremely* inefficient. The seq command doesn't do this repetitive reconstruction, but deals with each element in newlist *once and only once*.

Sequential Access

Another efficiency problem that occurs when using lists is that of *sequential access*. When an element of a list is accessed with the [ ] syntax, Maple must search through each and every element of that list occurring before the desired element.

To illustrate this problem, redo the above example, but this time the values to be contained in newlist are the elements at position 1, 4, 7, 10, ... of an existing 2000-element list, oldlist; and look at *n* values of 100, 250, and 500. The code segments for this example are identical to those in the previous example, except that oldlist[1+3*(i-1)] is substituted for 1+3*(i-1).

(We'll leave out the timing for the $ operator, as this is really just another internal implementation of the seq command, and their efficiencies are very close.)

n	for loop	seq
100	0.800	0.750
250	2.134	1.816
500	4.666	3.684

It is difficult to see, but the for loop method is still *exponential* and the seq method is still *linear*. The reason that the timings are so close for varying values of *n* is that the large majority of the computation time is being used for accessing the individual elements of oldlist, which must be done in either case. There are relatively small savings with the seq command here.

In fact, the amount of time taken up in accessing elements from a list is so great that, for lists of sufficient size, it is more efficient to:

- Convert the list to an array. An array is a special form of the table structure, the elements of which are much more efficient to access.
- Perform the accessing operations on the elements of the array.
- Convert the array back to a list structure, if necessary.

Of course, all this conversion is only necessary if you are initially given a list as input and require the final output to be a list as well. The overhead involved in making the conversions is small compared to the amount of time saved. To illustrate this, perform the earlier example for $n = 1000$ and an original oldlist containing 5000 elements. Then do the same computation using arrays instead of lists and making the needed conversions. The code for the new for loop construction is:

```
oldarray := convert(oldlist, array):
newlist := []:
for i from 1 to 1000 do
    newlist := [op(newlist), oldarray[1+3*(i-1)]]:
od:
```

and the code for the new seq method is:

```
oldarray := convert(oldlist, array):
newlist2 := [seq(oldarray[1+3*(j-1)], j=1..1000)]:
```

The timings are contained in the following table.

	for loop	seq
list access	22.484	18.083
array access	8.117	3.783

The larger the lists you are dealing with, the greater the savings using arrays.

Conclusion

In conclusion, the following points have been made.

1. Use a seq command instead of a for/from/to/do/od construct whenever possible.
2. Accessing individual elements of a list is very CPU-intensive.
3. When accessing many elements from a large list, convert the list to an array before proceeding.

CHAPTER 5

ExpressionTools

It is a rare user that will always be satisfied with the answers Maple produces exactly as they are presented. It is not uncommon that you will want to pick apart an expression or selected pieces of an expression in order to perform further operations on that selection. Because of this, learning to navigate through and operate upon Maple expressions is of paramount importance.

Every structure in Maple is made up of individual parts, or *operands*, strung together by various *operators*. Structures, or expressions, can be as simple as single-element values, or can have hundreds of operands each of which has dozens of levels of complexity. Regardless of their size, the keys to understanding and therefore manipulating Maple expressions are always the same.

The structure of an expression can be modeled after a tree. Every expression is made up of one or more subexpressions, called operands, and each of these operands itself is constructed out of one or more such operands. This progression continues down each "branch" of the tree, creating new offshoots that eventually end in single-operand nodes. Pictorially, such a tree structure would look like:

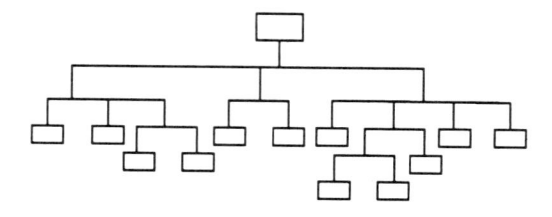

These tree models are also known as *directed acyclic graphs* or *DAGs*.

What Maple Has

While Maple contains the basic tools necessary for examination of expressions, using these tools effectively can be tricky and cumbersome.

Basic Expression Tools

The most basic tool for exploring the DAG of an expression is the op command. Every expression is made up of a sequence of operands at the highest level. Have a look at this operand sequence for a relatively simple expression.

> myexpr := 3*x^2/(y-2) + sin(z+1/3) - 2.5;

$$myexpr := 3\frac{x^2}{y-2} + \sin\left(z + \frac{1}{3}\right) - 2.5$$

> op(myexpr);

$$3\frac{x^2}{y-2}, \sin\left(z + \frac{1}{3}\right), -2.5$$

myexpr is initially made up of *three* operands. You can access the individual operands by supplying another parameter to op.

> op(1, myexpr);

$$3\frac{x^2}{y-2}$$

> op(2, myexpr);

$$\sin\left(z + \frac{1}{3}\right)$$

> op(3, myexpr);

$$-2.5$$

The op command also takes a range as its first parameter.

> op(2..3, myexpr);

$$\sin\left(z + \frac{1}{3}\right), -2.5$$

Additionally, the command nops tells you how many first-level operands (not including the zeroth operand) there are in an expression, without actually listing them.

```
> nops(myexpr);
```

$$3$$

These three operands are connected together with (in this case) arithmetic operators. While there is no way to always directly determine the exact operators used, the *type* of operation can be determined by using the whattype command.

```
> whattype(myexpr);
```

$$+$$

myexpr is of type + (a sum). A rule that helps you visualize the structure of expressions is that operands at the same level are always connected to one another with operators of the same type. For example, the first-level operands of an expression cannot be joined by both a + *and* a *.

whattype always returns a basic data type, which can be any one of the following:

'+'	'*'	'^'	'='	'<>'
'<'	'<='	'.'	'..'	'and'
'or'	'not'	exprseq	float	fraction
function	indexed	integer	list	procedure
series	set	string	table	uneval

If you look more closely at the first operand of myexpr above, you will see that it has a rather complicated structure itself. To look at the operands of this operand, use nested op commands.

```
> op(op(1, myexpr));
```

$$3, x^2, \frac{1}{y-2}$$

```
> op(2, op(1, myexpr));
```

$$x^2$$

And again, this subexpression can be broken down further.

```
> op(op(2, op(1, myexpr)));
```

$$x, 2$$

Already, the syntax for exploring and manipulating myexpr is getting out of hand. Imagine working with an expression that stretches over several screens—it is *not* unusual to be working with such huge structures. The tools provided in *ExpressionTools* go a long way towards alleviating these situations, in most cases freeing you from having to use the op command at all.

There are other built-in commands for investigating and manipulating Maple structures. The subsop command replaces a specified operand in an expression with a new subexpression. For example, to change the third operand of myexpr, -2.5, to -5/2, do the following:

> subsop(3=-5/2, myexpr);

$$3\frac{x^2}{y-2} + \sin\left(z + \frac{1}{3}\right) - \frac{5}{2}$$

Only first-level operands can be accessed with subsop. For a better, more flexible alternative, see the Utility command subsexpr.

The commands has and hastype allow you to search an expression's internal tree for an occurrence of either a specific subexpression or a specific *type* of subexpression.

> myexpr;

$$3\frac{x^2}{y-2} + \sin\left(z + \frac{1}{3}\right) - 2.5$$

> has(myexpr, x);

true

> has(myexpr, 1/3);

true

> hastype(myexpr, `^`);

true

> hastype(myexpr, list);

false

Again, the Utility commands showtype, whattypes, and findexpr build upon these facilities, providing much more flexible and powerful tools.

Some Words of Caution

Unfortunately, providing you with tools to facilitate exploration of large Maple structures does *not* free you from having to be aware of some "idiosyncrasies" in the way Maple creates and stores its structures. Some of the more unintuitive behaviors of Maple are demonstrated here and examples are given in the rest of this chapter to show how you might get tripped up if you are not careful.

The Zeroth Operand

One "oddity" in Maple that needs special attention is the concept of a *zeroth* operand. Most types of expression have a zeroth operand,[1] but usually this operand only contains type information—as can be found with whattype.

> myexpr;

$$3\frac{x^2}{y-2} + \sin\left(z + \frac{1}{3}\right) - 2.5$$

> op(0, myexpr);

$$+$$

There are data types where the zeroth operand contains special, needed information. The three types that fall into this category are function, series, and indexed. The following examples give you an idea of the structure of these data types.

> sin(57/58*Pi);

$$\sin\left(\frac{1}{58}\pi\right)$$

> op(");

$$\frac{1}{58}\pi$$

> op(0, "");

$$\sin$$

> series(exp(x), x=0);

$$1 + x + \frac{1}{2}x^2 + \frac{1}{6}x^3 + \frac{1}{24}x^4 + \frac{1}{120}x^5 + O(x^6)$$

> op(");

$$1, 0, 1, 1, \frac{1}{2}, 2, \frac{1}{6}, 3, \frac{1}{24}, 4, \frac{1}{120}, 5, O(1), 6$$

> op(0, "");

$$x$$

> fred[y+7];

$$fred_{y+7}$$

---

[1]Previous to Maple V Release 3, only a few data types had a zeroth operand.

```
> op(");
```
$$y + 7$$

```
> op(0, "");
```
$$\mathit{fred}$$

The commands in *ExpressionTools* ignore the existence of the zeroth operand, except in these three special cases.

Hidden −1s

Another Maple design decision that causes confusion is the existence of "hidden −1s." Take the following Maple expression for an example:

```
> anexpr := a - b;
```
$$anexpr := a - b$$

Does anexpr contain any integers? At first glimpse, you would say no; but that's not what the hastype command believes:

```
> hastype(anexpr, integer);
```
$$\mathit{true}$$

Use the op command to examine its internal structure.

```
> op(anexpr);
```
$$a, -b$$

```
> op(op(2, anexpr));
```
$$-1, b$$

```
> op(op(1, op(2, anexpr)));
```
$$-1$$

Maple stores -b as a product of -1 and b. At the same time, however, other "negative" values are not stored that way.

```
> has(a - 4, -1);
```
$$\mathit{false}$$

```
> has(a - 4.3, -1);
```
$$\mathit{false}$$

These "hidden −1s" can cause unexpected and usually undesired results if they are mistakenly lumped in with other −1s or general integers that you *can* see.

Negative Exponents

Another place where these unseen negative values occur is in rational values with unknowns in their denominators. Take a look at the following calls to has.

> has(a + 4/3, -1);

$$false$$

> has(a + b/3, -1);

$$false$$

> has(a + 4/b, -1);

$$true$$

> has(a + 4/b^2, -1);

$$false$$

What is going on here? The answer is that Maple stores the value 4/b as a product of 4 and 1/b. 1/b in turn is stored as the exponentiation of b and -1. Showing this in Maple commands:

> op(a + 4/b);

$$a, 4\frac{1}{b}$$

> whattype(op(2, a + 4/b));

$$*$$

> op(op(2, a + 4/b));

$$4, \frac{1}{b}$$

> whattype(op(2, op(2, a+4/b)));

$$\wedge$$

> op(op(2, op(2, a+4/b)));

$$b, -1$$

The lesson to be learned here is that you should *never* take for granted that what you see on the screen is representative of the way Maple stores an expression internally. The commands described in the following section provide you with simple ways of verifying these internal structures.

Utility Commands

The op command and its related tools can serve you well when dealing with small, simple expressions such as integer coefficient polynomials and the like. These Utility commands were designed to deal with larger, more complicated expressions, the type that are more likely to result from serious Maple calculations.

Visualizing the Structure

exprtree(expr)	view an expression's tree structure
isleaf(expr)	determine if an expression is indivisible
depth(expr)	determine a structure's maximal subexpression depth

In order to fully understand the DAG or *tree* structure of a Maple expression, it is necessary to view a pictorial representation of that structure. The exprtree command creates such a picture, using lprint statements stacked one upon the other. For more information on the complex algorithms used to create these tree representations, see the section *Programming Tips* on page 117.

Because it is easier to display a larger number of characters vertically, by scrolling the screen in that direction, than to do the same sort of thing horizontally, the result of exprtree is a tree whose root (or base) is to the left of the screen, and whose subsequent levels advance to the right.

Have a look at the result for myexpr, created earlier.

```
> with(utility):
```

```
> myexpr;
```

$$3\frac{x^2}{y-2} + \sin\left(z + \frac{1}{3}\right) - 2.5$$

```
> exprtree(myexpr);
            |--integer
     |--*--|
     |     |
     |     |     |--string
     |     |--^--|
     |     |     |--integer
     |     |
     |     |           |--string
     |     |     |--+--|
     |     |     |     |--integer
     |     |--^--|
```

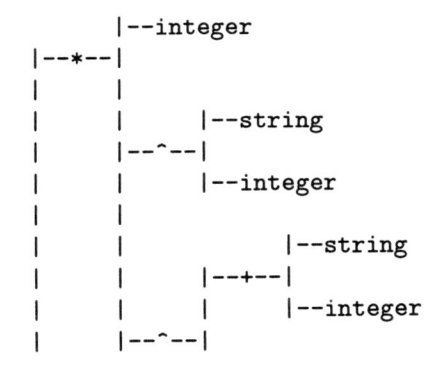

```
            |               |--integer
  +--|
     |                         |--string
     |               |--+--|
     |               |     |               |--integer
     |               |     |--fraction--|
     |               |                     |--integer
     |--function--|
     |
     |            |--integer
     |--float--|
                  |--integer
```

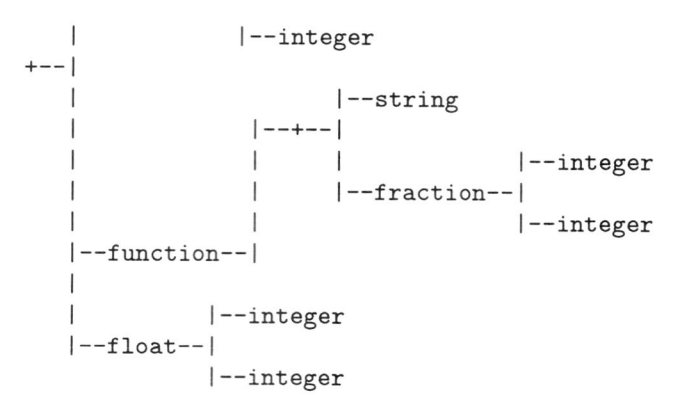

exprtree lists the types of each expression and subsequent subexpression in myexpr until types that cannot be broken down further (such as type integer, string)[2] are reached. The algorithms of exprtree automatically space the node of the tree so that there are no overlaps.[3]

The above result shows us that myexpr is, at its highest level, a sum of a product, a function, and a floating-point value. If you look at only the first operand, the product $3\frac{x^2}{y-2}$, in more detail you can see that it consists of three operands—an integer and two exponentiations (denoted by ^). In the same manner, you can travel up and down the rest of the tree structure.

As an exercise, what does the tree structure for exprtree tell us about Maple's internal representation of rational polynomials? Of a value such as $\frac{1}{y-2}$?

What if you want to know exactly what *value* corresponds to a certain *leaf* or endpoint of the tree? Supply exprtree with the optional parameter 'value'.

```
    > exprtree(myexpr, 'value');

                   |--(3)
          |--*--|
          |     |
          |     |       |--(x)
          |     |--^--|
          |     |       |--(2)
          |     |
          |     |                |--(y)
          |     |       |--+--|
          |     |       |     |--(-2)
```

---

[2]Actually, integer and string are the *only* two Maple types that cannot be broken down into smaller subexpressions.

[3]That is by far the most computationally intense task in exprtree, the lengthiest procedure in these Utilities.

```
            |      |--^--|
            |            |--(-1)
         +--|
            |                      |--(z)
            |            |--+--|
            |            |      |               |--(1)
            |            |      |--fraction--|
            |            |                      |--(3)
            |--(sin)--|
            |
            |            |--(-25)
            |--float--|
                         |--(-1)
```

If you compare closely the two previous tree representations of myexpr, you will see that it is not only the leaves that are replaced when the 'value' option is specified. The type name function in the second first-level operand is also replaced with sin, the actual function name. myexpr was designed in this way to provide access to the value of those special *zeroth* operands.[4]

Make sure that you don't mistake the optional parameter 'value' with the built-in Maple command value. Using the single forward quotes keeps them straight.

Another optional parameter for myexpr is 'numbered', which inserts the numbers of each operand and suboperand (prepended with the # character) into the tree structure. This is particularly useful when dealing with expressions with many operands on different levels.

```
> exprtree(myexpr, 'numbered');
                 |-#1-integer
     |-#1-*--|
     |        |
     |        |          |-#1-string
     |        |-#2-^--|
     |        |          |-#2-integer
     |        |
     |        |                    |-#1-string
     |        |          |-#1-+--|
     |        |          |        |-#2-integer
     |        |-#3-^--|
     |                   |-#2-integer
  +--|
     |                              |-#1-string
     |                    |-#1-+--|
     |          |-#1-+--|
```

---

[4]Therefore, type names series and indexed also get replaced with their values when 'value' is specified.

```
                |               |               |-#1-integer
                |               |-#2-fraction--|
                |               |               |-#2-integer
|-#2-function--|
                |
                |               |-#1-integer
                |-#3-float--|
                                |-#2-integer
```

Of course, these optional parameters can be combined.

```
> exprtree(myexpr, 'value', 'numbered');

            |-#1-(3)
|-#1-*--|
        |
        |               |-#1-(x)
        |-#2-^--|
        |       |-#2-(2)
        |
        |                       |-#1-(y)
        |               |-#1-+--|
        |               |       |-#2-(-2)
        |-#3-^--|
        |       |-#2-(-1)
+--|
    |                   |-#1-(z)
    |           |-#1-+--|
    |           |       |               |-#1-(1)
    |           |       |-#2-fraction--|
    |           |                       |-#2-(3)
    |-#2-(sin)--|
    |
    |           |-#1-(-25)
    |-#3-float--|
                |-#2-(-1)
```

But myexpr is a simple example, chosen for illustrative purposes; now try something more ambitious.

```
> newexpr := int(1/(1+x^4), x);
```

$newexpr :=$

$$\frac{1}{8}\sqrt{2}\ln\left(\frac{x^2+x\sqrt{2}+1}{x^2-x\sqrt{2}+1}\right) + \frac{1}{4}\sqrt{2}\arctan\left(x\sqrt{2}+1\right) + \frac{1}{4}\sqrt{2}\arctan\left(x\sqrt{2}-1\right)$$

```
> exprtree(newexpr);
                               |--integer
              |--fraction--|
              |               |--integer
    |--*--|
    |     |
    |     |         |--integer
    |     |--^--|
    |     |     |             |--integer
    |     |     |--fraction--|
    |     |                   |--integer
    |     |
    |     |                              |--string
    |     |                        |--^--|
    |     |                        |     |--integer
    |     |                  |--+--|
    |     |                  |     |
    |     |                  |     |        |--string
    |     |                  |     |--*--|
    |     |                  |     |     |        |--integer
    |     |                  |     |     |--^--|
    |     |                  |     |     |     |              |--integer
    |     |                  |     |     |     |--fraction--|
    |     |                  |     |     |                    |--integer
    |     |                  |     |
    |     |                  |     |--integer
    |     |            |--*--|
    |     |            |     |                    |--string
    |     |            |     |              |--^--|
    |     |            |     |              |     |--integer
    |     |            |     |        |--+--|
    |     |            |     |        |     |
    |     |            |     |        |     |--integer
    |     |            |     |        |--*--|
    |     |            |     |        |     |
    |     |            |     |        |     |--string
    |     |            |     |        |     |
    |     |            |     |        |     |              |--integer
    |     |            |     |        |     |--^--|
    |     |            |     |        |     |     |              |--integer
    |     |            |     |        |     |     |--fraction--|
    |     |            |     |        |     |                    |--integer
    |     |            |     |        |
    |     |            |     |        |--integer
    |     |            |     |--^--|
```

```
            |          |          |            |--integer
            |          |--function--|
     +--|
            |                      |--integer
            |          |--fraction--|
            |          |            |--integer
     |--*--|
            |          |
            |          |            |--integer
            |          |--^--|
            |          |     |            |--integer
            |          |     |--fraction--|
            |          |                  |--integer
            |          |
            |          |                        |--string
            |          |            |--*--|
            |          |            |     |            |--integer
            |          |            |     |--^--|
            |          |            |     |     |            |--integer
            |          |            |     |     |--fraction--|
            |          |            |     |                  |--integer
            |          |            |
            |          |            |--+--|
            |          |                  |--integer
            |          |--function--|
            |
            |                      |--integer
            |          |--fraction--|
            |          |            |--integer
     |--*--|
                       |
                       |            |--integer
                       |--^--|
                       |     |            |--integer
                       |     |--fraction--|
                       |                  |--integer
                       |
                       |                        |--string
                       |            |--*--|
                       |            |     |            |--integer
                       |            |     |--^--|
                       |            |     |     |            |--integer
                       |            |     |     |--fraction--|
                       |            |     |                  |--integer
                       |            |
                       |            |--+--|
                       |                  |--integer
                       |--function--|
```

This example shows how very quickly the complexity of Maple expressions grows. Imagine the tree for a much larger expression. When complete trees will obviously be too large to display, a non-negative integer value can be given to limit the depth to which the tree is explored.[5] For example, given the value 3, exprtree only advances three levels of subexpressions within the given expression.

```
> exprtree(newexpr, 3, 'numbered');

                                        |-#1-integer
                      |-#1-fraction--|
                      |                 |-#2-integer
      |-#1-*--|
      |       |                 |-#1-integer
      |       |-#2-^--|
      |       |                 |-#2-fraction--|
      |       |                                |-#1-*--|
      |       |-#3-function--|
  +--|
      |                                |-#1-integer
      |       |-#1-fraction--|
      |       |                 |-#2-integer
      |-#2-*--|
      |       |                 |-#1-integer
      |       |-#2-^--|
      |       |                 |-#2-fraction--|
      |       |                                |-#1-+--|
      |       |-#3-function--|
      |
      |                                |-#1-integer
      |       |-#1-fraction--|
      |       |                 |-#2-integer
      |-#3-*--|
              |                 |-#1-integer
              |-#2-^--|
              |                 |-#2-fraction--|
              |                                |-#1-+--|
              |-#3-function--|
```

---

[5]This depth option cannot be used in conjunction with the 'value' option.

A branch of the tree ending in the characters --| means that the tree has been "truncated" at that point (i.e., there are more undisplayed levels below).

Using the results of exprtree, you can determine what combination of op commands is necessary to extract a particular subexpression. For example, $x\sqrt{2} + 1$ is the first operand of the third operand of the second operand of newexpr. As a Maple command:

```
> op(1, op(3, op(2, newexpr)));
```
$$x\sqrt{2} + 1$$

This is still a somewhat unwieldy way to pick apart large expressions. A more intuitive way is given in the section *Accessing Subexpressions* on page 101.

Two other simpler tools which are also provided are isleaf and depth. As its name implies, isleaf takes an expression and determines whether or not it is indivisible; i.e., whether it would be at the end of one of the branches displayed by exprtree.

```
> isleaf(myexpr);
```
false

```
> isleaf(3.2);
```
false

```
> isleaf(32);
```
true

Since only objects of type integer and string are truly indivisible, isleaf is very much like a structured type command.

The depth command takes an expression and travels its tree structure, keeping track of the maximal subexpression depth encountered.

```
> depth(myexpr);
```
$$4$$

```
> depth(newexpr);
```
$$9$$

Searching for Particular Expression Types

whattypes(expr)	find all the types present in an expression
showtype(typename, expr)	find *all* subexpressions of a particular type

The commands whattypes and showtype are used for locating particular classes or *types* of subexpressions. This can be helpful in understanding how Maple sees expressions internally.

whattypes is an extension of the built-in Maple command whattype. As noted earlier, whattype takes a Maple expression and determines its type at the highest possible level (i.e., *not* the type(s) of its subexpressions). whattypes, on the other hand, returns a set containing all the *basic data types* present in an expression at *all* levels.

> myexpr;

$$3\frac{x^2}{y-2} + \sin\left(z + \frac{1}{3}\right) - 2.5$$

> whattypes(myexpr);

$$\{+, \textit{integer}, *, \hat{\,}, \textit{float}, \textit{string}, \textit{fraction}, \textit{function}\}$$

To come up with its results, whattypes explores all the branches and leaves in the tree structure of an expression. A list of basic data types is available by entering ?whattype.

Keep in mind that there are other sorts of data types, called *structured data types*, that can be tested for as well. whattypes does not return these types. For example, the type polynom represents a polynomial, and while it is not included in the above result, the built-in command hastype shows that myexpr does indeed contain a polynomial.

> hastype(myexpr, polynom);

true

For more information on basic and structured types, see the on-line help pages for type and type[structured].

whattypes can also take some optional parameters. If a non-negative integer, *n*, is supplied, the search for types is only carried out to the nth level of the expression. As with exprtree, supplying 0 examines only the expression as a whole. If the parameter 'count' is given, then a set of *two-element lists* is returned. The first element of each list is a positive integer representing frequency, and the second element is a set of type names which all occur with that frequency.[6]

> whattypes(myexpr, 'count');

$$[[8, \{\textit{integer}\}], [3, \{+, \textit{string}\}], [2, \{\hat{\,}\}], [1, \{*, \textit{float}, \textit{fraction}, \textit{function}\}]]$$

---

[6]The resulting list is in the same format as that returned by the frequency command in ListTools.

The command showtype is a more highly focussed version of whattypes. Given an expression and a particular type name (which can be a basic or structured type), showtype returns a set of all the subexpressions of that type present. Using the larger expression newexpr, you can find all its fractions.

> newexpr;

$$\frac{1}{8}\sqrt{2}\ln\left(\frac{x^2 + x\sqrt{2} + 1}{x^2 - x\sqrt{2} + 1}\right) + \frac{1}{4}\sqrt{2}\arctan\left(x\sqrt{2} + 1\right) + \frac{1}{4}\sqrt{2}\arctan\left(x\sqrt{2} - 1\right)$$

> showtype(fraction, ");

$$\left\{\frac{1}{2}, \frac{1}{8}, \frac{1}{4}\right\}$$

Where does the value of $\frac{1}{2}$ come from? Again, it is a case of the way Maple displays an expression being different from how it is stored internally. Examine the following:

> op(sqrt(2));

$$2, \frac{1}{2}$$

By returning a *set* of values, showtype pares down the multiple occurrences of the fractions $\frac{1}{2}$ and $\frac{1}{4}$ to only one entry each.

The optional parameters for showtype are similar to those for whattypes, but have subtle differences. If a non-negative integer, n, is supplied, the search for examples of the particular type is only continued until n *unique* subexpressions are found. The search for subexpressions is conducted using a *depth-first* method.[7] If the parameter 'count' is given, then a set of *two-element lists* is returned. The first element of each list is a positive integer representing frequency, and the second element is a set of subexpressions of the desired type all of which occur with that frequency. While the two optional parameters of whattypes can be used in unison, only one optional parameter can be used in each call to showtype.

> showtype(fraction, newexpr, 'count');

$$\left[\left[7, \left\{\frac{1}{2}\right\}\right], \left[2, \left\{\frac{1}{4}\right\}\right], \left[1, \left\{\frac{1}{8}\right\}\right]\right]$$

---

[7]For more information on depth-first searches, see the *Programming Tips* section later in this chapter.

```
> showtype('*', newexpr, 4);
```

$$\left\{ x\sqrt{2}, \frac{x^2 + x\sqrt{2} + 1}{x^2 - x\sqrt{2} + 1}, -x\sqrt{2}, \frac{1}{8}\sqrt{2}\ln\left(\frac{x^2 + x\sqrt{2} + 1}{x^2 - x\sqrt{2} + 1}\right) \right\}$$

The result of the last call to showtype illustrates that results of this command can easily be wholly contained one within another.

Accessing Subexpressions

findexpr(subexpr, expr)	locate a subexpression within the tree structure
type(expr, loclist)	determine if a locator list is valid for an expression
showexpr(llist, expr, n)	extract a subexpression given a locator list
markexpr(llist, expr, n)	mark a subexpression within its parent expression
findtype(typename, expr)	locate a subexpression of a particular type

All of the work you have been doing in this chapter has been leading up to the use of the commands findexpr, showexpr, and markexpr. These are the commands that will prove the most useful to you in your exploration of Maple structures. They eliminate the need to use the op command and its built-in companions when dealing with large expressions.

The commands in this section are meant to be used together. For example, rarely will you use showexpr or markexpr without having used findexpr first. Because of the inter-connectivity of these commands, their functionality is described not one command at a time, but as you would learn them through constructive use. Because of this, you will need to read through this entire section to determine the *full* functionality of any one of the commands.

Before going into details, use Maple to create a result that is complicated and difficult to handle with the built-in tools.

```
> Int((x+exp(a*(x+b)))/(x^8),x);
```

$$\int \frac{x + e^{(a(x+b))}}{x^8}\, dx$$

```
> largeexpr := value(");
```

$$largeexpr := \left(\frac{\frac{1}{7}\dfrac{ab}{(-a(x+b)+ab)^7} - \frac{1}{6}\dfrac{1}{(-a(x+b)+ab)^6}}{a}\right) + \frac{1}{7}\frac{b}{(a(x+b)-ab)^7}$$
$$-\frac{1}{7}\frac{e^{(a(x+b))}}{(a(x+b)-ab)^7} - \frac{1}{42}\frac{e^{(a(x+b))}}{(a(x+b)-ab)^6} - \frac{1}{210}\frac{e^{(a(x+b))}}{(a(x+b)-ab)^5}$$

$$-\frac{1}{840}\frac{e^{(a(x+b))}}{(a(x+b)-ab)^4} - \frac{1}{2520}\frac{e^{(a(x+b))}}{(a(x+b)-ab)^3} - \frac{1}{5040}\frac{e^{(a(x+b))}}{(a(x+b)-ab)^2}$$

$$\left. -\frac{1}{5040}\frac{e^{(a(x+b))}}{a(x+b)-ab} - \frac{1}{5040}e^{(ab)}\operatorname{Ei}(1,-a(x+b)+ab) \right) a^7$$

This is an interesting result; many of the terms in the main summation have the subexpression $a(b+x) - ab$ in their denominator. Suppose that you are particularly interested in the term that has this value raised to the power 5. How can you extract that subexpression and do further work with it?

- You could examine the subexpression on the screen and attempt to retype it in from scratch. But that is prone to errors, especially when you are dealing with even larger subexpressions.

- You could try to find out, using exprtree, precisely which internal operand this subexpression is, and then construct a complicated op command to extract it. But this would be no quicker or easier than retyping the whole thing.

How did you visually find this subexpression? Probably, first the $(a(b+x) - ab)^5$ value caught your eye, and then you expanded from there to see the term in which it was contained. The Utility commands we have created work in much the same way.

First, use findexpr to determine the location of $(a(b+x) - ab)^5$.

> findexpr((a*(b+x) - a*b)^5, largeexpr);

$$[\,]$$

No such subexpression was found. This is because findexpr can only search for subexpressions that are specified exactly as Maple stores them internally. Earlier you saw that Maple stores rational expressions with unknowns as the product of the numerator and one over the denominator, or $\frac{1}{(a(b+x)-ab)^5}$ in this case. Now try findexpr again, using the new search criteria.

> llist := findexpr(1/(a*(b+x) - a*b)^5, largeexpr);

$$llist := [3, 5, 1]$$

The result is a list of positive integers. This list is called a *locator list* and contains (in reverse order) the integer values that would be contained in the complicated nested op command to extract that exact subexpression.

An extension of the built-in type command has been provided to determine whether a given list is a valid candidate to be a locator list.

```
> type([3,5,1], loclist);
```

true

In this form, the first parameter is simply determined to be a list of *any* positive integers. This list still may or may not make sense combined with certain expressions. An extension to the loclist parameter can be used to see if the given locator list is valid for a specific expression.

```
> type([3,5,1], loclist(largeexpr));
```

true

```
> type([3,5,1], loclist(x^2+3));
```

false

Getting back to using the locator list returned by findexpr, it is not really necessary to understand how to convert it into an op command, because the command showexpr is provided to do this for you.

```
> showexpr(llist, largeexpr);
```

$$\frac{1}{(a(x+b)-ab)^5}$$

Of course, doing all this just to find $\frac{1}{(a(b+x)-ab)^5}$ doesn't make much sense—you had to type that entire subexpression into findexpr in the first place. But remember that what you were really interested in was finding the *term* in the main sum of largeexpr that *contained* $(a(b+x)-ab)^5$. Using the model of a tree structure, this term would be found by traveling "up" the tree[8] a few levels. A third parameter can be passed to showexpr to specify the number of levels you want to ascend.

```
> showexpr(llist, largeexpr, 1);
```

$$-\frac{1}{210}\frac{e^{(a(x+b))}}{(a(x+b)-ab)^5}$$

There is your term. You can now assign it to some name and do further work with it. Is there any easier way to find the same term? It still seems as if you are typing a lot of Maple syntax within the findexpr command.

Looking at the expression as a whole, you see that our desired term contains the only occurrence of the integer 210. Use that subexpression to extract the term.

---

[8]Or to the left in the tree representation created by exprtree.

```
> findexpr(210, largeexpr);
```

$$[2,1,5,1]$$

```
> showexpr(", largeexpr, 3);
```

$$\frac{1}{7}\frac{ab}{(-a(x+b)+ab)^7} - \frac{1}{6}\frac{1}{(-a(x+b)+ab)^6} + \frac{1}{7}\frac{b}{(a(x+b)-ab)^7}$$
$$- \frac{1}{7}\frac{e^{(a(x+b))}}{(a(x+b)-ab)^7} - \frac{1}{42}\frac{e^{(a(x+b))}}{(a(x+b)-ab)^6} - \frac{1}{210}\frac{e^{(a(x+b))}}{(a(x+b)-ab)^5}$$
$$- \frac{1}{840}\frac{e^{(a(x+b))}}{(a(x+b)-ab)^4} - \frac{1}{2520}\frac{e^{(a(x+b))}}{(a(x+b)-ab)^3} - \frac{1}{5040}\frac{e^{(a(x+b))}}{(a(x+b)-ab)^2}$$
$$- \frac{1}{5040}\frac{e^{(a(x+b))}}{a(x+b)-ab} - \frac{1}{5040}e^{(ab)}\text{Ei}(1, -a(x+b)+ab)$$

What happened here? You obviously went too far up the expression tree.

```
> showexpr("", largeexpr, 2);
```

$$-\frac{1}{210}\frac{e^{(a(x+b))}}{(a(x+b)-ab)^5}$$

Getting completely comfortable with the combination of the findexpr and showexpr tools takes a little effort; but they are so powerful that it is well worth the time.

You can also use findexpr to find *multiple* occurrences of specific subexpressions. By default, findexpr returns only the first occurrence.[9]

```
> findexpr(5040, largeexpr);
```

$$[2,1,8,1]$$

By adding a positive integer value as the third parameter (much as in showtype in the previous section), the first *n* appropriate locator lists are returned within another list.

```
> findexpr(5040, largeexpr, 2);
```

$$[[2,1,8,1],[2,1,9,1]]$$

The value infinity can be used to ensure that locator lists for *all* occurrences are returned.

---

[9]That is, as found by a *depth-first* search.

```
> allocc := findexpr(5040, largeexpr, infinity);
```
$$allocc := [[2,1,8,1],[2,1,9,1],[2,1,10,1]]$$

Each internal list is a locator list for a specific occurrence of the subexpression. (The lists are presented in the order they were found in the depth-first search.)

showexpr can then be used to display all the relevant subexpressions.

```
> showexpr(allocc, largeexpr);
```
$$[5040, 5040, 5040]$$

Of course, that combination of parameters in showtype doesn't provide you with any new information. Adding a third parameter to go up some levels does.

```
> showexpr(allocc, largeexpr, 2);
```
$$\left[-\frac{1}{5040} \frac{e^{(a(x+b))}}{(a(x+b)-ab)^2}, -\frac{1}{5040} \frac{e^{(a(x+b))}}{a(x+b)-ab}, \right.$$
$$\left. -\frac{1}{5040} e^{(ab)} \operatorname{Ei}(1, -a(x+b)+ab) \right]$$

One of the foremost reasons for using the multiple occurrence option of findexpr is that, in large enough expressions, you might not be able to find any subexpression of the particular subexpression you are interested in that is unique within the entire expression.

Once you have computed the list of locator lists, you can use showexpr (as demonstrated above) to determine which of the multiple occurrences you were specifically searching for, or you can use markexpr to redisplay the entire expression with the specific subexpressions enclosed in a call to the non-existent MARK command.

```
> markexpr(allocc, largeexpr);
```
$$\left(\frac{\frac{1}{7} \frac{ab}{(-a(x+b)+ab)^7} - \frac{1}{6} \frac{1}{(-a(x+b)+ab)^6}}{a} + \frac{1}{7} \frac{b}{(a(x+b)-ab)^7} \right.$$
$$-\frac{1}{7} \frac{e^{(a(x+b))}}{(a(x+b)-ab)^7} - \frac{1}{42} \frac{e^{(a(x+b))}}{(a(x+b)-ab)^6} - \frac{1}{210} \frac{e^{(a(x+b))}}{(a(x+b)-ab)^5}$$
$$-\frac{1}{840} \frac{e^{(a(x+b))}}{(a(x+b)-ab)^4} - \frac{1}{2520} \frac{e^{(a(x+b))}}{(a(x+b)-ab)^3}$$
$$-\frac{e^{(a(x+b))}}{\operatorname{MARK}(5040)(a(x+b)-ab)^2} - \frac{e^{(a(x+b))}}{\operatorname{MARK}(5040)(a(x+b)-ab)}$$

$$-\frac{e^{(ab)}\operatorname{Ei}(1,-a(x+b)+ab)}{\operatorname{MARK}(5040)}\Bigg)a^7$$

markexpr can also take the previously discussed positive integer parameter to back up the structure tree n levels before performing the marking.

```
> markexpr(allocc, largeexpr, 2);
```

$$\Bigg(\frac{\frac{1}{7}\frac{ab}{(-a(x+b)+ab)^7} - \frac{1}{6}\frac{1}{(-a(x+b)+ab)^6}}{a} + \frac{1}{7}\frac{b}{(a(x+b)-ab)^7}$$

$$-\frac{1}{7}\frac{e^{(a(x+b))}}{(a(x+b)-ab)^7} - \frac{1}{42}\frac{e^{(a(x+b))}}{(a(x+b)-ab)^6} - \frac{1}{210}\frac{e^{(a(x+b))}}{(a(x+b)-ab)^5}$$

$$-\frac{1}{840}\frac{e^{(a(x+b))}}{(a(x+b)-ab)^4} - \frac{1}{2520}\frac{e^{(a(x+b))}}{(a(x+b)-ab)^3}$$

$$+\operatorname{MARK}\left(-\frac{1}{5040}\frac{e^{(a(x+b))}}{(a(x+b)-ab)^2}\right) + \operatorname{MARK}\left(-\frac{1}{5040}\frac{e^{(a(x+b))}}{a(x+b)-ab}\right)$$

$$+\operatorname{MARK}\left(-\frac{1}{5040}e^{(ab)}\operatorname{Ei}(1,-a(x+b)+ab)\right)\Bigg)a^7$$

In this example, you can easily count along the markers to choose a particular one. For example, if you are interested in the term containing the second 5040, then it can be extracted with:

```
> showexpr(allocc[2], largeexpr, 2);
```

$$-\frac{1}{5040}\frac{e^{(a(x+b))}}{a(x+b)-ab}$$

Unfortunately, in much larger expressions (which take up pages and pages) it may not be as easy to manually count along. In that case, markexpr can take the option 'numbered', which indicates that the values 1, 2, ... are to be appended to the name MARK.

```
> markexpr(allocc, largeexpr, 2, 'numbered');
```

$$\Bigg(\frac{\frac{1}{7}\frac{ab}{(-a(x+b)+ab)^7} - \frac{1}{6}\frac{1}{(-a(x+b)+ab)^6}}{a} + \frac{1}{7}\frac{b}{(a(x+b)-ab)^7}$$

$$-\frac{1}{7}\frac{e^{(a(x+b))}}{(a(x+b)-ab)^7} - \frac{1}{42}\frac{e^{(a(x+b))}}{(a(x+b)-ab)^6} - \frac{1}{210}\frac{e^{(a(x+b))}}{(a(x+b)-ab)^5}$$

$$-\frac{1}{840}\frac{e^{(a(x+b))}}{(a(x+b)-ab)^4} - \frac{1}{2520}\frac{e^{(a(x+b))}}{(a(x+b)-ab)^3}$$

$$+ \text{MARK1}\left(-\frac{1}{5040}\frac{e^{(a(x+b))}}{(a(x+b)-ab)^2}\right) + \text{MARK2}\left(-\frac{1}{5040}\frac{e^{(a(x+b))}}{a(x+b)-ab}\right)$$

$$+ \text{MARK3}\left(-\frac{1}{5040}e^{(ab)}\text{Ei}(1,-a(x+b)+ab)\right)\Bigg)a^7$$

The numbers displayed correspond directly to the locator lists in allocc.

```
> showexpr(allocc[3], largeexpr, 2);
```

$$-\frac{1}{5040}e^{(ab)}\text{Ei}(1,-a(x+b)+ab)$$

One final parameter allows you to change the unevaluated function name if you don't want to use MARK.

```
> markexpr(allocc, largeexpr, 2, 'Term', 'numbered');
```

$$\left(\frac{1}{7}\frac{ab}{(-a(x+b)+ab)^7} - \frac{1}{6}\frac{1}{(-a(x+b)+ab)^6} + \frac{1}{7}\frac{b}{(a(x+b)-ab)^7}\right)$$

$$-\frac{1}{7}\frac{e^{(a(x+b))}}{(a(x+b)-ab)^7} - \frac{1}{42}\frac{e^{(a(x+b))}}{(a(x+b)-ab)^6} - \frac{1}{210}\frac{e^{(a(x+b))}}{(a(x+b)-ab)^5}$$

$$-\frac{1}{840}\frac{e^{(a(x+b))}}{(a(x+b)-ab)^4} - \frac{1}{2520}\frac{e^{(a(x+b))}}{(a(x+b)-ab)^3}$$

$$+ \text{Term1}\left(-\frac{1}{5040}\frac{e^{(a(x+b))}}{(a(x+b)-ab)^2}\right) + \text{Term2}\left(-\frac{1}{5040}\frac{e^{(a(x+b))}}{a(x+b)-ab}\right)$$

$$+ \text{Term3}\left(-\frac{1}{5040}e^{(ab)}\text{Ei}(1,-a(x+b)+ab)\right)\Bigg)a^7$$

There is yet another way to home in on a particular subexpression. Even if that subexpression does not contain any *one* further subexpression that is unique to itself, it may contain a *combination* of subexpressions that separates it from all others. For example, observe what supplying the following list of subexpressions produces in findexpr.

```
> findexpr([7, exp(a*(x+b))], largeexpr);
```

$$[3,1]$$

> showexpr(", largeexpr);

$$-\frac{1}{7}\frac{e^{(a(x+b))}}{(a(x+b)-ab)^7}$$

Notice that the above call to showexpr does not contain the third parameter n. This is to demonstrate that when given a list of subexpressions, findexpr searches for the smallest proper subexpression such that *all* the given values are contained within. The 7 present in the exponent is stored internally as a -7, so findexpr uses the 7 found in $-\frac{1}{7}$. The smallest subexpression that has both that 7 and $e^{a(x+b)}$ within it is the entire term we were searching for.

The last command in this section, findtype, is identical in operation to findexpr, except that it searches for subexpressions that are of a specific *type* instead of those of an exactly specified value. For example, to find the first fraction in largeexpr call

> findtype(fraction, largeexpr);

$$[1,1,1,1,1]$$

The result is a locator list which specifies a subexpression. Therefore, the command showexpr can be used on it.

> showexpr(", largeexpr);

$$\frac{1}{7}$$

All the optional parameters that are valid for findexpr can also be used in findtype.

> findtype('^', largeexpr, 5);

$$[[4,1,1,1,1],[2,2,1,1,1],[2,1,1],[2,2,1],[3,3,1]]$$

> markexpr(", largeexpr, 'numbered');

$$\left(\left(\frac{1}{7}ab\,\text{MARK1}\left(\frac{1}{(-a(x+b)+ab)^7}\right)-\frac{1}{6}\text{MARK2}\left(\frac{1}{(-a(x+b)+ab)^6}\right)\right)\right)$$

$$\text{MARK3}\left(\frac{1}{a}\right)+\frac{1}{7}\text{MARK4}\left(\frac{1}{(a(x+b)-ab)^7}\right)b$$

$$-\frac{1}{7}e^{(a(x+b))}\text{MARK5}\left(\frac{1}{(a(x+b)-ab)^7}\right)-\frac{1}{42}\frac{e^{(a(x+b))}}{(a(x+b)-ab)^6}$$

$$-\frac{1}{210}\frac{e^{(a(x+b))}}{(a(x+b)-ab)^5}-\frac{1}{840}\frac{e^{(a(x+b))}}{(a(x+b)-ab)^4}-\frac{1}{2520}\frac{e^{(a(x+b))}}{(a(x+b)-ab)^3}$$

$$-\frac{1}{5040}\frac{e^{(a(x+b))}}{(a(x+b)-ab)^2} - \frac{1}{5040}\frac{e^{(a(x+b))}}{a(x+b)-ab}$$

$$\left. -\frac{1}{5040}e^{(ab)}\operatorname{Ei}(1,-a(x+b)+ab)\right)a^7$$

Notice that the *a* in the denominator of the first large fraction of largeexpr has been pulled out to become the third expression of type '⌢' marked.

```
> findtype([function, fraction], largeexpr);
```

$$[9,1]$$

```
> showexpr(", largeexpr);
```

$$-\frac{1}{5040}\frac{e^{(a(x+b))}}{a(x+b)-ab}$$

Replacing Subexpressions

subsexpr(llist = subexpr$_{new}$, expr)	substitute for a subexpression defined by a locator list
mapexpr(fnc, [llist$_1$, ..., llist$_n$], expr)	map a function onto selected subexpressions

In the previous section, you learned how to compute *locator lists* which pinpoint the location of a subexpression in a larger expression, and how to make use of those lists in commands like showexpr and markexpr to extract and display some desired value.

Another obvious use of the information in locator lists is to alter the value of the larger expression by substituting a new value in for the specified subexpressions. While there are several built-in tools in Maple for making substitutions, there are some specialized tasks that cannot be done easily with these tools. The Utility commands subsexpr and mapexpr were designed to fill in these gaps.

First, a review of the existing commands. The subs command searches for *every* occurrence at *all* levels of a given subexpression in the larger expression and switches them with a new value. This may be the the most common kind of substitution that you will do.

```
> subs(x+b=x, largeexpr);
```

$$\left(\frac{\frac{1}{7}\frac{ab}{(-ax+ab)^7} - \frac{1}{6}\frac{1}{(-ax+ab)^6}}{a} + \frac{1}{7}\frac{b}{(ax-ab)^7} - \frac{1}{7}\frac{e^{(ax)}}{(ax-ab)^7} - \frac{1}{42}\frac{e^{(ax)}}{(ax-ab)^6}\right.$$

$$-\frac{1}{210}\frac{e^{(ax)}}{(ax-ab)^5} - \frac{1}{840}\frac{e^{(ax)}}{(ax-ab)^4} - \frac{1}{2520}\frac{e^{(ax)}}{(ax-ab)^3} - \frac{1}{5040}\frac{e^{(ax)}}{(ax-ab)^2}$$

$$-\frac{1}{5040}\frac{e^{(ax)}}{ax-ab} - \frac{1}{5040}e^{(ab)}\text{Ei}(1,-ax+ab)\bigg)a^7$$

Unfortunately, there is no way to specify that you only want a *one particular* occurrence of a subexpression to be switched.

The subsop command has a syntax very similar to subs, except that the left-hand side of the first parameter equation must be a non-negative integer value. subsop then switches the *first-level* operand of the expression that corresponds to this integer value with the new value. This allows you to circumvent some of the shortcomings of subs, as the following example shows.

> 3*x^2 - x - 7;

$$3x^2 - x - 7$$

> subsop(2=y, "");

$$3x^2 + y - 7$$

One particular x has been changed. Unfortunately, subsop only works on first-level operands. This means that if you want to switch the x in $3x^2$, you must enter the entire new subexpression, instead of just y.

> subsop(1=3*y^2, "");

$$3y^2 - x - 7$$

For such a small subexpression, retyping is not a problem, but imagine trying to use the same command on one particular $x + b$ in largeexpr.[10]

subsexpr takes care of many of these problems. In its simplest form, subsexpr replaces a subexpression that is completely determined by a locator list (as found by findexpr). For example, take another look at largeexpr.

> largeexpr;

$$\bigg(\frac{1}{7}\frac{ab}{(-a(x+b)+ab)^7} - \frac{1}{6}\frac{1}{(-a(x+b)+ab)^6} + \frac{1}{7}\frac{b}{(a(x+b)-ab)^7}$$

$$-\frac{1}{7}\frac{e^{(a(x+b))}}{(a(x+b)-ab)^7} - \frac{1}{42}\frac{e^{(a(x+b))}}{(a(x+b)-ab)^6} - \frac{1}{210}\frac{e^{(a(x+b))}}{(a(x+b)-ab)^5}$$

---

[10]More information on the subs commands, its uses, its shortcomings, and how the Utilities deal with them is available throughout the *PatternTools* chapter.

$$-\frac{1}{840}\frac{e^{(a(x+b))}}{(a(x+b)-ab)^4}-\frac{1}{2520}\frac{e^{(a(x+b))}}{(a(x+b)-ab)^3}-\frac{1}{5040}\frac{e^{(a(x+b))}}{(a(x+b)-ab)^2}$$
$$-\frac{1}{5040}\frac{e^{(a(x+b))}}{a(x+b)-ab}-\frac{1}{5040}e^{(ab)}\operatorname{Ei}(1,-a(x+b)+ab)\bigg)a^7$$

Say you want to replace the numerator $e^{a(x+b)}$ of the term with the $-\frac{1}{42}$ constant with the variable c. First, use findexpr to create locator lists for all the occurrences of $e^{a(x+b)}$.

> `loclists := findexpr(exp(a*(x + b)), largeexpr, infinity);`

$$loclists := [[2,3,1],[2,4,1],[2,5,1],[2,6,1],[2,7,1],[2,8,1],[2,9,1]]$$

By visual methods, you can see that the $e^{a(x+b)}$ you want is the second one in largeexpr, so use that one in subsexpr.

> `subsexpr(loclists[2] = c, largeexpr);`

$$\Bigg(\frac{\frac{1}{7}\frac{ab}{(-a(x+b)+ab)^7}-\frac{1}{6}\frac{1}{(-a(x+b)+ab)^6}}{a}+\frac{1}{7}\frac{b}{(a(x+b)-ab)^7}$$
$$-\frac{1}{7}\frac{e^{(a(x+b))}}{(a(x+b)-ab)^7}-\frac{1}{42}\frac{c}{(a(x+b)-ab)^6}-\frac{1}{210}\frac{e^{(a(x+b))}}{(a(x+b)-ab)^5}$$
$$-\frac{1}{840}\frac{e^{(a(x+b))}}{(a(x+b)-ab)^4}-\frac{1}{2520}\frac{e^{(a(x+b))}}{(a(x+b)-ab)^3}-\frac{1}{5040}\frac{e^{(a(x+b))}}{(a(x+b)-ab)^2}$$
$$-\frac{1}{5040}\frac{e^{(a(x+b))}}{a(x+b)-ab}-\frac{1}{5040}e^{(ab)}\operatorname{Ei}(1,-a(x+b)+ab)\Bigg)a^7$$

If you are unable to tell which locator list you need by viewing the entire expression, the command markexpr with the optional parameter 'numbered' can be very helpful.

Once you are comfortable with all the expression tools, you will be able to make a substitution for a large subexpression with very few command calls. For example, to replace the last term in the greatest sum in largeexpr (i.e., the one containing e^{ab}) with the value $\frac{\pi}{20}$, you could use the following two commands.

> `myll := findexpr(exp(a*b), largeexpr);`

$$myll := [2,10,1]$$

> subsexpr(myll=Pi/20, largeexpr, 1);

$$\left(\frac{1}{7}\frac{ab}{(-a(x+b)+ab)^7} - \frac{1}{6}\frac{1}{(-a(x+b)+ab)^6} + \frac{1}{7}\frac{b}{(a(x+b)-ab)^7}\right.$$
$$- \frac{1}{7}\frac{e^{(a(x+b))}}{(a(x+b)-ab)^7} - \frac{1}{42}\frac{e^{(a(x+b))}}{(a(x+b)-ab)^6} - \frac{1}{210}\frac{e^{(a(x+b))}}{(a(x+b)-ab)^5}$$
$$- \frac{1}{840}\frac{e^{(a(x+b))}}{(a(x+b)-ab)^4} - \frac{1}{2520}\frac{e^{(a(x+b))}}{(a(x+b)-ab)^3} - \frac{1}{5040}\frac{e^{(a(x+b))}}{(a(x+b)-ab)^2}$$
$$\left.- \frac{1}{5040}\frac{e^{(a(x+b))}}{a(x+b)-ab} + \frac{1}{20}\pi\right)a^7$$

subsexpr also takes a third parameter that allows you to move up the tree structure a certain number of levels before performing the substitution. The key to this efficient result is noticing that the only occurrence of e^{ab} in largeexpr is in the desired subexpression.

The mapexpr command performs a similar task. Instead of substituting completely new values for the specified subexpression, that subexpression is passed through a Maple function and the result of that operation is substituted in place of the original subexpression.

From the previous examples of subsexpr, if instead of substituting c for that particular occurrence of $e^{a(b+x)}$, you instead want to expand that value, you could use

> mapexpr(expand, loclists[2], largeexpr);

$$\left(\frac{1}{7}\frac{ab}{(-a(x+b)+ab)^7} - \frac{1}{6}\frac{1}{(-a(x+b)+ab)^6} + \frac{1}{7}\frac{b}{(a(x+b)-ab)^7}\right.$$
$$- \frac{1}{7}\frac{e^{(a(x+b))}}{(a(x+b)-ab)^7} - \frac{1}{42}\frac{e^{(ax)}e^{(ab)}}{(a(x+b)-ab)^6} - \frac{1}{210}\frac{e^{(a(x+b))}}{(a(x+b)-ab)^5}$$
$$- \frac{1}{840}\frac{e^{(a(x+b))}}{(a(x+b)-ab)^4} - \frac{1}{2520}\frac{e^{(a(x+b))}}{(a(x+b)-ab)^3} - \frac{1}{5040}\frac{e^{(a(x+b))}}{(a(x+b)-ab)^2}$$
$$\left.- \frac{1}{5040}\frac{e^{(a(x+b))}}{a(x+b)-ab} - \frac{1}{5040}e^{(ab)}\operatorname{Ei}(1,-a(x+b)+ab)\right)a^7$$

And, to simplify the term containing e^{ab} (which cancels the ab values from the call to Ei) you could use

> mapexpr(simplify, myll, largeexpr, 1);

$$\left(\frac{1}{7}\frac{ab}{(-a(x+b)+ab)^7} - \frac{1}{6}\frac{1}{(-a(x+b)+ab)^6}\right. \\ \left. + \frac{1}{7}\frac{b}{(a(x+b)-ab)^7} \right.$$
$$-\frac{1}{7}\frac{e^{(a(x+b))}}{(a(x+b)-ab)^7} - \frac{1}{42}\frac{e^{(a(x+b))}}{(a(x+b)-ab)^6} - \frac{1}{210}\frac{e^{(a(x+b))}}{(a(x+b)-ab)^5}$$
$$-\frac{1}{840}\frac{e^{(a(x+b))}}{(a(x+b)-ab)^4} - \frac{1}{2520}\frac{e^{(a(x+b))}}{(a(x+b)-ab)^3} - \frac{1}{5040}\frac{e^{(a(x+b))}}{(a(x+b)-ab)^2}$$
$$\left. -\frac{1}{5040}\frac{e^{(a(x+b))}}{a(x+b)-ab} - \frac{1}{5040}e^{(ab)}\text{Ei}(1,-ax)\right)a^7$$

mapexpr also takes the same optional parameters as maplists (and all the other maplike commands) that allow you to specify which parameter of the function is substituted and what constant values, if any, should be applied.[11]

Both subsexpr and mapexpr allow you to pass lists of locator lists in order to operate on several subexpressions. For example, to simplify all the terms containing $e^{a(b+x)}$ you can enter

> mapexpr(simplify, loclists, largeexpr, 1);

$$\left(\frac{1}{7}\frac{ab}{(-a(x+b)+ab)^7} - \frac{1}{6}\frac{1}{(-a(x+b)+ab)^6} + \frac{1}{7}\frac{b}{(a(x+b)-ab)^7} - \frac{1}{7}\frac{e^{(a(x+b))}}{a^7 x^7}\right.$$
$$-\frac{1}{42}\frac{e^{(a(x+b))}}{a^6 x^6} - \frac{1}{210}\frac{e^{(a(x+b))}}{a^5 x^5} - \frac{1}{840}\frac{e^{(a(x+b))}}{a^4 x^4} - \frac{1}{2520}\frac{e^{(a(x+b))}}{a^3 x^3}$$
$$\left. -\frac{1}{5040}\frac{e^{(a(x+b))}}{a^2 x^2} - \frac{1}{5040}\frac{e^{(a(x+b))}}{ax} - \frac{1}{5040}e^{(ab)}\text{Ei}(1,-a(x+b)+ab)\right)a^7$$

A slightly more ambitious example is to replace each of the same terms with the value of c.

> subsexpr(loclists=c, largeexpr, 1);

$$\left(\frac{1}{7}\frac{ab}{(-a(x+b)+ab)^7} - \frac{1}{6}\frac{1}{(-a(x+b)+ab)^6} + \frac{1}{7}\frac{b}{(a(x+b)-ab)^7} + 7c\right.$$

---

[11] See the section *Mapping Lists* in the *ListTools* chapter for more details.

$$-\frac{1}{5040}\,\mathrm{e}^{(ab)}\,\mathrm{Ei}(\,1,-a\,(\,x+b\,)+a\,b\,)\bigg)\,a^7$$

This appears to have worked exactly as desired. subsexpr had to perform some special "tricks" to keep the first two substitutions (i.e., the ones replacing terms with constants $-\frac{1}{7}$ and $-\frac{1}{42}$) from resulting in an automatic simplification to *2c before* the remainder of the substitutions were performed. If these tricks weren't performed, then the remaining locator lists would no longer point to the proper subexpressions and subsexpr would have either failed or produced an incorrect result. For more details on this code, see the section *Controlling Evaluation* on page 128.

Examples

Restructuring an Expression

An integral table in a popular German formula handbook[12] lists the following equation:

$$\int \frac{x^2\,dx}{(a+x)\,(b+x)^2} = \frac{b^2}{(b-a)\,(b+x)} + \frac{a^2}{(a-b)^2}\ln(a+x) + \frac{(b^2-2\,ab)}{(b-a)^2}\ln(b+x)$$

What does Maple give for the solution to this integral?

> Int(x^2/((a+x)*(b+x)^2), x);

$$\int \frac{x^2}{(\,a+x\,)(\,x+b\,)^2}\,dx$$

> mapleval := value(");

$$mapleval :=$$

$$\frac{a^2\ln(\,a+x\,)}{-2\,a\,b+b^2+a^2} - 2\,\frac{b\ln(\,x+b\,)\,a}{-2\,a\,b+b^2+a^2} + \frac{b^2\ln(\,x+b\,)}{-2\,a\,b+b^2+a^2} + \frac{b^2}{(\,b-a\,)(\,x+b\,)}$$

That looks *similar* to the answer supplied in the table. There are several reasons why you might want to manipulate an expression to look more like the published answer, including:

- It is not always possible to use Maple to verify that two expressions with different representations are actually equal to each other. Simplifying a complicated expression to 0 is a difficult task. By performing

---

[12] *Taschenbuch mathematischer Formeln und moderner Verfahren*, H. Stöcker, Verlag Harri Duetsch, p. 749, (1992).

manipulations on an expression that do not affect its value (e.g., simplification, factoring, expansion, etc.), you can perhaps get it close enough to the desired form that you can convince yourself visually that the two expressions are indeed equal.

- You might want to publish the result in a paper or book in a format closer to the already published value. Again, by performing operations on the Maple result that don't change its value, you can ensure the validity of your result.
- You might want the result in a format closer to the already published value so you can apply certain functions to the restructured terms.

So, how can mapleval be restructured to look more like the published value?

Maple has an internal ordering for all expressions, which depends on the order in which the variables were first encountered. To show this, create a Maple expression tableval by typing in the published result exactly as it is presented.

```
> tableval := b^2/((b-a)*(b+x))+(a^2/(a-b)^2)*ln(a+x)+
>      ((b^2-2*a*b)/(b-a)^2)*ln(b+x);
```

$$tableval := \frac{b^2}{(b-a)(x+b)} + \frac{a^2 \ln(a+x)}{(a-b)^2} + \frac{(-2ab+b^2)\ln(x+b)}{(b-a)^2}$$

The result Maple produces has two small differences from what was typed in; the logarithm terms have been added to the numerators of their respective terms.

Looking closer at mapleval and tableval, you can see that the two terms in mapleval which contain $ln(b+x)$ need to be combined into a single term. This can be obtained with the built-in collect command.

```
> mapleval := collect(mapleval, ln(b+x));
```

$$mapleval := \left(-2\frac{ba}{-2ab+b^2+a^2} + \frac{b^2}{-2ab+b^2+a^2}\right)\ln(x+b) + \frac{a^2 \ln(a+x)}{-2ab+b^2+a^2}$$
$$+ \frac{b^2}{(b-a)(x+b)}$$

Ok, now both values have three terms. The third term in mapleval is identical to the first term in tableval (except for the signs of some values). The "coefficient" of the $ln(x + b)$ term in mapleval needs to be altered significantly. First, using findexpr and markexpr, try to get a valid pointer to the entire coefficient.

> `markexpr(findexpr(b^2, mapleval), mapleval, 3);`

$$\left(\text{MARK}\left(-2\frac{ba}{-2ab+b^2+a^2}\right)+\frac{b^2}{-2ab+b^2+a^2}\right)\ln(x+b)+\frac{a^2\ln(a+x)}{-2ab+b^2+a^2}$$
$$+\frac{b^2}{(b-a)(x+b)}$$

> `markexpr(findexpr(b^2, mapleval), mapleval, 4);`

$$\text{MARK}\left(-2\frac{ba}{-2ab+b^2+a^2}+\frac{b^2}{-2ab+b^2+a^2}\right)\ln(x+b)+\frac{a^2\ln(a+x)}{-2ab+b^2+a^2}$$
$$+\frac{b^2}{(b-a)(x+b)}$$

Now, using mapexpr, apply the simplify command to that coefficient.

> `mapleval := mapexpr(simplify, findexpr(b^2, mapleval), mapleval, 4);`

$$mapleval := \frac{b(-2a+b)\ln(x+b)}{-2ab+b^2+a^2}+\frac{a^2\ln(a+x)}{-2ab+b^2+a^2}+\frac{b^2}{(b-a)(x+b)}$$

This is much closer. The next step could be to factor the values $-2ab+a^2+b^2$ into (hopefully) $(a-b)^2$. Try applying factor to the entire expression.

> `factor(mapleval);`

$$(b^3\ln(x+b)+b^3-2b^2\ln(x+b)a-ab^2+b^2\ln(x+b)x-2b\ln(x+b)ax$$
$$+a^2\ln(a+x)b+a^2\ln(a+x)x)\Big/\left((x+b)(b-a)^2\right)$$

That did far too much. Using findexpr together with mapexpr, only the occurrences of $-2ab+a^2+b^2$ can be factored.

> `findexpr(-2*a*b+a^2+b^2, mapleval, infinity);`

$$[[1,3,1],[1,1,2]]$$

> `mapleval := mapexpr(factor, ", mapleval);`

$$mapleval := \frac{b(-2a+b)\ln(x+b)}{(b-a)^2}+\frac{a^2\ln(a+x)}{(b-a)^2}+\frac{b^2}{(b-a)(x+b)}$$

Now the second terms in mapleval and tableval match exactly. As well, the $ln(x+b)$ terms are similar enough for you to be satisfied that they are indeed equal.

Reviewing the two expressions shows how similar they now are overall.

> `tableval;`

$$\frac{b^2}{(b-a)(x+b)} + \frac{a^2 \ln(a+x)}{(a-b)^2} + \frac{(-2ab+b^2)\ln(x+b)}{(b-a)^2}$$

> `mapleval;`

$$\frac{b(-2a+b)\ln(x+b)}{(b-a)^2} + \frac{a^2 \ln(a+x)}{(b-a)^2} + \frac{b^2}{(b-a)(x+b)}$$

This is as much as can be done easily with the commands in *ExpressionTools*. Further manipulation can be done with the tools in the *PatternTools* chapter.

Programming Tips

The coding and data structures used in *ExpressionTools* are by far the most complicated in *The Practical Approach Utilities for Maple*. Some of the techniques used in creating these commands (e.g., the extensive use of linked lists), are far beyond most Maple users' programming skills. For that reason, we do not delve too deeply into the actual code written for *ExpressionTools*, but instead focus on simplified examples of some of the algorithms you might use when writing your own expression manipulation routines. Of course, if you want to view the actual code for our commands, you can do so. Just refer to the section *Viewing a Procedure's Code* on page 77 for more details.

In the following sections, three examples are used to illustrate several techniques that might prove useful to you.

In the first example, a rudimentary version of the showtype command is constructed. In its simplest form, showtype takes an expression, expr, and the name of a Maple type, typename, and returns a set of *all* the subexpressions of type typename in expr.

In the second example, the type checking and error checking used in the showexpr command is examined. showexpr takes a locator list (or list of locator lists), an expression, and a non-negative integer, and returns a list of expressions.

By using these two examples to illustrate several points, we hope to give you an idea how a procedure grows as it is being constructed; showing how errors and omissions affect the final product.

The final example illustrates how to avoid some problems caused by *automatic simplification* when performing multiple substitutions on a single expression.

Searching the Tree

Every expression in Maple is stored in a structure called a *directed acyclic graph* or *DAG*, which is in the shape of a tree with a root, branches, and leaves. To demonstrate, use the exprtree command to show the tree structure of the expression $x^2 \sin(y) + b^3 \cos(x+3)$.

```
> myexpr := x^2*sin(y) + b^3*cos(x+3);
```

$$myexpr := x^2 \sin(y) + b^3 \cos(x+3)$$

```
> exprtree(myexpr);
```

```
                    |--string
            |--^--|
            |       |--integer
    |--*--|
    |       |             |--string
    |       |--function--|
+--|
    |             |--string
    |       |--^--|
    |       |       |--integer
    |--*--|
    |             |             |--string
    |             |       |--+--|
    |             |       |       |--integer
    |             |--function--|
```

In the command showtype, you are looking for *all* subexpressions of a certain type; this means that you must search through every *node* (branching point and end point) of the tree. There are two types of searches that can be used—*depth-first* and *breadth-first*. A depth-first search method has been chosen for the coding for *ExpressionTools*, and will be used in our example.

A depth-first search involves checking the first subexpression (operand) of the complete expression, then checking the first subexpression of that subexpression, and so on. Whenever a subexpression that cannot be further subdivided is encountered, the search goes back up one level and advances one operand to the right (pictorially speaking). Eventually, in this manner, the entire tree is searched.

The only reasonable method to use for such a search is *recursion*. For a primer on the theory of recursion, see the section *Recursion* on page 79. Using this method, a compact command can be written that works equally well on expressions of all sizes.

Since the result you want showtype to return is a set, start the procedure off with an empty set and use the union command to add newly found elements of the indicated type. Comments are added to the code using the # character, which tells Maple to view everything on a line after this character as text, not code.

```
> showtype := proc(t, expr)
>     # Declare local variables.
>     local i, outset, numops;
>
>     # Initialize values.
>     outset := {};
>     numops := nops(expr);
>
>     # Check the expression for type.
>     if type(expr, t) then
>         outset := {expr};
>     fi;
>
>     # If there are no further subexpressions to investigate, quit!
>     if numops = 1 then
>         RETURN(outset);
>     fi;
>
>     # Otherwise, call showtype recursively on each subexpression.
>     for i from 1 to numops do
>         outset := outset union showtype(t, op(i, expr));
>     od;
>     RETURN(outset);
> end;

showtype :=

    proc(t,expr)
    local i,outset,numops;
        outset := {};
        numops := nops(expr);
        if type(expr,t) then outset := {expr} fi;
        if numops = 1 then RETURN(outset) fi;
        for i to numops do  outset := outset union showtype(t,op(i,expr)) od;
        RETURN(outset)
    end
```

As you can see, the RETURN command is being used to exit from each call to showtype. This is still quite a simple procedure, but let's check it on myexpr to see if it works:

```
> myexpr;
```
$$x^2 \sin(y) + b^3 \cos(x+3)$$

```
> showtype('^', myexpr);
```

$$\{b^3, x^2\}$$

Yes, that seems to work just fine. How about searching for sums in myexpr?

```
> showtype('+', myexpr);
```

$$\{x^2 \sin(y) + b^3 \cos(x+3)\}$$

showexpr only returned the entire expression, which *is* a sum. But what about the $x + 3$ in $cos(x + 3)$? Why wasn't it found?

Checking the Special Cases

The above code for showexpr doesn't appear to be working in all cases. Often, when dealing with the structure of Maple expressions, you will run into classes of expressions or subexpressions that don't follow the same sets of rules that other classes do. When faced with a command that works in one instance but not in another, the best thing to do is try out the individual tests made by that command on the troublesome expression. In this case,

```
> type(x+3, '+');
```

true

```
> nops(x+3);
```

2

These both work as expected—maybe the problem is that we're never getting to this point in the algorithm.

```
> nops(cos(x+3));
```

1

There's our problem; because showexpr determines that cos(x+3) has only *one* operand, the algorithm investigates no further. Actually, cos(x+3) has *two* operands, a first operand and a *zeroth* operand, because Maple uses the zeroth operand to store information about this expression.

```
> op(1, cos(x+3));
```

$$x + 3$$

```
> op(0, cos(x+3));
```

cos

So, obviously it is not sufficient to simply check if nops returns 1, although the zeroth operand, in most but not all cases, contains only the type of the expression.

```
> op(0, 5);
```

integer

```
> op(0, Fred);
```

string

These basic expressions don't need to be investigated more thoroughly. Only those types of expressions whose zeroth operand contains special information need special treatment. Those types are function, indexed, and series. Let's make the changes that will cause showtype to investigate these special expressions further.

```
> showtype := proc(t, expr)
>     # Declare local variables.
>     local i, outset, numops;
>
>     # Initialize values.
>     outset := {};
>     numops := nops(expr);
>
>     # Check the expression for type.
>     if type(expr, t) then
>         outset := {expr};
>     fi;
>
>     # If there are no further subexpressions to investigate
>     # and expr is not of one of three special types, quit!
>     if not member(whattype(expr), {'function', 'indexed', 'series'}) then
>         if numops = 1 then
>             RETURN(outset);
>         fi;
>     fi;
>
>     # Otherwise, call showtype recursively on each subexpression.
>     for i from 1 to numops do
>         outset := outset union showtype(t, op(i, expr));
>     od;
>     RETURN(outset);
> end:
```

Now try to find all the sums in myexpr.

```
> showtype('+', myexpr);
```
$$\{x + 3, x^2 \sin(y) + b^3 \cos(x + 3)\}$$

That's better! Use this new command to investigate a series data structure.

```
> myseries := series(sin(x), x=0);
```
$$myseries := x - \frac{1}{6}x^3 + \frac{1}{120}x^5 + O(x^6)$$

```
> showtype(integer, myseries);
```
$$\{-1, 1, 3, 5, 6, 120\}$$

```
> showtype(string, myseries);
```
$$\{\,\}$$

That last result is incorrect. The string x is part of myseries. But what part?

```
> op(myseries);
```
$$1, 1, \frac{-1}{6}, 3, \frac{1}{120}, 5, O(1), 6$$

```
> op(0, myseries);
```
$$x$$

It is apparent that you also need to pass the zeroth operand through showtype in these special cases. The revamped code looks like:

```
> showtype := proc(t, expr)
>    # Declare local variables.
>    local i, outset, numops;
>
>    # Initialize values.
>    outset := {};
>    numops := nops(expr);
>
>    # Check the expression for type.
>    if type(expr, t) then
>       outset := {expr};
>    fi;
>
>    # Check if expr is one of three special types.
>    # If not, and there is only one operand, quit.
>    # Else, check the zeroth operand and continue on.
>    if not member(whattype(expr), {'function', 'indexed', 'series'}) then
>       if numops = 1 then
>          RETURN(outset);
>       fi;
```

```
>     else
>         outset := outset union showtype(t, op(0, expr));
>     fi;
>
>     # Call showtype recursively on each subexpression.
>     for i from 1 to numops do
>         outset := outset union showtype(t, op(i, expr));
>     od;
>     RETURN(outset);
> end:
```

Now that bug should be fixed.

```
> showtype(string, myseries);
```

$$\{O, x\}$$

It turns out that O (the Order term indicator) is a string as well.

Initial Type and Error Checking

Along with checking for the special cases, as seen in the previous section, it is also necessary to ensure that your procedures are passed the proper type(s) and combination(s) of parameters. While some Maple commands, such as op, accept *any* type of parameter, the large majority of procedures have some restrictions on the types of object with which they can work. As well, even if all the individual parameters are of valid type, they may, in combination, cause an untenable situation.

Typically, this checking is performed at the beginning of a procedure, with the idea that if errors have been made it is wasteful, and possibly dangerous, to continue with computations. A third stage of checking involves investigation of the number of parameters passed to a procedure. This is dealt with in the section *Varying the Number of Parameters* on page 296.

For an illustrative example, let's look at some of the checking that needs to be done for the showexpr command. showexpr takes three parameters with the following type restrictions:

1. a *locator list*, which is a list of zero or more non-negative integers, or a list of such lists (which can all have differing numbers of elements),
2. any expression,
3. an optional non-negative integer value (default value = 0).

The following is Maple code that ensures that these criteria are met. (Any checking for incorrect numbers of parameters passed is left out at this point.)

```
> showexpr := proc(llist, expr)
```

```
>    local i, n;
>    # Is the first parameter a list?
>    if not type(llist, list) then
>       ERROR('first parameter must be a list', llist);
>    else
>       # Are all the elements of llist non-negative integers?
>       # The map command applies type to all elements, and the
>       # member command checks to see if any type command returned false.
>       if member(false, map(type, llist, nonnegint)) then
>          # Check each element of llist with a do loop. If any is not
>          # a list of non-negative integers, send an error message.
>          for i from 1 to nops(llist) do
>             if type(llist[i], list) then
>                if member(false, map(type, llist[i], nonnegint)) then
>                   ERROR('each internal list must contain only non-negative
>                   integer values', llist[i]);
>                fi;
>             # If you've gotten this far you have an element of llist that
>             # is neither a list or a non-negative integer.
>             else
>                ERROR('elements of the first parameter must be all
>                non-negative integers or all lists of non-negative
>                integers', llist);
>             fi;
>          od;
>       fi;
>    fi;
>
>    # Is the third parameter given and is it a non-negative integer?
>    if nargs > 2 then
>       if type(args[3], nonnegint) then
>          n := args[3];
>       else
>          ERROR('third parameter must be a non-negative integer', n);
>       fi;
>    else
>       n := 0;
>    fi;
> end:
```

The ERROR command forces an exit from the procedure and displays an error message containing the values passed to it as parameters.

The test command if member(false, map(type, llist, nonnegint)) ... performs all the following steps.

1. Using the map command, each element (say elemi) of llist is entered in the command type(elemi, nonnegint). The results of all these tests (i.e.,

values of true and false) are put together in a list of the same length as llist.
2. Using the member command, the above result is checked for *any* values of false.
3. If any false values were found, then the if criteria was passed and the code immediately following is executed. Otherwise the code following the related else is executed, if it exists.

Try out the code on some obviously incorrect parameter sequences.

```
> showexpr([1,2,3,s], myexpr, 3);
```

Error, (in showexpr) elements of the first parameter must be all
            non-negative integers or all lists of non-negative
            integers, [1, 2, 3, s]

```
> showexpr([[0,2,3], [4], 10, [9,1]], myexpr, 3);
```

Error, (in showexpr) elements of the first parameter must be all
            non-negative integers or all lists of non-negative
            integers, [[0, 2, 3], [4], 10, [9, 1]]

```
> showexpr([1,2,3,4,5,6], myexpr, -1);
```

Error, (in showexpr) third parameter must be a non-negative integer, n

If you choose a valid input and follow the above code through carefully, you will notice that you safely traverse all the code, and reach the final end statement. Where possible, try to keep error messages close to their related tests.

While this is a large section of code for type-testing one procedure, the information returned is concise and useful. Intelligible error messages are extremely important. If you want to write shorter code and are willing to forgo customized error messages, there is a method called *automatic type checking* that allows you to specify what types are needed directly in the proc() statement. The following code performs the same type checking as above.

```
> showexpr := proc(llist:{list(nonnegint), list(list(nonnegint))}, expr,
>                  n:nonnegint);
> end:
```

The indicator list(nonnegint) checks for a list of non-negative integers, while list(list(nonnegint)) checks for a list of lists of non-negative integers. Curly brackets { } in this context enclose multiple valid type specifications for a single parameter. Standardized error messages are returned; and some of them are less than illuminating to the beginning Maple user.

```
> showexpr([1,2,3,s], myexpr, 3);
```

Error, showexpr expects its 1st argument, llist, to be of type {list(nonnegint)
, list(list(nonnegint))}, but received [1, 2, 3, s]

```
> showexpr([[0,2,3], [4], 10, [9,1]], myexpr, 3);
```

Error, showexpr expects its 1st argument, llist, to be of type {list(nonnegint)
, list(list(nonnegint))}, but received [[0, 2, 3], [4], 10, [9, 1]]

```
> showexpr([1,2,3,4,5,6], myexpr, -1);
```

Error, showexpr expects its 3rd argument, n, to be of type nonnegint,
but received -1

While automatic type checking can handle most instances of type checking, it cannot deal with initial error checking; that is, checking for errors caused by unwanted *combinations* of initial parameters.

In the above example, the third parameter, n, cannot be strictly greater than the length of the *shortest* list of non-negative integers passed to the procedure.[13]

In order to verify the parameters, use the map command again.

```
> showexpr := proc(llist, expr, n)
>    local minlength;
>    # Determine the minimum length of locator lists.
>    if type(llist, list(nonnegint)) then
>       minlength := nops(llist);
>    # Check each internal locator list using map and min.
>    # The op command around map must be used because min does
>    # not take a list as input.
>    else
>       minlength := min(op(map(nops, llist)));
>    fi;
>    # Display the error message, if appropriate.
>    if n > minlength then
>       ERROR('third parameter', n, 'is greater than length of shortest list');
>    fi;
> end:
```

Putting the error checking and the type checking together (without comments) results in

```
> showexpr := proc(llist, expr, n)
>    local i, minlength;
```

---

[13]To see the reason for this, turn to the discussion of the showexpr command earlier in this chapter.

```
>     if not type(llist, list) then
>         ERROR('first parameter must be a list', llist);
>     else
>         if member(false, map(type, llist, nonnegint)) then
>             for i from 1 to nops(llist) do
>                 if type(llist[i], list) then
>                     if member(false, map(type, llist[i], nonnegint)) then
>                         ERROR('each internal list must contain only non-negative
>                             integer values', llist[i]);
>                     fi;
>                 else
>                     ERROR('elements of the first parameter must be all
>                         non-negative integers or all lists of non-negative
>                         integers', llist);
>                 fi;
>             od;
>         fi;
>     fi;
>
>     if nargs > 2 then
>         if type(args[3], nonnegint) then
>             n := args[3];
>         else
>             ERROR('third parameter must be a non-negative integer', n);
>         fi;
>     else
>         n := 0;
>     fi;
>
>     if type(llist, list(nonnegint)) then
>         minlength := nops(llist);
>     else
>         minlength := min(op(map(nops, llist)));
>     fi;
>     if n > minlength then
>         ERROR('third parameter', n, 'is greater than length of shortest list');
>     fi;
> end:
```

Notice that the type checking is placed first. There is no point in doing the error checking if the types don't work out.

In cases where the algorithm for the actual computation that a command performs is relatively straightforward, the initial checking can take up much more than half the code. While this may seem excessive to you, taking the trouble to thoroughly check the input *does* make for better commands, and anyone using your code will thank you for it.

As an exercise, use interface(verboseproc=2) to view the complete code for showexpr. Determine what other tests were made and what percentage of the code actually performs the computation.

Controlling Evaluation

Certain details in the way Maple evaluates expressions can cause some rather interesting and difficult to track problems with the operation of the Utility commands subsexpr and mapexpr when they have to deal with multiple substitutions. To understand these problem, you first need some information about Maple evaluation in general.

In most cases, Maple follows the rule of *full evaluation*, meaning that expressions are typically evaluated as far as they possibly can be, at the earliest possible opportunity. One important exception to this rule is produced by Maple's built-in commands subs and subsop.[14]

These substitution commands return a result wherein the new values they inserted are *not* allowed to cause further evaluation. As a very simple example, take the following commands.

```
> simexpr := sin(x);
```

$$simexpr := \sin(x)$$

```
> subs(x=0, simexpr);
```

$$\sin(0)$$

Normally, if sin(0) were entered as a Maple command, it would automatically simplify to 0, but here it remained as sin(0). Full evaluation can easily be performed on the result by simply displaying (and therefore evaluating) it a second time.

```
> ";
```

$$0$$

Not *all* automatic substitutions are delayed by subs and subsop. For example, collecting like terms is performed right away.

```
> simexpr2 := x + y + z;
```

$$simexpr2 := x + y + z$$

```
> subsop(1=z, simexpr2);
```

$$2z + y$$

---

[14] Another prominent exception to *full evaluation* occurs with arrays. See the chapter *ArrayTools* for more details.

What has all this got to do with subsexpr and mapexpr? This simplification of like terms can wreak havoc when multiple substitutions are being performed, because the locator lists[15] near the end of the first parameter no longer point to the proper subexpressions.

For an example, let's revisit the last example from the section *Replacing Subexpressions*. Every term in the large summation which contained $e^{a(b+x)}$ was to be replaced by the constant c.

```
> largeexpr;
```

$$\left(\frac{\frac{1}{7} \frac{ab}{(-a(x+b)+ab)^7} - \frac{1}{6} \frac{1}{(-a(x+b)+ab)^6}}{a} + \frac{1}{7} \frac{b}{(a(x+b)-ab)^7} \right.$$

$$- \frac{1}{7} \frac{e^{(a(x+b))}}{(a(x+b)-ab)^7} - \frac{1}{42} \frac{e^{(a(x+b))}}{(a(x+b)-ab)^6} - \frac{1}{210} \frac{e^{(a(x+b))}}{(a(x+b)-ab)^5}$$

$$- \frac{1}{840} \frac{e^{(a(x+b))}}{(a(x+b)-ab)^4} - \frac{1}{2520} \frac{e^{(a(x+b))}}{(a(x+b)-ab)^3} - \frac{1}{5040} \frac{e^{(a(x+b))}}{(a(x+b)-ab)^2}$$

$$\left. - \frac{1}{5040} \frac{e^{(a(x+b))}}{a(x+b)-ab} - \frac{1}{5040} e^{(ab)} \operatorname{Ei}(1, -a(x+b)+ab) \right) a^7$$

```
> newll := findexpr(exp(a*(x + b)), largeexpr, infinity);
```

$$newll := [\,[\,2,3,1\,],[\,2,4,1\,],[\,2,5,1\,],[\,2,6,1\,],[\,2,7,1\,],[\,2,8,1\,],[\,2,9,1\,]\,]$$

```
> subsexpr(newll=c, largeexpr, 1);
```

$$\left(\frac{\frac{1}{7} \frac{ab}{(-a(x+b)+ab)^7} - \frac{1}{6} \frac{1}{(-a(x+b)+ab)^6}}{a} + \frac{1}{7} \frac{b}{(a(x+b)-ab)^7} + 7c \right.$$

$$\left. - \frac{1}{5040} e^{(ab)} \operatorname{Ei}(1, -a(x+b)+ab) \right) a^7$$

As you can see, subsexpr did the job perfectly, replacing all seven terms with c. Automatic collecting of like terms was *then* performed.

But how exactly did subsexpr get around the problems caused by automatic collection of those like terms? Did it just call itself seven times? Using the subsexpr command itself, step through the seven substitutions indicated by newll one at a time, and examine closely each new result.

---

[15]Remember, *locator lists* are lists of non-negative integers that specify the location of a subexpression within a given tree structure.

> `subsexpr(newll[1]=c, largeexpr, 1);`

$$\left(\frac{\frac{1}{7}\frac{ab}{(-a(x+b)+ab)^7} - \frac{1}{6}\frac{1}{(-a(x+b)+ab)^6}}{a} + \frac{1}{7}\frac{b}{(a(x+b)-ab)^7} + c\right.$$

$$- \frac{1}{42}\frac{e^{(a(x+b))}}{(a(x+b)-ab)^6} - \frac{1}{210}\frac{e^{(a(x+b))}}{(a(x+b)-ab)^5} - \frac{1}{840}\frac{e^{(a(x+b))}}{(a(x+b)-ab)^4}$$

$$- \frac{1}{2520}\frac{e^{(a(x+b))}}{(a(x+b)-ab)^3} - \frac{1}{5040}\frac{e^{(a(x+b))}}{(a(x+b)-ab)^2} - \frac{1}{5040}\frac{e^{(a(x+b))}}{a(x+b)-ab}$$

$$\left.- \frac{1}{5040}e^{(ab)}\,\mathrm{Ei}(1,-a(x+b)+ab)\right)a^7$$

That worked just fine. Try the next one.

> `subsexpr(newll[2]=c, ", 1);`

$$\left(\frac{\frac{1}{7}\frac{ab}{(-a(x+b)+ab)^7} - \frac{1}{6}\frac{1}{(-a(x+b)+ab)^6}}{a} + \frac{1}{7}\frac{b}{(a(x+b)-ab)^7} + 2c\right.$$

$$- \frac{1}{210}\frac{e^{(a(x+b))}}{(a(x+b)-ab)^5} - \frac{1}{840}\frac{e^{(a(x+b))}}{(a(x+b)-ab)^4} - \frac{1}{2520}\frac{e^{(a(x+b))}}{(a(x+b)-ab)^3}$$

$$- \frac{1}{5040}\frac{e^{(a(x+b))}}{(a(x+b)-ab)^2} - \frac{1}{5040}\frac{e^{(a(x+b))}}{a(x+b)-ab}$$

$$\left.- \frac{1}{5040}e^{(ab)}\,\mathrm{Ei}(1,-a(x+b)+ab)\right)a^7$$

Again, that appeared to work appropriately. Notice, however, that the two c terms (which were originally the terms with constants of $-\frac{1}{7}$ and $-\frac{1}{42}$) have been combined into $2c$.

> `subsexpr(newll[3]=c, ", 1);`

$$\left(\frac{\frac{1}{7}\frac{ab}{(-a(x+b)+ab)^7} - \frac{1}{6}\frac{1}{(-a(x+b)+ab)^6}}{a} + \frac{1}{7}\frac{b}{(a(x+b)-ab)^7} + 3c\right.$$

$$- \frac{1}{210}\frac{e^{(a(x+b))}}{(a(x+b)-ab)^5} - \frac{1}{2520}\frac{e^{(a(x+b))}}{(a(x+b)-ab)^3} - \frac{1}{5040}\frac{e^{(a(x+b))}}{(a(x+b)-ab)^2}$$

$$\left. -\frac{1}{5040}\frac{e^{(a(x+b))}}{a(x+b)-ab} - \frac{1}{5040} e^{(ab)} \text{Ei}(1, -a(x+b)+ab) \right) a^7$$

The 2c has changed to 3c, but knowing that the elements in newll are stored in the order they appear in largeexpr, why was the term with the $-\frac{1}{840}$ constant substituted for instead of the term with the $-\frac{1}{210}$ constant? The reason is that the previous collection of like terms into 2c has changed the overall structure of the large expression by changing the number of terms in that particular summation. This can be demonstrated by applying markexpr to the penultimate result.

```
> markexpr(newll[3], "", 1);
```

$$\left(\frac{1}{7}\frac{ab}{(-a(x+b)+ab)^7} - \frac{1}{6}\frac{1}{(-a(x+b)+ab)^6} \right) \Big/ a + \frac{1}{7}\frac{b}{(a(x+b)-ab)^7} + 2c$$
$$-\frac{1}{210}\frac{e^{(a(x+b))}}{(a(x+b)-ab)^5} + \text{MARK}\left(-\frac{1}{840}\frac{e^{(a(x+b))}}{(a(x+b)-ab)^4} \right)$$
$$-\frac{1}{2520}\frac{e^{(a(x+b))}}{(a(x+b)-ab)^3} - \frac{1}{5040}\frac{e^{(a(x+b))}}{(a(x+b)-ab)^2} - \frac{1}{5040}\frac{e^{(a(x+b))}}{a(x+b)-ab}$$
$$\left. -\frac{1}{5040} e^{(ab)} \text{Ei}(1, -a(x+b)+ab) \right) a^7$$

In other words, the locator lists produced from the original largeexpr no longer point to the proper places. For a while, subsexpr can be fooled because the subsequent locator lists still point to valid subexpressions, but that doesn't last for long.

```
> subsexpr(newll[4]=c, "", 1);
```

$$\left(\frac{1}{7}\frac{ab}{(-a(x+b)+ab)^7} - \frac{1}{6}\frac{1}{(-a(x+b)+ab)^6} \right) \Big/ a + \frac{1}{7}\frac{b}{(a(x+b)-ab)^7} + 4c$$
$$-\frac{1}{210}\frac{e^{(a(x+b))}}{(a(x+b)-ab)^5} - \frac{1}{2520}\frac{e^{(a(x+b))}}{(a(x+b)-ab)^3} - \frac{1}{5040}\frac{e^{(a(x+b))}}{a(x+b)-ab}$$
$$\left. -\frac{1}{5040} e^{(ab)} \text{Ei}(1, -a(x+b)+ab) \right) a^7$$

```
> subsexpr(newll[5]=c, ", 1);
```

$$\left(\frac{1}{7}\frac{ab}{(-a(x+b)+ab)^7} - \frac{1}{6}\frac{1}{(-a(x+b)+ab)^6} + \frac{1}{7}\frac{b}{(a(x+b)-ab)^7} + 5c \right.$$

$$\left. - \frac{1}{210}\frac{e^{(a(x+b))}}{(a(x+b)-ab)^5} - \frac{1}{2520}\frac{e^{(a(x+b))}}{(a(x+b)-ab)^3} - \frac{1}{5040}\frac{e^{(a(x+b))}}{a(x+b)-ab} \right) a^7$$

Here, the last term of the sum, one that doesn't even contain $e^{a(x+b)}$, is incorrectly replaced. The following substitution produces an error message.

```
> subsexpr(newll[6]=c, ", 1);

Error, (in subsexpr) [8, 1], is not a valid locator list for , ((1/7*a*b/(-a*(
x+b)+a*b)^7-1/6/(-a*(x+b)+a*b)^6)/a+1/7/(a*(x+b)-a*b)^7*b+5*c-1/210*exp(a*(x+b)
)/(a*(x+b)-a*b)^5-1/2520*exp(a*(x+b))/(a*(x+b)-a*b)^3-1/5040*exp(a*(x+b))/(a*(x
+b)-a*b))*a^7

> type(newll[6], loclist("));
```

$$false$$

One method for circumventing this problem is to hold off the automatic simplification until the very end of the procedure by using unevaluated functions containing the final value to be substituted. Try this using the function name _z_z[16] and performing the substitutions one at a time as before.

```
> subsexpr(newll[1]=_z_z(c), largeexpr, 1);
```

$$\left(\frac{1}{7}\frac{ab}{(-a(x+b)+ab)^7} - \frac{1}{6}\frac{1}{(-a(x+b)+ab)^6} + \frac{1}{7}\frac{b}{(a(x+b)-ab)^7} + \_z\_z(c) \right.$$

$$- \frac{1}{42}\frac{e^{(a(x+b))}}{(a(x+b)-ab)^6} - \frac{1}{210}\frac{e^{(a(x+b))}}{(a(x+b)-ab)^5} - \frac{1}{840}\frac{e^{(a(x+b))}}{(a(x+b)-ab)^4}$$

$$- \frac{1}{2520}\frac{e^{(a(x+b))}}{(a(x+b)-ab)^3} - \frac{1}{5040}\frac{e^{(a(x+b))}}{(a(x+b)-ab)^2} - \frac{1}{5040}\frac{e^{(a(x+b))}}{a(x+b)-ab}$$

$$\left. - \frac{1}{5040} e^{(ab)} \text{Ei}(1, -a(x+b)+ab) \right) a^7$$

---

[16]This name was chosen because it is unlikely to coincide with any user defined value or procedure name.

```
> subsexpr(newll[2]=_z_z(c), ", 1);
```

$$\left(\frac{1}{7}\frac{ab}{(-a(x+b)+ab)^7} - \frac{1}{6}\frac{1}{(-a(x+b)+ab)^6}\right)\Big/a + \frac{1}{7}\frac{b}{(a(x+b)-ab)^7} + 2\_z\_z(c)$$

$$-\frac{1}{210}\frac{e^{(a(x+b))}}{(a(x+b)-ab)^5} - \frac{1}{840}\frac{e^{(a(x+b))}}{(a(x+b)-ab)^4} - \frac{1}{2520}\frac{e^{(a(x+b))}}{(a(x+b)-ab)^3}$$

$$-\frac{1}{5040}\frac{e^{(a(x+b))}}{(a(x+b)-ab)^2} - \frac{1}{5040}\frac{e^{(a(x+b))}}{a(x+b)-ab}$$

$$-\frac{1}{5040}e^{(ab)}\operatorname{Ei}(1,-a(x+b)+ab)\bigg)a^7$$

```
> subsexpr(newll[3]=_z_z(c), ", 1);
```

$$\left(\frac{1}{7}\frac{ab}{(-a(x+b)+ab)^7} - \frac{1}{6}\frac{1}{(-a(x+b)+ab)^6}\right)\Big/a + \frac{1}{7}\frac{b}{(a(x+b)-ab)^7} + 3\_z\_z(c)$$

$$-\frac{1}{210}\frac{e^{(a(x+b))}}{(a(x+b)-ab)^5} - \frac{1}{2520}\frac{e^{(a(x+b))}}{(a(x+b)-ab)^3} - \frac{1}{5040}\frac{e^{(a(x+b))}}{(a(x+b)-ab)^2}$$

$$-\frac{1}{5040}\frac{e^{(a(x+b))}}{a(x+b)-ab} - \frac{1}{5040}e^{(ab)}\operatorname{Ei}(1,-a(x+b)+ab)\bigg)a^7$$

You still have exactly the same problem. Collection of like terms also applies to the expression _z_z(c); so, no progress has been made. In order to avoid this simplification in *all* cases, it is necessary to use *unique* function names for each unevaluated function. The following loop performs the substitutions, appending different integer values to _z_z in each circumstance.

```
> lexpr2 := largeexpr:
> for i from 1 to nops(newll) do
>     lexpr2 := subsexpr(newll[i]=cat(_z_z,i)(c), lexpr2, 1):
> od:
```

Let's have a look at the overall result.

```
> lexpr2;
```

$$\left(\frac{1}{7}\frac{ab}{(-a(x+b)+ab)^7} - \frac{1}{6}\frac{1}{(-a(x+b)+ab)^6}\right)\Big/a + \frac{1}{7}\frac{b}{(a(x+b)-ab)^7} + \_z\_z1(c)$$

$$+ \_z\_z2(c) + \_z\_z3(c) + \_z\_z4(c) + \_z\_z5(c) + \_z\_z6(c) + \_z\_z7(c)$$
$$-\frac{1}{5040} e^{(ab)} \operatorname{Ei}(1, -a(x+b) + ab) \Bigg) a^7$$

Now, to finish the job, using the built-in subs command, each of the unevaluated functions names _z_z1 through _z_z7 must be replaced by the eval command (which simply *eval*uates their parameters).

```
> for i from 1 to nops(newll) do
>    lexpr2 := subs(cat(_z_z,i)=eval, lexpr2):
> od:
```

Now, by displaying the final result, all the evaluations are performed and you get the correct answer.

```
> lexpr2;
```

$$\left(\frac{1}{7} \frac{ab}{(-a(x+b)+ab)^7} - \frac{1}{6} \frac{1}{(-a(x+b)+ab)^6} + \frac{1}{7} \frac{b}{(a(x+b)-ab)^7} + 7c \right.$$
$$\left. - \frac{1}{5040} e^{(ab)} \operatorname{Ei}(1, -a(x+b) + ab) \right) a^7$$

This general method of controlling evaluation has been built into both subsexpr and mapexpr. Its implementation is more complicated than the above code, but should still be accessible to you if you view the source code.

CHAPTER 6

PatternTools

The commands in *PatternTools* build on the philosophy, structure, and capabilities of the last chapter, *ExpressionTools*. While commands such as findexpr, subsexpr, and mapexpr are very powerful expression manipulation tools, the extent of their power is defined by the internal, tree-like representation of all Maple objects. In other words, they (and built-in commands like op and subs) can only work on subexpressions that are *whole parts* of this internal structure.

This limitation gives rise to several situations where tools are needed that transcend the internal representation. Three of the more obvious examples are:

- How do you replace something that is built up of adjacent objects in the visual representation of an object, but which is not a single subexpression in terms of the tree-like internal structure? For example, replace the x*y in x*y*z* with another value (e.g., (x+y)).

- How do you replace something that, by itself, is not a valid (i.e., parsable) Maple structure? For example, change every occurrence of cos(2* in a large expression with cos((2+e)*, without affecting any other values.

- How do you replace something that is a parsable structure, but whose definition contains some areas where values of different length are all valid? For example, simplify all the unevaluated calls to cos in an expression, but only those that contain somewhere within them the variable x.

While it is true that the commands provided in *PatternTools* are not representative of true *pattern matching* in the broadest sense of the phrase, they do allow you to accomplish all three of the specific examples provided above, and much more. Maple is not designed for pattern matching; its basic construction leans more towards *procedural programming*. Trying to make a complete pattern matching facility for Maple would be like using a glove as a sock—you could probably accomplish it, but it really wouldn't fit.

The best way to discover the power that is provided in *PatternTools* is to read on and try the examples given.

What Maple Has

Given the lack of *real* pattern tools in Maple, this section is used to introduce the basic concept used in creating the expression manipulation commands in *PatternTools* and the two built-in Maple procedures that are used most frequently throughout.

Converting Between Expressions and Strings

It is of paramount importance that you understand thoroughly how Maple converts typical expressions to string form and back again. These two conversions are at the very heart of the commands in *PatternTools*.

The built-in **convert** command can transform *any* valid Maple expression into its string equivalent.

> convert(a+b+c, string);

$$(a) + (b) + (c)$$

Why are the extra parentheses provided around each term in the summation?[1] This idiosyncrasy does lead to some problems later on, but none that can't be handled once you are aware of them. These extra characters can become rather daunting within larger expressions.

> convert(int(1/(1+x^4), x), string);

$$((1/8)*((2)^{\wedge}(1/2))*(ln((((x)^{\wedge}(2)) + ((x)*((2)^{\wedge}(1/2))) + (1))*((((x)^{\wedge}(2)) + ((-1)*(x)\backslash$$
$$*((2)^{\wedge}(1/2))) + (1))^{\wedge}(-1)))) + ((1/4)*((2)^{\wedge}(1/2))*(arctan(((x)*((2)^{\wedge}(1/2)))\backslash$$
$$+(1)))) + ((1/4)*((2)^{\wedge}(1/2))*(arctan(((x)*((2)^{\wedge}(1/2))) + (-1))))$$

As you can see, the first parameter to **convert** is always evaluated fully before the conversion takes place. The result is a one-dimensional string

---

[1] We've never been able to get a satisfactory answer to this question from the Maple people, but we have been assured that in future versions there will be a way around this side effect.

of characters, not unlike that returned by the lprint command—but don't confuse the two; they are *not* identical.

```
> lprint(");
```

((1/8)*((2)^(1/2))*(ln((((x)^(2))+((x)*((2)^(1/2)))+(1))*((((x)^(2))+((-1)*(x)\
((2)^(1/2)))+(1))^(-1)))))+((1/4)((2)^(1/2))*(arctan(((x)*((2)^(1/2)))+(1)))\
)+((1/4)*((2)^(1/2))*(arctan(((x)*((2)^(1/2)))+(-1))))

```
> lprint(int(1/(1+x^4), x));
```

1/8*2^(1/2)*ln((x^2+x*2^(1/2)+1)/(x^2-x*2^(1/2)+1))+1/4*2^(1/2)*arctan(x*2^(1/2
)+1)+1/4*2^(1/2)*arctan(x*2^(1/2)-1)

Up until Maple V Release 2, there was no way to convert a string back into a Maple expression. At that time, the parse command was added for just that purpose.

```
> parse('a+b+(c)');
```

$$a + b + c$$

```
> anexpr := expand((x+2)^5);
```

$$anexpr := x^5 + 10\,x^4 + 40\,x^3 + 80\,x^2 + 80\,x + 32$$

```
> astr := convert(anexpr, string);
```

$$astr := ((x)^\wedge(5)) + ((10) * ((x)^\wedge(4))) + ((40) * ((x)^\wedge(3))) + ((80) * ((x)^\wedge(2))) + ((80) * (x)) + (32)$$

```
> parse(astr);
```

$$x^5 + 10\,x^4 + 40\,x^3 + 80\,x^2 + 80\,x + 32$$

The string is passed to Maple's internal parser, where superfluous parentheses are automatically removed. If the contents of the string are not parsable (i.e., they do not represent a valid Maple expression), then an error message is returned.

```
> parse('a*b+c-');
```

Error, incorrect syntax in parse

This message doesn't tell you much, other than that an error occurred.

For more detail on the finer workings of parse, see its on-line help page.

A Matter of Structure

As explained earlier, non-string expressions have an internal tree-like structure that dictates, to a large extent, the type of operations that can be performed upon them. Strings, on the other hand, are stored simply as the juxtaposition of many characters, without information as to the meaning of those characters.

By putting an entire expression into string form, searching for smaller substrings within that string, and then performing some operation upon that substring, tasks that are impossible within expression form become simple. There are several potential pitfalls for those who use these tools unwisely; but in the following sections we attempt to point out these dangers and steer you around them.

One danger to avoid is the overuse of the commands in *PatternTools*. A large majority of the expression manipulation tasks you will need to perform are within the capabilities of the *ExpressionTools*, and since they are based on the more intuitive, mathematically-based internal structure of expressions, they are easier to use and to understand. These new tools are meant to be used when other tools fail.

Because the large majority of manipulations done by the commands in *PatternTools* are performed upon strings, it is a good idea for you read the *StringTools* chapter to review Maple's built-in capabilities in this area and the Utility commands provided before you proceed.

Utility Commands

The discussion in this section begins with a look at five tools whose design directly mimics commands in *ExpressionTools*. At first, the patterns (strings) being searched for are simple and straightforward, explicitly defined within the parameter sequence. Later, more ambitious "pattern matching" capabilities are explored.

Finding, Displaying, and Replacing Basic Patterns

findpat(pat, expr)	locate a pattern within an expression
showpat(patrng, expr)	extract a pattern given a pattern range
markpat(patrng, expr)	mark a subexpression within its parent expression
subspat(patrng = expr$_{new}$, expr)	substitute a new value for a pattern
mappat(fnc,[patrng$_1$,...,patrng$_n$], expr)	map a function onto selected subexpressions

In the preceding sections, a pattern has been introduced as a *string* representing some part of a Maple expression. In the findpat command, on which the other four commands in this section are based, a string is a valid first parameter. To demonstrate this, create the following large trigonometric expression.

> `with(utility):`

> `myexpr := expand(sin(2*x+y*x)*cos(2*y+x*y));`

$$myexpr := 4\cos(yx)^2 \sin(x)\cos(x)\cos(y)^2 - 2\cos(yx)^2 \sin(x)\cos(x)$$
$$- 4\cos(yx)\sin(x)\cos(x)\sin(yx)\sin(y)\cos(y)$$
$$+ 4\sin(yx)\cos(x)^2 \cos(yx)\cos(y)^2 - 2\sin(yx)\cos(x)^2 \cos(yx)$$
$$- 4\sin(yx)^2 \cos(x)^2 \sin(y)\cos(y) - 2\sin(yx)\cos(yx)\cos(y)^2$$
$$+ \sin(yx)\cos(yx) + 2\sin(yx)^2 \sin(y)\cos(y)$$

Say you want to find every occurrence of $\sin(x)\cos(x)$ in myexpr. Use the built-in convert command to transform this "subexpression" [2] into string representation.

> `findpat(convert(sin(x)*cos(x), string), myexpr);`

$$27..43$$

The result is an integer range. This *pattern range* specifies the character positions in the converted (to a string) myexpr where you can find the first occurrence of the string representing $\sin(x)\cos(x)$. As with the locator lists returned by findexpr, you do not really need to know how the resulting range is applied to point out the desired subexpression—other commands such as showpat, subspat, and mappat completely understand these ranges when they are used directly as input.

Also similar to findexpr, findpat can take an optional parameter specifying how many occurrences of the pattern are to be found. Adding the value infinity finds all occurrences.

> `findpat(convert(sin(x)*cos(x), string), myexpr, 2);`

$$[27..43, 88..104]$$

> `allranges := findpat(convert(sin(x)*cos(x), string), myexpr, infinity);`

$$allranges := [27..43, 88..104, 128..144]$$

Typing in the convert command seems inefficient. What would happen if you simply enclosed the desired subexpression in backquotes?

---

[2]The term subexpression is put in quotes because although $\sin(x)\cos(x)$ appears several times in myexpr, it is *not* a true subexpression within the internal tree-like structure of the Maple expression. (That is, it could not be found by findexpr.)

> findpat('sin(x)*cos(x)', myexpr);

$$( )..( )$$

findpat returned a NULL range (i.e., ( )..( )), indicating that it didn't find any occurrences of $\sin(x)\cos(x)$, although they obviously are there. When any of the commands in this section are given an *explicit* string to search for, they take it that you have entered the string in exactly the same form as the convert(,string) command would produce. In this case, that is very different from what was previously input.

> convert(sin(x)*cos(x), string);

$$(sin(x)) * (cos(x))$$

To get around this problem and the unwanted typing of the convert command, enter the pattern simply as the subexpression itself.

> myrange := findpat(sin(x)*cos(x), myexpr);

$$myrange := 27..43$$

When findpat determines that it has been passed a non-string to search for, it first converts it using convert(,string). Unfortunately, this technique does not work in all cases. For example, try to find the pattern matching $\cos(y) + 4\sin(yx)$. Typing this expression directly into findpat produces a NULL range, even though the expression can be clearly seen near the middle of myexpr.

> findpat(cos(y)+4*sin(y*x), myexpr);

$$( )..( )$$

The problem here is again attributable to extra (or missing) parentheses. Because convert(,string) puts an extra set of parentheses around entire sums and products, and $\cos(y)$ and $4\sin(yx)$ are the last and first terms, respectively, of two *different* products, the string produced when the first parameter of the last command is converted is different than the desired substring in the larger expression.

> convert(cos(y)+4*sin(y*x), string);

$$(cos(y)) + ((4) * (sin((y) * (x))))$$

> extractstring(convert(myexpr, string), 170..198);

$$(cos(y))) + ((4) * (sin((y) * (x)))$$

If you look carefully, there is an extra right parenthesis directly before the + in the second string. Also, there is one less right parenthesis on the end of that string. Put this new string into a call to findpat.[3]

> findpat(", myexpr, infinity);

$$170..198$$

Once you have determined a pattern range, the showpat command can be used to display that pattern.

> showpat(", myexpr);

$$(cos(y))) + ((4) * (sin((y) * (x))))$$

> showpat(myrange, myexpr);

$$(sin(x)) * (cos(x))$$

The patterns returned by showpat are always in string form.[4] To convert it to an expression, use parse.

> parse(");

$$\sin(x)\cos(x)$$

Of course, like showexpr, showpat can be applied to a list of several pattern ranges.

> map(parse, showpat(allranges, myexpr));

$$[\sin(x)\cos(x), \sin(x)\cos(x), \sin(x)\cos(x)]$$

If you want to display the pattern within the larger expression, markpat encloses it with an unevaluated call to MARK.

> markpat(myrange, myexpr);

$$4\cos(yx)^2 \text{MARK}(\sin(x)\cos(x))\cos(y)^2 - 2\cos(yx)^2 \sin(x)\cos(x)$$
$$- 4\cos(yx)\sin(x)\cos(x)\sin(yx)\sin(y)\cos(y)$$
$$+ 4\sin(yx)\cos(x)^2 \cos(yx)\cos(y)^2 - 2\sin(yx)\cos(x)^2 \cos(yx)$$
$$- 4\sin(yx)^2 \cos(x)^2 \sin(y)\cos(y) - 2\sin(yx)\cos(yx)\cos(y)^2$$
$$+ \sin(yx)\cos(yx) + 2\sin(yx)^2 \sin(y)\cos(y)$$

---

[3] Using findpat with a range determined in this way is a little wasteful, since you have already determined the necessary pattern range. If there is more than one occurrence of the pattern in the larger expression, however, it is worth the effort.

[4] The reasons for this will become more apparent shortly.

You might have noticed that in this case markpat returned a *parsed* expression, not a string as with showpat. This demonstrates the first part of a general rule regarding the input and output forms of the commands markpat, subspat, and mappat:

1. If the expression from which the pattern emerges is entered in non-string form, then the result is automatically passed through parse before it is returned.

Other optional features available in markexpr can also be supplied, including multiple pattern ranges, alternate function names, and numbered functions.

> markpat(allranges, myexpr, 'SPOT', 'numbered');

$4\cos(yx)^2 \text{SPOT1}(\sin(x)\cos(x))\cos(y)^2 - 2\cos(yx)^2 \text{SPOT2}(\sin(x)\cos(x))$
$- 4\cos(yx)\text{SPOT3}(\sin(x)\cos(x))\sin(yx)\sin(y)\cos(y)$
$+ 4\sin(yx)\cos(x)^2\cos(yx)\cos(y)^2 - 2\sin(yx)\cos(x)^2\cos(yx)$
$- 4\sin(yx)^2\cos(x)^2\sin(y)\cos(y) - 2\sin(yx)\cos(yx)\cos(y)^2$
$+ \sin(yx)\cos(yx) + 2\sin(yx)^2\sin(y)\cos(y)$

subspat can be used to replace the specified patterns with new values. As with findpat, entering an expression and letting the command do the conversion to a string works best.

> subspat(allranges = C(x), myexpr);

$4\cos(yx)^2 C(x)\cos(y)^2 - 2\cos(yx)^2 C(x)$
$- 4\cos(yx)C(x)\sin(yx)\sin(y)\cos(y)$
$+ 4\sin(yx)\cos(x)^2\cos(yx)\cos(y)^2 - 2\sin(yx)\cos(x)^2\cos(yx)$
$- 4\sin(yx)^2\cos(x)^2\sin(y)\cos(y) - 2\sin(yx)\cos(yx)\cos(y)^2$
$+ \sin(yx)\cos(yx) + 2\sin(yx)^2\sin(y)\cos(y)$

mappat works similarly, except that the substituted values are the results of passing the individually parsed patterns through the function given as the first parameter.

> mappat(diff, allranges, myexpr, 1, {2=x});

$2\cos(yx)^2\cos(x)^2 - \sin(x)^2\cos(y)^2 - \sin(x)^2 - 4\cos(yx)\cos(x)^2$
$- \sin(x)^2\sin(yx)\sin(y)\cos(y) + 4\sin(yx)\cos(x)^2\cos(yx)\cos(y)^2$
$- 2\sin(yx)\cos(x)^2\cos(yx) - 4\sin(yx)^2\cos(x)^2\sin(y)\cos(y)$
$- 2\sin(yx)\cos(yx)\cos(y)^2 + \sin(yx)\cos(yx) + 2\sin(yx)^2\sin(y)\cos(y)$

As demonstrated, the parameters specifying which parameter is being mapped to and the values of other static parameters are also available in mappat.

Unparsable Patterns

In the previous section, the action of the five basic commands in *PatternTools* when dealing with parsable patterns was discussed. What happens when the pattern you are searching for is *definitely not* a parsable Maple expression? For example, what if you want to find all occurrences of cos(y in myexpr?

First you must be able to pass cos(y to findpat. Entering it as a "halfexpression" causes a syntax error.

```
> findpat(cos(y, myexpr,infinity);

syntax error:
findpat(cos(y, myexpr,infinity);
             ^
```

Enclosing it directly in backquotes seems to work.

```
> pats1 := findpat(`cos(y`, myexpr, infinity);
```

$pats1 := [\,47..51, 171..175, 232..236, 350..354, 397..401, 479..483\,]$

Are those really the only patterns that we want? Try using markpat to display the patterns specified in pats1.

```
> markpat(pats1, myexpr);
```

$4\cos(yx)^2 \sin(x)\cos(x)\,\text{MARK}(\cos(y))^2 - 2\cos(yx)^2 \sin(x)\cos(x)$

$- 4\cos(yx)\sin(x)\cos(x)\sin(yx)\sin(y)\,\text{MARK}(\cos(y))$

$+ 4\sin(yx)\cos(x)^2\cos(yx)\,\text{MARK}(\cos(y))^2 - 2\sin(yx)\cos(x)^2\cos(yx)$

$- 4\sin(yx)^2\cos(x)^2\sin(y)\,\text{MARK}(\cos(y))$

$- 2\sin(yx)\cos(yx)\,\text{MARK}(\cos(y))^2 + \sin(yx)\cos(yx)$

$+ 2\sin(yx)^2 \sin(y)\,\text{MARK}(\cos(y))$

The substitution for cos(y has caused the replacement of several occurrences of cos(y) with MARK(cos(y)). (Can you tell which of the closing parentheses in MARK(cos(y)) came from the original expression, and which came from the call to MARK?)

As mentioned earlier, when markpat is passed the non-string expression myexpr, it automatically parses the final result. The result here was parsable, so a Maple expression was returned. If the result was not parsable, an error message would have been generated. The standing rule needs to be changed, and a new one added as follows:

1. If the expression from which the pattern emerges is entered in non-string form, then the result is automatically passed through parse before it is returned. If the result is unparsable, an error message is returned.

2. If the expression from which the pattern emerges is entered in string form, then the result is not parsed, but returned in string form.

Applying the second rule to markpat results in:

> `markpat(pats1, convert(myexpr, string));`

$((4) * ((cos((y) * (x)))^\wedge(2)) * (sin(x)) * (cos(x)) * ((MARK(cos(y)))^\wedge(2))) + ((-2) * ((cos((y) * (x)))^\wedge(2)) * (sin(x)) * (cos(x))) + ((-4) * (cos((y) * (x))) * (sin(x)) * (cos(x)) * (sin((y) * (x))) * (sin(y)) * (MARK(cos(y)))) + ((4) * (sin((y) * (x))) * ((cos(x))^\wedge(2)) * (cos((y) * (x))) * ((MARK(cos(y)))^\wedge(2))) + ((-2) * (sin((y) * (x))) * ((cos(x))^\wedge(2)) * (cos((y) * (x)))) + ((-4) * ((sin((y) * (x)))^\wedge(2)) * ((cos(x))^\wedge(2)) * (sin(y)) * (MARK(cos(y)))) + ((-2) * (sin((y) * (x))) * (cos((y) * (x))) * ((MARK(cos(y)))^\wedge(2))) + ((sin((y) * (x))) * (cos((y) * (x)))) + ((2) * ((sin((y) * (x)))^\wedge(2)) * (sin(y)) * (MARK(cos(y))))$

Looking at the earlier result, you can see that pats1 did not include the desired patterns for cos(yx). How does Maple represent that value in string form?

> `convert(cos(y*x), string);`

$cos((y) * (x))$

In order to catch those patterns, you must add a left parenthesis to your search string.

> `pats2 := findpat('cos((y', myexpr, infinity);`

$pats2 := [8..13, 69..74, 114..119, 216..221, 283..288, 381..386, 428..433]$

Using appendlist from *ListTools*, try to use the two pattern range lists in a call to subspat.

> `subspat(appendlist(pats1, pats2)='COS(y', myexpr);`

`Error, (in subspat) incorrect syntax in parse`

What happened here? Replacing the strings 'cos((y' from pats2 with 'COS(y' created an unparsable string. You could pass myexpr as a string, but you really want the final result to be an expression.

What about using mappat? As seen in the last section, in most cases, mappat expects the individual patterns to be parsable. A third rule gets you around this problem.

1. If the expression from which the patterns emerge is entered in non-string form, then the result is automatically passed through parse before it is returned. If the result is unparsable, an error message is returned.
2. If the expression from which the patterns emerge is entered in string form, then the result is not parsed, but returned in string form.
3. In mappat, if the expression from which the patterns emerge is entered in non-string form, then *each* individual pattern is also parsed before being passed to the given function. If the expression from which the patterns emerge is entered in string form, then the individual patterns are passed in string form, and the given function must act upon strings.

Using these rules and the Utility command uppercase,[5] you can now perform the desired substitution.

```
> mappat(uppercase, appendlist(pats1, pats2), convert(myexpr,string),
> 1, {2=1..3});
```

$((4) * ((COS((y) * (x)))^{(2)}) * (sin(x)) * (cos(x)) * ((COS(y))^{(2)})) + ((-2) * ((COS((y \backslash$
$) * (x)))^{(2)}) * (sin(x)) * (cos(x))) + ((-4) * (COS((y) * (x))) * (sin(x)) * (cos(x)) * \backslash$
$(sin((y) * (x))) * (sin(y)) * (COS(y))) + ((4) * (sin((y) * (x))) * ((cos(x))^{(2)}) * (C \backslash$
$OS((y) * (x))) * ((COS(y))^{(2)})) + ((-2) * (sin((y) * (x))) * ((cos(x))^{(2)}) * (CO \backslash$
$S((y) * (x)))) + ((-4) * ((sin((y) * (x)))^{(2)}) * ((cos(x))^{(2)}) * (sin(y)) * (COS(y) \backslash$
$)) + ((-2) * (sin((y) * (x))) * (COS((y) * (x))) * ((COS(y))^{(2)})) + ((sin((y) * (x))) \backslash$
$*(COS((y) * (x)))) + ((2) * ((sin((y) * (x)))^{(2)}) * (sin(y)) * (COS(y)))$

```
> parse(");
```

$$4 COS(yx)^2 \sin(x) \cos(x) COS(y)^2 - 2 COS(yx)^2 \sin(x) \cos(x)$$
$$- 4 COS(yx) \sin(x) \cos(x) \sin(yx) \sin(y) COS(y)$$
$$+ 4 \sin(yx) \cos(x)^2 COS(yx) COS(y)^2 - 2 \sin(yx) \cos(x)^2 COS(yx)$$
$$- 4 \sin(yx)^2 \cos(x)^2 \sin(y) COS(y) - 2 \sin(yx) COS(yx) COS(y)^2$$
$$+ \sin(yx) COS(yx) + 2 \sin(yx)^2 \sin(y) COS(y)$$

---

[5] See the *StringTools* chapter for more information on uppercase.

Patterns Containing Unknown Characters

pattern([expr$_1$, ..., expr$_n$])	represent a pattern
nchars(n)	represent a character string of length n
anychars()	represent a character string of any length

Continuing the example from the previous section, what if you want to actually perform some sort of mathematical operation upon the calls to cos which have y as a parameter? The string-form patterns determined earlier can't be passed to mappat as expressions.

The three commands in this section allow you create more ambitious patterns, containing "wildcard characters" representing zero or more unknown characters. While each of the commands in this section always returns an unevaluated command call to itself,[6] some simplification of the entered parameters does take place.

The nchars command accepts a non-negative integer, n, as its first parameter and represents a string of exactly n characters. If you pass it a real constant that is not an integer, the value is truncated to an integer value.

```
> nchars(3);
```
$$\text{nchars}(\,3\,)$$

```
> nchars(Pi);
```
$$\text{nchars}(\,3\,)$$

The anychars command, which needs no parameters, represents a string of any non-negative length.

```
> anychars();
```
$$\text{anychars}(\,)$$

The pattern command binds them all together. pattern takes a list as its first parameter, whose internal elements can each be any of the following:

1. a Maple string

2. a Maple expression—in which case it gets converted to a string using convert(,string)

3. a call to nchars, or anychars

Any adjacent elements from categories 1) or 2) above are concatenated together to create a larger string. For example, the following are all valid calls to pattern.

---

[6]Except if an error message is triggered.

```
> pattern([ 'cos(', x*y, ')' ]);
```
$$cos((y)*(x))$$
```
> pattern([ 'cos(', nchars(5), ')' ]);
```
$$\mathrm{pattern}([\,cos(,\mathrm{nchars}(\,5\,),)\,])$$
```
> pattern([ 'cos(', y, anychars(), ')' ]);
```
$$\mathrm{pattern}([\,cos(y,\mathrm{anychars}(\,),)\,])$$

Now that you know how to create more complex patterns, try using them to find all the patterns for either $\sin(x)$ or $\cos(x)$ in myexpr.

```
> mypat := pattern([ nchars(3), '(', x, ')' ]);
```
$$mypat := \mathrm{pattern}([\,\mathrm{nchars}(\,3\,),(x)\,])$$
```
> findpat(mypat, myexpr, infinity);
```
$$[13..18, 28..33, 37..42, 74..79, 89..94, 98..103, 119..124, 129..134,$$
$$138..143, 152..157, 191..196, 202..207, 221..226, 258..263,$$
$$269..274, 288..293, 311..316, 327..332, 371..376, 386..391,$$
$$418..423, 433..438, 455..460]$$

Now use markexpr to verify that you have found *all* the desired patterns.

```
> markpat(", myexpr);
```
$$4\cos(\mathrm{MARK}(y)x)^2\,\mathrm{MARK}(\sin(x))\,\mathrm{MARK}(\cos(x))\cos(y)^2$$
$$-2\cos(\mathrm{MARK}(y)x)^2\,\mathrm{MARK}(\sin(x))\,\mathrm{MARK}(\cos(x))-4$$
$$\cos(\mathrm{MARK}(y)x)\,\mathrm{MARK}(\sin(x))\,\mathrm{MARK}(\cos(x))\sin(\mathrm{MARK}(y)x)\sin(y)$$
$$\cos(y)+4\sin(\mathrm{MARK}(y)x)\,\mathrm{MARK}(\cos(x))^2\cos(\mathrm{MARK}(y)x)\cos(y)^2$$
$$-2\sin(\mathrm{MARK}(y)x)\,\mathrm{MARK}(\cos(x))^2\cos(\mathrm{MARK}(y)x)$$
$$-4\sin(\mathrm{MARK}(y)x)^2\,\mathrm{MARK}(\cos(x))^2\sin(y)\cos(y)$$
$$-2\sin(\mathrm{MARK}(y)x)\cos(\mathrm{MARK}(y)x)\cos(y)^2$$
$$+\sin(\mathrm{MARK}(y)x)\cos(\mathrm{MARK}(y)x)+2\sin(\mathrm{MARK}(y)x)^2\sin(y)\cos(y)$$

It looks as if some "extra" patterns were picked up—basically all the occurrences of the string '(y)(x)', which also fit the search criteria.

A little more challenging example: replace the first subexpression that is a call to cos which contains y as part of its single parameter with the value π.

First, create a pattern satisfying the given criteria:

> `newpat := pattern([ 'cos(', anychars(), y, anychars(), ')' ]);`

$$newpat := \text{pattern}([\,cos(, anychars(\,), y, anychars(\,),)\,])$$

Now call findpat:

> `pats3 := findpat(newpat, myexpr);`

$$pats3 := 8..14$$

Finally, perform the desired substitution.

> `subspat(pats3=Pi, myexpr);`

`Error, (in subspat) incorrect syntax in parse`

Why did a parsing error occur? Display the pattern with showpat:

> `showpat(pats3, myexpr);`

$$cos((y)$$

This pattern, which is *part* of the cos (*yx*) in the first term, is not parsable. Count the number of left and right parentheses to verify this. What has happened is that the given call to pattern has caused the "extra" right parenthesis directly after the y to be chosen as the final character of the pattern.

The only way to ensure that the correct parenthesis gets chosen in such cases in to stipulate that any pattern returned by findpat be parsable. An optional parameter 'parsable' can be added to the end of the pattern command itself.

> `newpat := pattern([ 'cos(', anychars(), y, anychars(), ')' ], parsable);`

$$newpat := \text{pattern}([\,cos(, anychars(\,), y, anychars(\,),)\,], parsable\,)$$

> `pats3 := findpat(newpat, myexpr);`

$$pats3 := 8..19$$

> `showpat(pats3, myexpr);`

$$cos((y)*(x))$$

Now you can be assured that subspat will work.

> `subspat(pats3=Pi, myexpr);`

$$4\pi^2 \sin(x)\cos(x)\cos(y)^2 - 2\cos(yx)^2 \sin(x)\cos(x)$$
$$- 4\cos(yx)\sin(x)\cos(x)\sin(yx)\sin(y)\cos(y)$$

$$+ 4 \sin(yx) \cos(x)^2 \cos(yx) \cos(y)^2 - 2 \sin(yx) \cos(x)^2 \cos(yx)$$
$$- 4 \sin(yx)^2 \cos(x)^2 \sin(y) \cos(y) - 2 \sin(yx) \cos(yx) \cos(y)^2$$
$$+ \sin(yx) \cos(yx) + 2 \sin(yx)^2 \sin(y) \cos(y)$$

The 'parsable' option can be added to the end of any individual call to pattern, nchars, or anychars to ensure that the pattern represented by *that call alone* is parsable. Also, 'parsable' can be added to the end of the findpat command to ensure that each *entire* pattern returned is parsable.

Examples

Finding All Occurrences of a Function

Write a procedure, named allcalls, that takes a function name (e.g., cos) and any expression, and returns a set containing each unique occurence of that function in the expression.

First, create a large expression (similar to another created earlier in this chapter) for testing purposes.

```
> lexpr := expand(sin(2*sin(x)+cos(y)*x)*cos(2*sin(y)+cos(x)*y));
```

$$lexpr := 4\cos(\cos(y)x)\sin(\sin(x))\cos(\sin(x))\cos(\cos(x)y)\cos(\sin(y))^2$$
$$- 2\cos(\cos(y)x)\sin(\sin(x))\cos(\sin(x))\cos(\cos(x)y) - 4$$
$$\cos(\cos(y)x)\sin(\sin(x))\cos(\sin(x))\sin(\cos(x)y)\sin(\sin(y))\cos(\sin(y))$$
$$+ 4\sin(\cos(y)x)\cos(\sin(x))^2\cos(\cos(x)y)\cos(\sin(y))^2$$
$$- 2\sin(\cos(y)x)\cos(\sin(x))^2\cos(\cos(x)y)$$
$$- 4\sin(\cos(y)x)\cos(\sin(x))^2\sin(\cos(x)y)\sin(\sin(y))\cos(\sin(y))$$
$$- 2\sin(\cos(y)x)\cos(\cos(x)y)\cos(\sin(y))^2 + \sin(\cos(y)x)\cos(\cos(x)y)$$
$$+ 2\sin(\cos(y)x)\sin(\cos(x)y)\sin(\sin(y))\cos(\sin(y))$$

In order to display the actual unevaluated calls to cos in lexpr, findpat and showpat must be called in combination.

```
> allcos := showpat(
>     findpat(
>     pattern(['cos(', anychars(), ')'], parsable),
>     lexpr, infinity),
>     lexpr);
```

$$allcos := [cos((cos(y)) * (x)), cos(y), cos(sin(x)), cos((cos(x)) * (y)), cos(x),$$

$cos(sin(y)), cos((cos(y)) * (x)), cos(y), cos(sin(x)), cos((cos(x)) * (y)), cos(x),$
$cos((cos(y)) * (x)), cos(y), cos(sin(x)), cos(x), cos(sin(y)), cos(y), cos(sin(x)),$
$cos((cos(x)) * (y)), cos(x), cos(sin(y)), cos(y), cos(sin(x)), cos((cos(x)) * (y)),$
$cos(x), cos(y), cos(sin(x)), cos(x), cos(sin(y)), cos(y), cos((cos(x)) * (y)),$
$cos(x), cos(sin(y)), cos(y), cos((cos(x)) * (y)), cos(x), cos(y), cos(x), cos(sin(y))]$

> {op(allcos)};

$\{ cos(sin(x)), cos(sin(y)), cos((cos(x)) * (y)), cos(x), cos((cos(y)) * (x)), cos(y) \}$

Enclosing all the individual patterns in set braces eliminates repeated occurrences.

Even the calls to cos that themselves contain unevaluated command calls were found. However, showpat has left the patterns as strings. Using map and parse, convert the strings into expressions.

> map(parse, ");

$\{ cos(y), cos(x), cos(sin(x)), cos(cos(x)y), cos(cos(y)x), cos(sin(y)) \}$

Now you can easily combine this functionality in a procedure that works for *any* unevaluated function.

```
> allcalls := proc(fnc, expr)
>    local allpats;
>
>    allpats := findpat(pattern([
>       convert(fnc, string), '(', anychars(), ')'], parsable),
>       expr, infinity);
>    {op(map(parse, showpat(allpats, expr)))};
> end:
```

Test allcalls on each of the unevaluated functions in lexpr.

> allcalls(cos, lexpr);

$\{ cos(y), cos(x), cos(sin(x)), cos(cos(x)y), cos(cos(y)x), cos(sin(y)) \}$

> allcalls(sin, lexpr);

$\{ sin(y), sin(x), sin(sin(x)), sin(cos(y)x), sin(cos(x)y), sin(sin(y)) \}$

Programming Tips

Most of the techniques used in programming the *PatternTools* have already been discussed. The basic built-in tools, convert(,string), substring, parse, etc., were detailed earlier in this chapter. More complicated programming techniques used here are similar to those explained in the *Programming Tips* section of the *ExpressionTools* chapter.

The following section investigates a common programming practice used throughout many areas of *The Practical Approach Utilities for Maple*.

Trapping Errors

Typically, when a Maple error message is generated, that message stops all computations not only in the command that generated it, but also in the command that called that command, and in the command that called that command, and so on right to the top level of the session. At that point the actual error message is displayed.

In some cases, you do not want the generation of an error message to force you to the top level of computation. Two of the more common reasons are:

1. You want to examine the error message generated in a deeper level in the context of the current command, so that a more meaningful message can be passed to the user.
2. The possibility of the error situation has been forseen, and alternate computations can be performed in that case.

The example discussed in this section fits more into the latter category. In either case, to "trap" the error, use the built-in command, traperror. When passed a call to another command, traperror returns the result of that command, if no error occurred, or the string representing the error message, if an error did occur. Either way, control then passes to the next statement in the current level.

```
> traperror(int(x));
```

wrong number (or type) of arguments

What if the command passed to traperror actually produces a string as valid output? How then do you know whether an error occurred? The global variable lasterror always holds the string created by the most recent call to ERROR. So, compare the result of traperror to lasterror. The following small procedure demonstrates this comparison.

```
> littleproc := proc(fnc, param)
>     local res;
>
>     res := traperror(fnc);
>     if res = lasterror then
>         print('An error was encountered')
```

```
>         else
>            res;
>         fi;
> end:

> littleproc(int, x);
```

An error was encountered

```
> littleproc(reversestring, 'rrorE');
```

Erorr

In the Utility command findpat, it is often the case that you want to find a pattern that is parsable (i.e., able to stand on its own when converted to a Maple expression). In order to determine whether a pattern (string) is parsable, it must be passed to the built-in parse command.

```
> parse('sin(x)');
```

$$\sin(x)$$

```
> parse('x^2+3*y-');
```

Error, incorrect syntax in parse

If a loop is set up to test various patterns, you certainly don't want the process being aborted every time an unparsable pattern is encountered. The following simple procedure, npat, takes a positive integer, n, and an expression as input. The expression is converted to a string and then each n-character long substring, starting with the first n characters, is tested to see if it is parsable. Once a parsable string is found, it is returned.[7]

```
> npat := proc(n, expr)
>    local i, str, isparsable;
>
>    str := convert(expr, string);
>    for i from 1 to length(str)-n+1 do
>       isparsable := traperror(parse(substring(str, i..i+n-1)));
>       if isparsable = lasterror then
>          next;
>       else
>          RETURN(isparsable);
>       fi;
>    od;
> end:
```

---

[7]This process is contained within the code for findpat, but is much more difficult to see within all the other code.

Test this procedure out on a large expression.

```
> myexpr := int(1/(1+x^4), x);
```

$$myexpr :=$$
$$\frac{1}{8}\sqrt{2}\ln\left(\frac{x^2+x\sqrt{2}+1}{x^2-x\sqrt{2}+1}\right)+\frac{1}{4}\sqrt{2}\arctan\left(x\sqrt{2}+1\right)+\frac{1}{4}\sqrt{2}\arctan\left(x\sqrt{2}-1\right)$$

```
> npat(6, myexpr);
```

$$\text{arctan}$$

Looking closely at the string form of myexpr, you can see that this is indeed the first parsable six-character substring.

```
> convert(myexpr, string);
```

$$((1/8) * ((2)^\hat{}(1/2)) * (ln((((x)^\hat{}(2)) + ((x) * ((2)^\hat{}(1/2))) + (1)) * ((((x)^\hat{}(2)) + ((-1) * (x))\backslash$$
$$*((2)^\hat{}(1/2))) + (1))^\hat{}(-1)))) + ((1/4) * ((2)^\hat{}(1/2)) * (arctan(((x) * ((2)^\hat{}(1/2)))\backslash$$
$$+(1)))) + ((1/4) * ((2)^\hat{}(1/2)) * (arctan(((x) * ((2)^\hat{}(1/2))) + (-1))))$$

Using seq, you can then determine the first parsable substrings of length from one to twenty characters.

```
> seq(npat(i, myexpr), i=1..20);
```

$$1, \ln, \frac{1}{8}, 1, \frac{1}{8}, \arctan, x^2, -x, \sqrt{2}, \sqrt{2}, x\sqrt{2}, \frac{1}{8}\sqrt{2}, x\sqrt{2}, -x\sqrt{2}$$

There don't appear to be twenty results here.

```
> nops(["]);
```

$$14$$

Obviously, some of the integer values didn't find any parsable substrings. But for which values? Adding a line after the for/do/od loop in npat inserts a value of FAIL in the appropriate places.

```
> npat := proc(n, expr)
>     local i, str, isparsable;
>
>     str := convert(expr, string);
>     for i from 1 to length(str)-n+1 do
>         isparsable := traperror(parse(substring(str, i..i+n-1)));
>         if isparsable = lasterror then
>             next;
>         else
>             RETURN(isparsable);
```

```
>         fi;
>       od;
>       RETURN(FAIL);
> end:
```

```
> seq(npat(i, myexpr), i=1..20);
```

$$1, \ln, \frac{1}{8}, 1, \frac{1}{8}, \arctan, x^2, -x, \sqrt{2}, \textit{FAIL}, \sqrt{2}, \textit{FAIL}, \textit{FAIL}, \textit{FAIL}, x\sqrt{2}, \textit{FAIL}, \frac{1}{8}\sqrt{2},$$
$$x\sqrt{2}, \textit{FAIL}, -x\sqrt{2}$$

```
> nops(["]);
```

$$20$$

CHAPTER 7
ArrayTools

Arrays are Maple structures that, in their most common usage, form the backbone for Maple's representation of vectors and matrices. While Maple may not *entirely* revolve around vectors and matrices like some other computational tools (MATLAB in particular), they are involved in the majority of linear algebra calculations and have a myriad of uses in other areas as well. For more information on those uses, refer to any basic introduction to Maple, or, more specifically, to a text on Maple's uses in linear algebra.

For a structure that is used so often in Maple, arrays can be notoriously difficult to understand. It is hoped that this chapter will give you a better feel for how to deal with them, and that the accompanying Utility functions will make the job easier still.

What Maple Has

Basic Rules for Arrays

Arrays are high-level structures (of one or more dimensions) which contain a well-ordered collection of elements. Each individual dimension of an array has a *predefined* range.

Although one-dimensional arrays can be thought of as special lists, two-dimensional arrays as lists of lists, and so on, there are some important differences between the two types of structures.[1]

---

[1] In future versions of Maple, these differences may for the most part disappear, making lists and arrays interchangeable in many cases.

Multiple-dimension arrays are always *rectangular* in nature. That is, you cannot create a two-dimensional array with three elements in the first row, two in the second row, and four in the third row.

Arrays can be created with the array command. The individual elements of an array can either be specified in the call to array or left as unknowns. The following is an example of an array with four rows and three columns (4×3) that contains twelve predefined elements.

```
> array(1..4, 1..3, [[a,b,34],[5/7,x+2,0],[exp(3^x),Fred,1],[.2,d,a*c]]);
```

$$\begin{bmatrix} a & b & 34 \\ \frac{5}{7} & x+2 & 0 \\ e^{(3^x)} & Fred & 1 \\ .2 & d & ac \end{bmatrix}$$

As you can see, *any* type of expression, no matter how large, is acceptable as an element in an array. In most practical cases, however, all elements of an array are of the same type.

When you don't want all or some of the elements predefined, simply leave out all or part of the list of lists and Maple fills in the missing elements with unknown placeholders.[2]

```
> array(1..4, 1..2, [[3,2],[5],[6,3]]);
```

$$\begin{bmatrix} 3 & 2 \\ 5 & ?_{2,2} \\ 6 & 3 \\ ?_{4,1} & ?_{4,2} \end{bmatrix}$$

Using this method, you can only leave out elements of a row starting with the rightmost element and moving to the left; you cannot leave out, for example, just the second element of a four-element row. Because of this syntactical stipulation, it is typical when leaving some elements undefined to use an alternative method for specifying the defined elements. Instead of a list of lists, the third parameter is a list of equations, where each equation has the index of an element on the left side and the value of that element on the right side.

```
> array(1..3, 1..3, [(1,2)=f, (3,1)=h, (2,3)=g]);
```

$$\begin{bmatrix} ?_{1,1} & f & ?_{1,3} \\ ?_{2,1} & ?_{2,2} & g \\ h & ?_{3,2} & ?_{3,3} \end{bmatrix}$$

---

[2]Note that supplying *too many* elements in any one row, or too many rows in an array, causes an error message.

Another way to complete the same task is to start with a completely undefined array and then add elements. To do this, it is helpful to first assign the empty array to a name.

> A := array(1..3, 1..3, []);

$$A := \text{array}(1..3, 1..3, [\ ])$$

Completely empty arrays are initially displayed as unevaluated calls to array. To assign values to elements of A, use the following square bracket notation.[3]

> A[1,2] := f;

$$A_{1,2} := f$$

> A[2,3] := g:
> A[3,1] := h:
> print(A);

$$\begin{bmatrix} A_{1,1} & f & A_{1,3} \\ A_{2,1} & A_{2,2} & g \\ h & A_{3,2} & A_{3,3} \end{bmatrix}$$

(The reason for using the print command will be revealed presently.)

The same square brackets containing the row and column values can be used to query the value of individual elements.

> A[2,3];

$$g$$

> A[1,1];

$$A_{1,1}$$

Having a completely empty array is just one instance where Maple does not use the special, easy-to-read display form. Another occasion is when an array has an index starting at a value other than one.[4] When this happens, the array is printed out in a form more representative of its internal structure (i.e., as the bounding function(s) and a *table* representing the elements).

> array(-3..0, [a,b,c,d]);

$$\text{array}(-3..0, [$$

---

[3]This is another difference between arrays and lists—you cannot assign values to a list in this way.
[4]The only rules for index values are that they be integer values and that the second value in each range be greater than or equal to the first.

$$(-3) = a$$
$$(-2) = b$$
$$(-1) = c$$
$$(0) = d$$
])

Last Name Evaluation

There is one major difference in the evaluation rules for arrays that set them apart from most other Maple structures and causes a lot of confusion among Maple users. If you assign an array to a variable name and then type in that name, the result displayed is not the array itself but the variable name to which it is assigned. This is called *last name evaluation*. Among the commands that force full evaluation to the elements of the array are eval, op, and print.

```
> A := array(1..2, 1..2, [[2,0],[0,-7]]);
```

$$A := \begin{bmatrix} 2 & 0 \\ 0 & -7 \end{bmatrix}$$

```
> A;
```

$$A$$

```
> eval(A);
```

$$\begin{bmatrix} 2 & 0 \\ 0 & -7 \end{bmatrix}$$

```
> op(A);
```

$$\begin{bmatrix} 2 & 0 \\ 0 & -7 \end{bmatrix}$$

```
> print(A);
```

$$\begin{bmatrix} 2 & 0 \\ 0 & -7 \end{bmatrix}$$

Last name evaluation also holds for procedures and other types of Maple tables. For a more thorough review of the rules and consequences of last name evaluation, see an introductory Maple text, such as *Introduction to Maple* or *First Leaves*.

Creating Vectors and Matrices

In the linalg package there exist commands that allow you to create a *vector* or a *matrix* data structure (the vector and matrix commands, respectively). These commands are simply specialized cases of the array command.

A *vector* is equivalent to a one-dimensional array with its range starting at one. Instead of having a range as the first parameter, vector uses an integer that represents the size.

> linalg[vector](3, [x1,y1,z1]);

$$[\; x1 \quad y1 \quad z1 \;]$$

While the representation of this structure may lead you to believe that it is a *row vector*, vectors defined in this manner are thought of as *column vectors* when performing calculations. If you want to represent a *row vector*, embed a column vector in a call to linalg[transpose] or use the matrix command with 1 as the first parameter.

> linalg[transpose](linalg[vector](4, [1,2,3,4]));

$$\text{transpose}([\; 1 \quad 2 \quad 3 \quad 4 \;])$$

That is how column vectors are represented, as *unevaluated* calls to transpose. To transform the above column vector into a row vector, transpose it once more.

> linalg[transpose](");

$$[\; 1 \quad 2 \quad 3 \quad 4 \;]$$

Row and column vectors are used throughout the Utility commands in this chapter, and there are many examples given later of both creating and using them.

A *matrix* is equivalent to a two-dimensional array with both indices starting at one. The matrix command also takes integer dimensions.

> linalg[matrix](2, 3, [1,2,3,4,5,6]);

$$\begin{bmatrix} 1 & 2 & 3 \\ 4 & 5 & 6 \end{bmatrix}$$

As you may have noticed, the third parameter to matrix is not a list of lists, but a one-level list containing *all* the elements. The command automatically fills the rows from left to right, top to bottom.[5]

---

[5] A list of lists can also be used as the third parameter if you want to leave elements undefined.

Other Available Array Tools

A very simple tool for accessing the elements of arrays is the entries command, which returns the elements as a sequence of one-element lists.

> entries(A);

$$[2],[0],[0],[-7]$$

The map command can also be used to apply a command or an operation to each element of an array. (For more information on map, see the *Getting Started With Maple* chapter on page 46.)

> eval(A);

$$\begin{bmatrix} 2 & 0 \\ 0 & -7 \end{bmatrix}$$

> map(isprime, A);

$$\begin{bmatrix} true & false \\ false & false \end{bmatrix}$$

> map(x -> x^2, A);

$$\begin{bmatrix} 4 & 0 \\ 0 & 49 \end{bmatrix}$$

The large majority of existing commands for dealing with arrays are contained in the linalg package. To use them efficiently, first load in pointers to all the commands.

> with(linalg);

Warning: new definition for   norm
Warning: new definition for   trace

[BlockDiagonal, GramSchmidt, JordanBlock, Wronskian, add, addcol, addrow, adj, adjoint, angle, augment, backsub, band, basis, bezout, blockmatrix, charmat, charpoly, col, coldim, colspace, colspan, companion, concat, cond, copyinto, crossprod, curl, definite, delcols, delrows, det, diag, diverge, dotprod, eigenvals, eigenvects, entermatrix, equal, exponential, extend, ffgausselim, fibonacci, frobenius, gausselim, gaussjord, genmatrix, grad, hadamard, hermite, hessian, hilbert, htranspose, ihermite, indexfunc, innerprod, intbasis, inverse, ismith, iszero, jacobian, jordan, kernel, laplacian, leastsqrs, linsolve, matrix, minor, minpoly, mulcol, mulrow,

multiply, norm, normalize, nullspace, orthog, permanent, pivot, potential, randmatrix, randvector, rank, ratform, row, rowdim, rowspace, rowspan, rref, scalarmul, singularvals, smith, stack, submatrix, subvector, sumbasis, swapcol, swaprow, sylvester, toeplitz, trace, transpose, vandermonde, vecpotent, vectdim, vector]

Some of these commands will be demonstrated in the sections describing the new Utility commands we have provided. Many more of the commands listed above (e.g., det, potential, and inverse) are mathematical in nature and are not described here—see the on-line help pages, *The Maple Handbook*, or a Maple in linear algebra application text for a more thorough description of these commands.

Others described here include:

- augment and stack allow you to combine two vectors or matrices (given that the dimensions match up) to form one larger array.

> A := matrix(2,3,[1$6]);

$$A := \begin{bmatrix} 1 & 1 & 1 \\ 1 & 1 & 1 \end{bmatrix}$$

> B := matrix(3,4,[2$12]);

$$B := \begin{bmatrix} 2 & 2 & 2 & 2 \\ 2 & 2 & 2 & 2 \\ 2 & 2 & 2 & 2 \end{bmatrix}$$

> C := matrix(2,4,[3$8]);

$$C := \begin{bmatrix} 3 & 3 & 3 & 3 \\ 3 & 3 & 3 & 3 \end{bmatrix}$$

> augment(A,C);

$$\begin{bmatrix} 1 & 1 & 1 & 3 & 3 & 3 & 3 \\ 1 & 1 & 1 & 3 & 3 & 3 & 3 \end{bmatrix}$$

> stack(C,B);

$$\begin{bmatrix} 3 & 3 & 3 & 3 \\ 3 & 3 & 3 & 3 \\ 2 & 2 & 2 & 2 \\ 2 & 2 & 2 & 2 \\ 2 & 2 & 2 & 2 \end{bmatrix}$$

- vectdim, rowdim, and coldim allow you to determine the dimensions of both vectors and matrices.

> rowdim(B);

$$3$$

> coldim(C);

$$4$$

- row and col allow you to extract (as *column* vectors) specific rows or columns of a matrix.

    > A2 := matrix(2,3,[a,b,c,d,e,f]);

    $$A2 := \begin{bmatrix} a & b & c \\ d & e & f \end{bmatrix}$$

    > row(A2, 2);

    $$[\, d \ \ e \ \ f \,]$$

    > col(A2, 1..2);

    $$[\, a \ \ d \,], [\, b \ \ e \,]$$

- delrows and delcols allow you to remove a range of rows or columns from a matrix.

    > delrows(A2, 2..2);

    $$[\, a \ \ b \ \ c \,]$$

    > delcols(A2, 2..3);

    $$\begin{bmatrix} a \\ d \end{bmatrix}$$

- extend allows you to enlarge the dimensions of an already existing matrix. Rows and columns are only added to the right and bottom of the matrix, respectively. copyinto allows you to copy the elements of one matrix into another, starting at a certain row and column position.

    > A3 := extend(A2, 2, 3, 0);

    $$A3 := \begin{bmatrix} a & b & c & 0 & 0 & 0 \\ d & e & f & 0 & 0 & 0 \\ 0 & 0 & 0 & 0 & 0 & 0 \\ 0 & 0 & 0 & 0 & 0 & 0 \end{bmatrix}$$

    > A4 := copyinto(A, A3, 3, 4);

    $$A4 := \begin{bmatrix} a & b & c & 0 & 0 & 0 \\ d & e & f & 0 & 0 & 0 \\ 0 & 0 & 0 & 1 & 1 & 1 \\ 0 & 0 & 0 & 1 & 1 & 1 \end{bmatrix}$$

- randvector and randmatrix allow you to quickly create vectors and matrices with random elements. These can be very useful for testing procedures.

> `randvector(5);`

$$[\ -85\ \ -55\ \ -37\ \ -35\ \ 97\ ]$$

> `randmatrix(3, 3);`

$$\begin{bmatrix} 50 & 79 & 56 \\ 49 & 63 & 57 \\ -59 & 45 & -8 \end{bmatrix}$$

- entermatrix provides an alternative mechanism for entering elements of matrices. Try it and see if it is, for you, simpler than using the complete Maple syntax.

For more information on any of these commands, see the appropriate reference material.

Special Types of Arrays

Normally, when defining an array, you need to enter every element in the array for it to be *fully* defined. However, there are a few special types of arrays (or matrices) in Maple that can be automatically generated from fewer than a full complement of elements. *Symmetric*, *antisymmetric*, *sparse*, *diagonal*, and *identity* matrices are all available. To create such matrices, define the necessary elements and add the matrix type as an additional option to the array command.

> `array(1..2, 1..2, identity);`

$$\begin{bmatrix} 1 & 0 \\ 0 & 1 \end{bmatrix}$$

> `array(1..2, 1..6, [(1,3)=p, (2,4)=r], sparse);`

$$\begin{bmatrix} 0 & 0 & p & 0 & 0 & 0 \\ 0 & 0 & 0 & r & 0 & 0 \end{bmatrix}$$

> `array(1..3, 1..3, [(1,3)=x^2, (2,1)=y/z, (2,3)=1], antisymmetric);`

$$\begin{bmatrix} 0 & -\dfrac{y}{z} & x^2 \\ \dfrac{y}{z} & 0 & 1 \\ -x^2 & -1 & 0 \end{bmatrix}$$

Utility Commands

Diagonals and Triangulars

diagonal(V)	create a matrix with elements of a vector on main diagonal
getdiagonal(M)	extract elements of main diagonal into a vector
sumdiagonal(M)	add the elements of main diagonal
proddiagonal(M)	multiply the elements of main diagonal
banded(V, a..b, n,m)	create a banded matrix using elements of a vector
uppertri(M)	convert a matrix to upper triangular form
lowertri(M)	convert a matrix to lower triangular form

Often when you are doing linear algebra computations, you want to focus on a *diagonal* of a matrix. In most cases, the *main* diagonal (the one which starts in the upper left corner of the matrix) is the one you want to study; but, on occasion, other diagonals either above or below the main diagonal are also desired.

The four Utility commands diagonal, getdiagonal, sumdiagonal, and proddiagonal focus on the main diagonal as their default behavior. In each of these commands, an optional parameter specifies which subdiagonal (below the main diagonal) or superdiagonal (above the main diagonal) is desired. A negative integer value describes the nth subdiagonal and a positive integer value the nth superdiagonal. Zero represents the main diagonal, and is always the default value.

The first command, diagonal, in its simplest form, takes only a vector as input. A new matrix is created and the elements of the vector are placed on its *main* diagonal.[6] All other elements of the matrix are initialized to 0.

```
> with(utility):
```

```
> with(linalg):
```

```
> V := vector(4, [a,b,c,d]);
```

$$V := [\ a\quad b\quad c\quad d\ ]$$

```
> diagonal(V);
```

$$\begin{bmatrix} a & 0 & 0 & 0 \\ 0 & b & 0 & 0 \\ 0 & 0 & c & 0 \\ 0 & 0 & 0 & d \end{bmatrix}$$

---

[6]In all these commands, the dimensions of the new matrix are such that the specified elements *exactly* fill the specified diagonal.

In this simplest of forms, diagonal always produces a *square* matrix. In fact, even if a subdiagonal or superdiagonal is specified, the result is still a square matrix, but one of larger dimension.

> diagonal(V, -2);

$$\begin{bmatrix} 0 & 0 & 0 & 0 & 0 & 0 \\ 0 & 0 & 0 & 0 & 0 & 0 \\ a & 0 & 0 & 0 & 0 & 0 \\ 0 & b & 0 & 0 & 0 & 0 \\ 0 & 0 & c & 0 & 0 & 0 \\ 0 & 0 & 0 & d & 0 & 0 \end{bmatrix}$$

> diagonal(V, 3);

$$\begin{bmatrix} 0 & 0 & 0 & a & 0 & 0 & 0 \\ 0 & 0 & 0 & 0 & b & 0 & 0 \\ 0 & 0 & 0 & 0 & 0 & c & 0 \\ 0 & 0 & 0 & 0 & 0 & 0 & d \\ 0 & 0 & 0 & 0 & 0 & 0 & 0 \\ 0 & 0 & 0 & 0 & 0 & 0 & 0 \\ 0 & 0 & 0 & 0 & 0 & 0 & 0 \end{bmatrix}$$

What if you don't want to have all other elements initialized to 0, but want to replace elements in the diagonal of an already existing matrix? By adding that matrix as the second parameter to diagonal, the job is done.

> M := matrix(4, 4, [$1..16]);

$$M := \begin{bmatrix} 1 & 2 & 3 & 4 \\ 5 & 6 & 7 & 8 \\ 9 & 10 & 11 & 12 \\ 13 & 14 & 15 & 16 \end{bmatrix}$$

> diagonal(V, M);

$$\begin{bmatrix} a & 2 & 3 & 4 \\ 5 & b & 7 & 8 \\ 9 & 10 & c & 12 \\ 13 & 14 & 15 & d \end{bmatrix}$$

Remember, of course, that to actually change the matrix M itself, you must reassign it to the result.

```
> eval(M);
```
$$\begin{bmatrix} 1 & 2 & 3 & 4 \\ 5 & 6 & 7 & 8 \\ 9 & 10 & 11 & 12 \\ 13 & 14 & 15 & 16 \end{bmatrix}$$

```
> M := diagonal(V, M):
> eval(M);
```
$$\begin{bmatrix} a & 2 & 3 & 4 \\ 5 & b & 7 & 8 \\ 9 & 10 & c & 12 \\ 13 & 14 & 15 & d \end{bmatrix}$$

diagonal complains if the dimensions of the vector and matrix do not match up.

```
> diagonal(V, M, -2);
Error, (in diagonal) invalid vector for this diagonal
> diagonal(vector(2, [g,h]), M, -2);
```
$$\begin{bmatrix} a & 2 & 3 & 4 \\ 5 & b & 7 & 8 \\ g & 10 & c & 12 \\ 13 & h & 15 & d \end{bmatrix}$$

The built-in command diag provides a small subset of the abilities of diagonal, plus one other valuable feature. If any of the elements[7] passed to diag are themselves *square* matrices, then these matrices get inserted on the diagonal as *blocks*. The best way to show how this works is with an example.

```
> linalg[diag](4/3, M, z^2, exp(y));
```
$$\begin{bmatrix} \frac{4}{3} & 0 & 0 & 0 & 0 & 0 & 0 \\ 0 & a & 2 & 3 & 4 & 0 & 0 \\ 0 & 5 & b & 7 & 8 & 0 & 0 \\ 0 & 9 & 10 & c & 12 & 0 & 0 \\ 0 & 13 & 14 & 15 & d & 0 & 0 \\ 0 & 0 & 0 & 0 & 0 & z^2 & 0 \\ 0 & 0 & 0 & 0 & 0 & 0 & e^y \end{bmatrix}$$

---

[7] diag actually doesn't take a vector of diagonal elements, but requires the elements to be passed as its *parameters*.

The next three commands *access* the elements of a diagonal, instead of creating them. getdiagonal is simply the opposite of diagonal; it extracts the elements of a specified matrix diagonal into a column vector.

> getdiagonal(M);

$$[\ a\quad b\quad c\quad d\ ]$$

> getdiagonal(M, 1);

$$[\ 2\quad 7\quad 12\ ]$$

In any of these commands, if you supply a diagonal specifier that is out of the range of the related matrix, an error message is returned.

> getdiagonal(M, -6);

Error, (in getdiagonal) the second parameter is out of range

The commands sumdiagonal and proddiagonal work exactly the same as getdiagonal, except that their result is the sum or product of the diagonal's elements.

> sumdiagonal(M);

$$a + b + c + d$$

> proddiagonal(M, 1);

168

The next command in this section is slightly more complicated than the last four. banded creates a *banded* matrix from the elements of a given vector. The built-in command band is similar, but less powerful, only allowing you to create square matrices whose bands are "centered" around the main diagonal.

> V := vector(5, [1/2, 1/3, 1/4, 1/5, 1/6]):

> band(V, 8);

$$\begin{bmatrix} \frac{1}{4} & \frac{1}{5} & \frac{1}{6} & 0 & 0 & 0 & 0 & 0 \\ \frac{1}{3} & \frac{1}{4} & \frac{1}{5} & \frac{1}{6} & 0 & 0 & 0 & 0 \\ \frac{1}{2} & \frac{1}{3} & \frac{1}{4} & \frac{1}{5} & \frac{1}{6} & 0 & 0 & 0 \\ 0 & \frac{1}{2} & \frac{1}{3} & \frac{1}{4} & \frac{1}{5} & \frac{1}{6} & 0 & 0 \\ 0 & 0 & \frac{1}{2} & \frac{1}{3} & \frac{1}{4} & \frac{1}{5} & \frac{1}{6} & 0 \\ 0 & 0 & 0 & \frac{1}{2} & \frac{1}{3} & \frac{1}{4} & \frac{1}{5} & \frac{1}{6} \\ 0 & 0 & 0 & 0 & \frac{1}{2} & \frac{1}{3} & \frac{1}{4} & \frac{1}{5} \\ 0 & 0 & 0 & 0 & 0 & \frac{1}{2} & \frac{1}{3} & \frac{1}{4} \end{bmatrix}$$

The Utility command banded overcomes both these limitations. The second parameter, an integer range, determines the diagonals to be initialized to the values in the vector. The third and fourth parameters specify the number of rows and columns in the resulting matrix, respectively.

> banded(V, -3..1, 5, 7);

$$\begin{bmatrix} \frac{1}{5} & \frac{1}{6} & 0 & 0 & 0 & 0 & 0 \\ \frac{1}{4} & \frac{1}{5} & \frac{1}{6} & 0 & 0 & 0 & 0 \\ \frac{1}{3} & \frac{1}{4} & \frac{1}{5} & \frac{1}{6} & 0 & 0 & 0 \\ \frac{1}{2} & \frac{1}{3} & \frac{1}{4} & \frac{1}{5} & \frac{1}{6} & 0 & 0 \\ 0 & \frac{1}{2} & \frac{1}{3} & \frac{1}{4} & \frac{1}{5} & \frac{1}{6} & 0 \end{bmatrix}$$

If the number of diagonals specified in the second parameter does not exactly match the number of elements in the vector, or if the stated matrix dimensions conflict with that range, then an error message is produced.

> banded(V, -1..4, 5, 7);

Error, (in banded) the specified range is invalid

```
> banded(V, -3..1, 3, 4);
```

Error, (in banded) Invalid range in rows specified

As with the previous four Utility commands, banded can also replace elements of an already existing matrix. In this case, the matrix is inserted as the second parameter, and the row and column dimensions are left out.

```
> M := matrix(6, 5, [$1..30]);
```

$$M := \begin{bmatrix} 1 & 2 & 3 & 4 & 5 \\ 6 & 7 & 8 & 9 & 10 \\ 11 & 12 & 13 & 14 & 15 \\ 16 & 17 & 18 & 19 & 20 \\ 21 & 22 & 23 & 24 & 25 \\ 26 & 27 & 28 & 29 & 30 \end{bmatrix}$$

```
> banded(V, M, -2..2);
```

$$\begin{bmatrix} \frac{1}{4} & \frac{1}{5} & \frac{1}{6} & 4 & 5 \\ \frac{1}{3} & \frac{1}{4} & \frac{1}{5} & \frac{1}{6} & 10 \\ \frac{1}{2} & \frac{1}{3} & \frac{1}{4} & \frac{1}{5} & \frac{1}{6} \\ 16 & \frac{1}{2} & \frac{1}{3} & \frac{1}{4} & \frac{1}{5} \\ 21 & 22 & \frac{1}{2} & \frac{1}{3} & \frac{1}{4} \\ 26 & 27 & 28 & \frac{1}{2} & \frac{1}{3} \end{bmatrix}$$

The commands banded and diagonal also share another optional parameter. By adding the string 'sparse' or 'full' at the end of either command's parameter sequence, you can force the resulting matrix to be created with either *sparse* or *full* internal representation. The default for both commands is *sparse* representation. For more information on these two storage options, see the section *Sparse and Full Representation* on page 176.

The last two commands in this section, uppertri and lowertri, take an existing matrix and create its related upper- or lower-triangular matrix. For example, if uppertri is used with just one parameter, all elements *strictly below* the main diagonal are set to 0.

> uppertri(M);

$$\begin{bmatrix} 1 & 2 & 3 & 4 & 5 \\ 0 & 7 & 8 & 9 & 10 \\ 0 & 0 & 13 & 14 & 15 \\ 0 & 0 & 0 & 19 & 20 \\ 0 & 0 & 0 & 0 & 25 \\ 0 & 0 & 0 & 0 & 0 \end{bmatrix}$$

> lowertri(M);

$$\begin{bmatrix} 1 & 0 & 0 & 0 & 0 \\ 6 & 7 & 0 & 0 & 0 \\ 11 & 12 & 13 & 0 & 0 \\ 16 & 17 & 18 & 19 & 0 \\ 21 & 22 & 23 & 24 & 25 \\ 26 & 27 & 28 & 29 & 30 \end{bmatrix}$$

The main diagonal is not affected by either of the above commands. If a value other than 0 is supplied as the second parameter, the elements strictly above or strictly below the specified diagonal are set to 0.

> uppertri(M, -1);

$$\begin{bmatrix} 1 & 2 & 3 & 4 & 5 \\ 6 & 7 & 8 & 9 & 10 \\ 0 & 12 & 13 & 14 & 15 \\ 0 & 0 & 18 & 19 & 20 \\ 0 & 0 & 0 & 24 & 25 \\ 0 & 0 & 0 & 0 & 30 \end{bmatrix}$$

> lowertri(M, -2);

$$\begin{bmatrix} 0 & 0 & 0 & 0 & 0 \\ 0 & 0 & 0 & 0 & 0 \\ 11 & 0 & 0 & 0 & 0 \\ 16 & 17 & 0 & 0 & 0 \\ 21 & 22 & 23 & 0 & 0 \\ 26 & 27 & 28 & 29 & 0 \end{bmatrix}$$

Acting on Rows and Columns

sumrows(M)	add together elements of each row
sumcols(M)	add together elements of each column
prodrows(M)	multiply together elements of each row
prodcols(M)	multiply together elements of each column
maprows(fnc, M)	pass each row as parameters to a function
mapcols(fnc, M)	pass each column as parameters to a function
fliprows(M)	reverse the order of the rows
flipcols(M)	reverse the order of the columns

In the last section, commands that dealt with diagonals of matrices were described. In this section, it is the *rows* and *columns* of matrices that are investigated.

The first four commands, similar to their counterparts sumdiagonal and proddiagonal, find the sums and products of the elements in the rows or columns of a matrix.

sumrows and sumcols, in their most basic form, return a vector containing the sums of each of the n rows or m columns of an $n \times m$ matrix.

```
> M := matrix(5, 3, [1,4,-2,6,3,-7,-6,8,4,-5,-6,4,-5,-3,4]);
```

$$M := \begin{bmatrix} 1 & 4 & -2 \\ 6 & 3 & -7 \\ -6 & 8 & 4 \\ -5 & -6 & 4 \\ -5 & -3 & 4 \end{bmatrix}$$

```
> sumrows(M);
```

$$[\ 3 \quad 2 \quad 6 \quad -7 \quad -4\ ]$$

```
> sumcols(M);
```

$$\text{transpose}([\ -9 \quad 6 \quad 3\ ])$$

Notice that the result of sumcols is returned as a *row vector*. Conversely, sumrows returns a typical *column vector*.[8] One reason for returning different types of vectors is that if you want to compute the sum of *all* the elements in a matrix, the most intuitive way to do so is to take the sum of the rows and then sum the column that is created. For example:

---

[8]It has been acknowledged previously that it is difficult to visually distinguish a column vector from a row vector. In the section *What Maple Has*, how unevaluated transpose commands are used to represent row vectors is discussed.

> sumcols(sumrows(M));

$$0$$

> sumrows(sumcols(M));

$$0$$

Obviously from the above, sumrows and sumcols are designed to work on vectors as well as matrices. If you are summing together the elements of a vector, make sure that you use the appropriate Utility command, otherwise you get an error message.

> sumrows(vector(3, [a, b, c]));

Error, (in sumrows) expecting an array or row vector as first parameter

> sumcols(vector(3, [a, b, c]));

$$a + b + c$$

If you want to add or multiply together less than all the rows or columns, append a positive integer or positive integer range as the second parameter.

> sumcols(M, 3);

$$\text{transpose}([\ 3\ ])$$

> sumrows(M, 2..4);

$$[\ 2\ \ 6\ \ -7\ ]$$

In the same manner, the commands prodrows and prodcols multiply together the elements in a matrix.

> prodrows(M), prodcols(M);

$$[\ -8\ \ -126\ \ -192\ \ 120\ \ 60\ ], \text{transpose}([\ -900\ \ 1728\ \ 896\ ])$$

> prodrows(prodcols(M));

$$-1393459200$$

> prodrows(M, 3..4);

$$[\ -192\ \ 120\ ]$$

The commands maprows and mapcols also process the elements of each row or column of a matrix. For these commands, however, the elements are passed as the input to the function provided as the first parameter. As before, the result of maprows is a *column* vector and the result of mapcols is a *row* vector.

The simplest functions which illustrate the working of these two commands are the built-in max and min.

> maprows(max, M);

$$[\ 4\quad 6\quad 8\quad 4\quad 4\ ]$$

> mapcols(min, M);

$$\text{transpose}([\ -6\quad -6\quad -7\ ])$$

Of course, vectors are also acceptable as input, so long as the appropriate command is used.

> maprows(min, ");

$$-7$$

There is a great difference between how maprows and mapcols and the built-in map command work on a matrix. map applies the given function to *each* element of M *individually*, while the Utility commands treat the individual rows and column as separate entities.

maprows and mapcols also take the same optional parameters as maplists (and all the other maplike commands) that allow you to specify which parameter of the function is substituted and what constant values, if any, should be applied.[9]

The last two commands in this section, fliprows and flipcols, create new matrices by flipping the order of rows or columns. In effect, the matrix is "mirrored" about a horizontal or vertical axis.

> M := matrix(4, 5, [$1..20]);

$$M := \begin{bmatrix} 1 & 2 & 3 & 4 & 5 \\ 6 & 7 & 8 & 9 & 10 \\ 11 & 12 & 13 & 14 & 15 \\ 16 & 17 & 18 & 19 & 20 \end{bmatrix}$$

> fliprows(M), flipcols(M);

$$\begin{bmatrix} 16 & 17 & 18 & 19 & 20 \\ 11 & 12 & 13 & 14 & 15 \\ 6 & 7 & 8 & 9 & 10 \\ 1 & 2 & 3 & 4 & 5 \end{bmatrix}, \begin{bmatrix} 5 & 4 & 3 & 2 & 1 \\ 10 & 9 & 8 & 7 & 6 \\ 15 & 14 & 13 & 12 & 11 \\ 20 & 19 & 18 & 17 & 16 \end{bmatrix}$$

As with the other commands, providing a range limits the area of activity.

---

[9]See the section *Mapping Lists* on page 70 for more details.

```
> flipcols(M, 2..4);
```

$$\begin{bmatrix} 1 & 4 & 3 & 2 & 5 \\ 6 & 9 & 8 & 7 & 10 \\ 11 & 14 & 13 & 12 & 15 \\ 16 & 19 & 18 & 17 & 20 \end{bmatrix}$$

With a little thought, you can see that fliprows must handle *column* vectors, and flipcols must handle *row* vectors to keep all these commands consistent.

```
> V := vector(6, [a,b,c,d,e,f]);
```

$$V := [\,a \quad b \quad c \quad d \quad e \quad f\,]$$

```
> fliprows(V, 1..3);
```

$$[\,c \quad b \quad a \quad d \quad e \quad f\,]$$

In the standard library, the commands linalg[swaprow] and linalg[swapcol] can be used to *switch* two rows or columns in a matrix representation.

Sorting by Row or Column

sortbyrow(M, n)	sort the columns according to the elements in a particular row
sortbycol(M, n)	sort the rows according to the elements in a particular column

Similar to the commands flipcols and fliprows, the commands in this section rearrange the rows or columns of an existing matrix to create a new matrix. sortbyrow takes as input a matrix and an integer representing the row to be used as a *sorting key*.

```
> M := matrix(4, 4, [1,-3,4,-6,3,5,0,-11,12,9,1,1,2,-4,16,5]);
```

$$M := \begin{bmatrix} 1 & -3 & 4 & -6 \\ 3 & 5 & 0 & -11 \\ 12 & 9 & 1 & 1 \\ 2 & -4 & 16 & 5 \end{bmatrix}$$

```
> sortbyrow(M, 1);
```

$$\begin{bmatrix} -6 & -3 & 1 & 4 \\ -11 & 5 & 3 & 0 \\ 1 & 9 & 12 & 1 \\ 5 & -4 & 2 & 16 \end{bmatrix}$$

The *columns* of M are rearranged by sortbyrow, such that the elements in the first row read in ascending order left to right. It is important to make the distinction that sortbyrow reorders the *columns*. Similarly, sortbycol rearranges the *rows* so that the values in a specified column ascend from top to bottom.

> sortbycol(M, 3);

$$\begin{bmatrix} 3 & 5 & 0 & -11 \\ 12 & 9 & 1 & 1 \\ 1 & -3 & 4 & -6 \\ 2 & -4 & 16 & 5 \end{bmatrix}$$

What if there are two identical values in the row or column you are using as a key? If you provide a *list* of index values as the second parameter to either command, any ties found in the key corresponding to the first element of the list are broken by elements in the key corresponding to the second element of the list, and so on. In the present matrix, M, the third row contains two 1s. Using the fourth row as the secondary key clears up the ambiguity.

> sortbyrow(M, [3,4]);

$$\begin{bmatrix} -6 & 4 & -3 & 1 \\ -11 & 0 & 5 & 3 \\ 1 & 1 & 9 & 12 \\ 5 & 16 & -4 & 2 \end{bmatrix}$$

If *any* of the elements in the row or column being used as a key is non-numeric in nature, then an alpha-numeric sorting technique is used.[10] This can be most useful when you have a table of data represented in a matrix. For example, take the following matrix of high and low temperature readings for a week in July.

> TempInCelcius := matrix(7, 3, [[July13,28,20],
>   [July14,26,15],[July16,22,14],[July15,27,22],
>   [July18,34,27],[July17,31,20],[July12,32,23]]);

$$TempInCelcius := \begin{bmatrix} July13 & 28 & 20 \\ July14 & 26 & 15 \\ July16 & 22 & 14 \\ July15 & 27 & 22 \\ July18 & 34 & 27 \\ July17 & 31 & 20 \\ July12 & 32 & 23 \end{bmatrix}$$

---

[10]Use caution—constants like Pi and Catalan are not of numeric type!

This data can be sorted by the dates in the first column.

> sortbycol(TempInCelcius, 1);

$$\begin{bmatrix} July12 & 32 & 23 \\ July13 & 28 & 20 \\ July14 & 26 & 15 \\ July15 & 27 & 22 \\ July16 & 22 & 14 \\ July17 & 31 & 20 \\ July18 & 34 & 27 \end{bmatrix}$$

Or, it can be sorted by daily high temperature in the second column.

> sortbycol(TempInCelcius, 2);

$$\begin{bmatrix} July16 & 22 & 14 \\ July14 & 26 & 15 \\ July15 & 27 & 22 \\ July13 & 28 & 20 \\ July17 & 31 & 20 \\ July12 & 32 & 23 \\ July18 & 34 & 27 \end{bmatrix}$$

Of course, your data is likely to be much more complicated than this.

Vectors may also have their elements sorted by these commands, but keep in mind that sortbycol only accepts column vectors and sortbyrow only accepts row vectors.

Sparse and Full Representation

density(M)	compute the density of non-zero elements in an array
convert(M, *sparse*)	convert an array to sparse representation
convert(M, *full*)	convert an array to full representation

Sparse matrices differ from normal matrices in their internal representation only. A normal (or *full*) matrix is represented by a table with an entry for every element. A sparse matrix is represented by a table with entries for non-zero elements only, and can be created with the array command, but not with matrix.

> M := matrix(4, 4, [0,0,1,0,0,0,2,3,0,0,0,0,0,0,0,1]);

$$M := \begin{bmatrix} 0 & 0 & 1 & 0 \\ 0 & 0 & 2 & 3 \\ 0 & 0 & 0 & 0 \\ 0 & 0 & 0 & 1 \end{bmatrix}$$

```
> op(");
```
$1..4, 1..4, [(4,4) = 1, (1,1) = 0, (3,1) = 0, (1,2) = 0, (4,1) = 0, (3,2) = 0,$
$(1,3) = 1, (4,2) = 0, (3,3) = 0, (4,3) = 0, (1,4) = 0, (2,1) = 0, (2,2) = 0,$
$(2,3) = 2, (2,4) = 3, (3,4) = 0]$

```
> array(1..4, 1..4, [(1,3)=1,(2,3)=2,(2,4)=3,(4,4)=1], sparse);
```

$$\begin{bmatrix} 0 & 0 & 1 & 0 \\ 0 & 0 & 2 & 3 \\ 0 & 0 & 0 & 0 \\ 0 & 0 & 0 & 1 \end{bmatrix}$$

```
> op(");
```
$sparse, 1..4, 1..4, [(4,4) = 1, (1,3) = 1, (2,3) = 2, (2,4) = 3]$

The internal representation of a sparse matrix is much more compact. This difference is even more pronounced with matrices of larger dimensions.

Apart from the issue of storage space, several of Maple's linear algebra commands take advantage of sparse representations to perform more efficient computations. There is, however, a point when representing a matrix as a sparse matrix ceases to pay off. A good rule of thumb is to use sparse representation when a matrix has fewer than 10% non-zero entries. The Utility command **density** provides a quick way to determine this density given either a full or sparse matrix.

```
> density(M);
```

.2500000000

This matrix has a density of 25%, and is best left in full representation.

The built-in **convert** command is special in that it allows new conversions to be added by the user by the addition of second-level procedures of the form 'convert/name'. Conversions of matrices to **sparse** and **full** representation have been added. Their use is quite straightforward.

```
> S := convert(M, sparse):
> op(op(S));
```
$sparse, 1..4, 1..4, [(4,4) = 1, (1,3) = 1, (2,3) = 2, (2,4) = 3]$

```
> density(S);
```

.2500000000

```
> Mnew := convert(S, full):
```

Examples

Verifying Magic Squares

How can the commands in *ArrayTools* be used to verify that a matrix represents a valid *magic square*?[11]

First, read a previously created matrix, A, into the session.

> read 'bigmat';

$$A := \begin{bmatrix} 92 & 99 & 1 & 8 & 15 & 67 & 74 & 51 & 58 & 40 \\ 98 & 80 & 7 & 14 & 16 & 73 & 55 & 57 & 64 & 41 \\ 4 & 81 & 88 & 20 & 22 & 54 & 56 & 63 & 70 & 47 \\ 85 & 87 & 19 & 21 & 3 & 60 & 62 & 69 & 71 & 28 \\ 86 & 93 & 25 & 2 & 9 & 61 & 68 & 75 & 52 & 34 \\ 17 & 24 & 76 & 82 & 90 & 42 & 49 & 26 & 33 & 65 \\ 23 & 5 & 83 & 89 & 91 & 48 & 30 & 32 & 39 & 66 \\ 79 & 6 & 13 & 95 & 97 & 29 & 31 & 38 & 45 & 72 \\ 10 & 12 & 94 & 96 & 78 & 35 & 37 & 44 & 46 & 53 \\ 11 & 18 & 100 & 77 & 84 & 36 & 43 & 50 & 27 & 59 \end{bmatrix}$$

Using sumrows, all the rows can be summed.

> sumrows(A);

[505 505 505 505 505 504 506 505 505 505]

All of the elements are 505, except the elements in the sixth and seventh positions. What does sumcols return?

> sumcols(A);

transpose([505 505 506 504 505 505 505 505 505 505])

Again, there are two differing elements, in the third and fourth positions. You may be able to intuit from the specific values that the elements A[6,4] and A[7,3] differ by 1 and should be switched with each other. Perform this operation in Maple through the use of a temporary variable.

> temp := A[6,4];

$$temp := 82$$

> A[6,4] := A[7,3];

$$A_{6,4} := 83$$

> A[7,3] := temp;

$$A_{7,3} := 82$$

---

[11] Magic squares are square matrices whose individual rows, columns, main diagonal, and reverse diagonal all contain elements that sum to the exact same value.

Now try sumrows and sumcols again.

```
> sumrows(A);
```

[505 505 505 505 505 505 505 505 505 505]

```
> sumcols(A);
```

transpose([505 505 505 505 505 505 505 505 505 505])

Now the diagonals must be checked to determine whether they sum to 505.

```
> sumdiagonal(A);
```

505

```
> sumdiagonal(linalg[transpose](A));
```

505

A can now be said to be a magic square. Put all these tests into a procedure named checkmagic.

```
> checkmagic := proc(M)
>     local correctsum;
>     if nops({op(convert(sumrows(M), list))}) > 1 then
>         RETURN('Error in rows');
>     else
>         correctsum := sumrows(M, 1)[1];
>     fi;
>     if {op(convert(sumcols(M), list))} <> {correctsum} then
>         RETURN('Error in cols');
>     fi;
>     if sumdiagonal(M) <> correctsum then
>         RETURN('Error in main diagonal');
>     fi;
>     if sumdiagonal(linalg[transpose](M)) <> correctsum then
>         RETURN('Error in reverse diagonal');
>     fi;
>     RETURN('Magic');
> end:
```

Read through this code carefully, paying particular attention to the subtle differences in each if/then statement.

```
> checkmagic(A);
```

Error in cols

But it has already been determined that A *is* a magic square. There must be an error somewhere in the test for the columns. Perhaps since sumcols returns a *row* vector, which is represented by an unevaluated call to transpose, the conversion to a list is not working as planned.

```
> convert(sumcols(A), list);
```

$$[[\ 505\quad 505\quad 505\quad 505\quad 505\quad 505\quad 505\quad 505\quad 505\quad 505\ ]]$$

There are two levels of list brackets here; a one-level list is what is wanted, as in the following:

```
> convert(sumrows(A), list);
```

$$[\,505, 505, 505, 505, 505, 505, 505, 505, 505, 505\,]$$

To get a result in this form, extract the first operand of the result of sumcols before it is converted.

```
> convert(op(1,sumcols(A)), list);
```

$$[\,505, 505, 505, 505, 505, 505, 505, 505, 505, 505\,]$$

Build this new logic into the code for checkmagic.

```
> checkmagic := proc(M)
>    local correctsum;
>    if nops({op(convert(sumrows(M), list))}) > 1 then
>       ERROR('Error in rows');
>    else
>       correctsum := sumrows(M, 1)[1];
>    fi;
>    if {op(convert(op(1, sumcols(M)), list))} <> {correctsum} then
>       ERROR('Error in cols');
>    fi;
>    if sumdiagonal(M) <> correctsum then
>       ERROR('Error in main diagonal');
>    fi;
>    if sumdiagonal(linalg[transpose](M)) <> correctsum then
>       ERROR('Error in reverse diagonal');
>    fi;
>    RETURN('Magic');
> end:
> checkmagic(A);
```

Magic

To further test checkmagic, load in the magic command from the *Share Library*.[12]

---

[12] For more information on the Share Library, refer to the help pages for share and share, contents.

> with(share):

See ?share and ?share,contents for information about the share library

> readshare(magic, linalg):

Build an 11×11 magic square and pass it through checkmagic.

> A2 := magic(11);

$$A2 := \begin{bmatrix} 68 & 81 & 94 & 107 & 120 & 1 & 14 & 27 & 40 & 53 & 66 \\ 80 & 93 & 106 & 119 & 11 & 13 & 26 & 39 & 52 & 65 & 67 \\ 92 & 105 & 118 & 10 & 12 & 25 & 38 & 51 & 64 & 77 & 79 \\ 104 & 117 & 9 & 22 & 24 & 37 & 50 & 63 & 76 & 78 & 91 \\ 116 & 8 & 21 & 23 & 36 & 49 & 62 & 75 & 88 & 90 & 103 \\ 7 & 20 & 33 & 35 & 48 & 61 & 74 & 87 & 89 & 102 & 115 \\ 19 & 32 & 34 & 47 & 60 & 73 & 86 & 99 & 101 & 114 & 6 \\ 31 & 44 & 46 & 59 & 72 & 85 & 98 & 100 & 113 & 5 & 18 \\ 43 & 45 & 58 & 71 & 84 & 97 & 110 & 112 & 4 & 17 & 30 \\ 55 & 57 & 70 & 83 & 96 & 109 & 111 & 3 & 16 & 29 & 42 \\ 56 & 69 & 82 & 95 & 108 & 121 & 2 & 15 & 28 & 41 & 54 \end{bmatrix}$$

> checkmagic(A2);

Magic

What happens to this magic square if its rows are reordered using sortbycol?

> sortbycol(A2, 1);

$$\begin{bmatrix} 7 & 20 & 33 & 35 & 48 & 61 & 74 & 87 & 89 & 102 & 115 \\ 19 & 32 & 34 & 47 & 60 & 73 & 86 & 99 & 101 & 114 & 6 \\ 31 & 44 & 46 & 59 & 72 & 85 & 98 & 100 & 113 & 5 & 18 \\ 43 & 45 & 58 & 71 & 84 & 97 & 110 & 112 & 4 & 17 & 30 \\ 55 & 57 & 70 & 83 & 96 & 109 & 111 & 3 & 16 & 29 & 42 \\ 56 & 69 & 82 & 95 & 108 & 121 & 2 & 15 & 28 & 41 & 54 \\ 68 & 81 & 94 & 107 & 120 & 1 & 14 & 27 & 40 & 53 & 66 \\ 80 & 93 & 106 & 119 & 11 & 13 & 26 & 39 & 52 & 65 & 67 \\ 92 & 105 & 118 & 10 & 12 & 25 & 38 & 51 & 64 & 77 & 79 \\ 104 & 117 & 9 & 22 & 24 & 37 & 50 & 63 & 76 & 78 & 91 \\ 116 & 8 & 21 & 23 & 36 & 49 & 62 & 75 & 88 & 90 & 103 \end{bmatrix}$$

> checkmagic(");

Magic

What if a subset of the rows is reordered using fliprows?

```
> fliprows(A2, 3..7);
```

$$\begin{bmatrix} 68 & 81 & 94 & 107 & 120 & 1 & 14 & 27 & 40 & 53 & 66 \\ 80 & 93 & 106 & 119 & 11 & 13 & 26 & 39 & 52 & 65 & 67 \\ 19 & 32 & 34 & 47 & 60 & 73 & 86 & 99 & 101 & 114 & 6 \\ 7 & 20 & 33 & 35 & 48 & 61 & 74 & 87 & 89 & 102 & 115 \\ 116 & 8 & 21 & 23 & 36 & 49 & 62 & 75 & 88 & 90 & 103 \\ 104 & 117 & 9 & 22 & 24 & 37 & 50 & 63 & 76 & 78 & 91 \\ 92 & 105 & 118 & 10 & 12 & 25 & 38 & 51 & 64 & 77 & 79 \\ 31 & 44 & 46 & 59 & 72 & 85 & 98 & 100 & 113 & 5 & 18 \\ 43 & 45 & 58 & 71 & 84 & 97 & 110 & 112 & 4 & 17 & 30 \\ 55 & 57 & 70 & 83 & 96 & 109 & 111 & 3 & 16 & 29 & 42 \\ 56 & 69 & 82 & 95 & 108 & 121 & 2 & 15 & 28 & 41 & 54 \end{bmatrix}$$

```
> checkmagic(");
Error, (in checkmagic) Error in main diagonal
```

Perform some other row or column manipulations on A2 and retest the results.

Programming Tips

The code for the commands in *ArrayTools* is not overly complicated, once you learn a few basic rules about the structure of arrays and tables.

Returning an Unevaluated Function

In many existing Maple commands, the result returned is often an unevaluated function call. When this happens, there are three possible explanations:

1. You have called a command that simply does not exist anywhere in Maple. Usually, a typing error has been made, or you have used a command name from another application.

    ```
    > mult(x, y);
    ```

    $$\text{mult}(x, y)$$

2. You have called a command that exists in a *package* of Maple, but you have not yet loaded in the pointer to that function.

    ```
    > leftsum(x^k*exp(x), x=0..5);
    ```

    $$\text{leftsum}(x^k e^x, x = 0..5)$$

3. The parameters passed to the command are valid, but the command cannot simplify its result to something other than an unevaluated function call. For example, sin (1) cannot be further simplified.

```
> sin(1);
```
$$\sin(1)$$

It is not always the case that *exactly* what you entered is what you get back. For example, sin (−1) is altered slightly.

```
> sin(-1);
```
$$-\sin(1)$$

While the first two cases above are examples of user error, the third is a valid and quite necessary part of any *symbolic* computation language.

Like Maple's built-in commands, some Utility commands must occasionally return unevaluated functions. It is not always the case that the *same* command as was initially called is the one that is returned. Take the example of the sumcols command; it takes a matrix as input and returns a *row vector* as output. As shown in several places throughout this chapter, Maple represents a row vector with an unevaluated call to linalg[transpose].

```
> M:=linalg[matrix](4,4,[2,5,-3,4,5,6,-1,-3,-2,-1,0,0,12,5,6,-6]);
```
$$M := \begin{bmatrix} 2 & 5 & -3 & 4 \\ 5 & 6 & -1 & -3 \\ -2 & -1 & 0 & 0 \\ 12 & 5 & 6 & -6 \end{bmatrix}$$

```
> sumcols(M);
```
$$\mathrm{transpose}([\ 17\ \ 15\ \ 2\ \ -5\ ])$$

Now look at a simplified version of the code for sumcols (which doesn't do any error checking and only accepts a two-dimensional array as input). A standard (column) vector is created as the sums are computed. Pay special attention to the second last line of code where transpose is called on the column vector to convert it to a row vector.

```
> sumcols := proc(mat)
>    local Vect, i, j;
>    Vect := linalg[vector](linalg[coldim](mat), []);
>    for i from 1 to linalg[coldim](M) do
>        Vect[i] := convert([seq(mat[j,i], j=1..linalg[rowdim](M))], '+');
>    od;
>    linalg[transpose](Vect);
> end:
```

Now call this command with M.

```
> sumcols(M);
```

$$\text{transpose}(\textit{Vect})$$

This is different from before. What happened? We forgot about the special evaluation rule for arrays, *last name evaluation*. In order to actually get the elements printed out inside the transpose call, you need to wrap the name Vect in a call to eval.

```
> sumcols := proc(mat)
>    local Vect, i, j;
>    Vect := linalg[vector](linalg[coldim](mat), []);
>    for i from 1 to linalg[coldim](M) do
>       Vect[i] := convert([seq(mat[j,i], j=1..linalg[rowdim](M))], '+');
>    od;
>    linalg[transpose](eval(Vect));
> end:
```

Try it now.

```
> sumcols(M);
```

$$\text{transpose}([\begin{array}{cccc} 17 & 15 & 2 & -5 \end{array}])$$

That *looks* fine, but think about what is actually happening here. You know that when transpose is called with a column vector that it is always going to return an unevaluated call to itself containing the given vector. If you know this, is there really any reason why sumcols should go through the motions of actually calling linalg[transpose]? Wouldn't it be more efficient to pass an *unevaluated* function call instead?[13] This can be done by using the single forward quote to delay evaluation. Rewriting the command, you get:

```
> sumcols := proc(mat)
>    local Vect, i, j;
>    Vect := linalg[vector](linalg[coldim](mat), []);
>    for i from 1 to linalg[coldim](M) do
>       Vect[i] := convert([seq(mat[j,i], j=1..linalg[rowdim](M))], '+');
>    od;
>    'transpose(eval(Vect))';
> end:
```

---

[13]It may not be a good idea to have this command return an unevaluated call to transpose. It could be argued that the extra overhead is justifiable because someday Maple might change the transpose command so that the transpose of a column vector is represented by something other than an unevaluated function call. Be that as it may, we do it here to illustrate some other points about returning unevaluated command calls.

```
> sumcols(M);
```

$$\text{transpose}(\text{eval}(\textit{Vect}))$$

That isn't what you want either. You still want the *input* to transpose to be fully evaluated. The solution is to place the single quotes around the command name only.

```
> sumcols := proc(mat)
>    local Vect, i, j;
>    Vect := linalg[vector](linalg[coldim](mat), []);
>    for i from 1 to linalg[coldim](M) do
>        Vect[i] := convert([seq(mat[j,i], j=1..linalg[rowdim](M))], '+');
>    od;
>    'transpose'(eval(Vect));
> end:
> sumcols(M);
```

$$\text{transpose}([\,17\quad 15\quad 2\quad -5\,])$$

This "single-quoting" of a resulting command call is especially imperative when the unevaluated command name is the same as the original function. Without the single quotes, you could very easily run into a situation where a command infinitely recurses on itself, causing a system crash.

Checking for an Unevaluated Function

As well as returning unevaluated functions as output, Maple commands must sometimes accept specific types of unevaluated functions as input. For example, the command sumrows accepts an unevaluated call to transpose as input. How do you check for such an input parameter? The obvious first step is to use the type command to check for a function. Let's write a small procedure, isrowvector, that simply checks if a valid row vector is passed.

```
> isrowvector := proc(v)
>    if type(v, function) then
>        true;
>    else
>        false;
>    fi;
> end;
```

```
isrowvector := proc(v) if type(v,function) then true else false fi end
```

Create a valid row vector and try it out.

```
> rowV := linalg[transpose](array(1..4, [a,b,c,d]));
```

$$rowV := \operatorname{transpose}([\begin{array}{cccc} a & b & c & d \end{array}])$$

```
> isrowvector(rowV);
```

true

```
> isrowvector(sin(1));
```

true

While the valid input passes, sin(1) should *not* pass. You need to make sure that the unevaluated function being passed is transpose. Where is that information stored in rowV? Look at its operands.

```
> op(rowV);
```

$$[\begin{array}{cccc} a & b & c & d \end{array}]$$

As was discussed in the chapter *ExpressionTools*, some Maple structures contain special information in a zeroth operand, which isn't accessed by the previous generic call to op.

```
> op(0, rowV);
```

transpose

Using the and operator, change the if statement in isrowvector.

```
> isrowvector := proc(v)
>    if type(v, function) and op(0, v) = 'transpose' then
>       true;
>    else
>       false;
>    fi;
> end:
> isrowvector(rowV);
```

true

```
> isrowvector(sin(1));
```

false

Are you finished yet? What about the actual parameter in the unevaluated call to transpose? In the following call, since the linalg package has not been loaded, the nonsense input parameter passes.

```
> transpose(4);
```

transpose(4)

```
> isrowvector(");
```

true

To counter this, make sure that the input parameter is a valid vector.

```
> isrowvector := proc(v)
>    if type(v, function) and op(0, v) = 'transpose'
>    and type(op(1, v), vector) then
>       true;
>    else
>       false;
>    fi;
> end:

> isrowvector(rowV);
```

true

```
> isrowvector(transpose(4));
```

false

Checking for valid input parameters can be a lot more complicated than it first appears to be.

Copying Matrices

Many commands in *ArrayTools* take an existing array and change it to some extent, returning a new matrix. One rule of good design for Maple commands is that *a command should not alter any parameters passed to it.*[14] Following this rule can be a little tricky when dealing with arrays. To illustrate, let's look at a simple procedure, dummy, that takes an array and doubles the first element in the first row.

```
> dummy := proc(A)
>    local newA;
>    newA := A;
>    newA[1,1] := newA[1,1]*2;
>    eval(newA);
> end:
```

---

[14]The one exception to this rule is when an unevaluated name is passed specifically to give it a value. Even taking this exception into account, the built-in code for Maple breaks this basic rule many times.

Testing this new procedure on a simple matrix, you get:

```
> M := linalg[matrix](2, 2, [1,2,3,4]);
```

$$M := \begin{bmatrix} 1 & 2 \\ 3 & 4 \end{bmatrix}$$

```
> dummy(M);
```

$$\begin{bmatrix} 2 & 2 \\ 3 & 4 \end{bmatrix}$$

That is the proper result; the only problem is that the input matrix M has been altered.

```
> eval(M);
```

$$\begin{bmatrix} 2 & 2 \\ 3 & 4 \end{bmatrix}$$

This a direct consequence of *last name evaluation*. For a more complete discussion of this issue, see section 17.2—*Last Name Evaluation* in *Introduction to Maple* by André Heck. Regardless of why it happens, the built-in command copy alleviates this problem. copy duplicates an array but breaks the evaluation chain that is normally created.

```
> dummy := proc(A)
>    local newA;
>    newA := copy(A);
>    newA[1,1] := newA[1,1]*2;
>    eval(newA);
> end:
> M := linalg[matrix](2, 2, [1,2,3,4]);
```

$$M := \begin{bmatrix} 1 & 2 \\ 3 & 4 \end{bmatrix}$$

```
> dummy(M);
```

$$\begin{bmatrix} 2 & 2 \\ 3 & 4 \end{bmatrix}$$

```
> eval(M);
```

$$\begin{bmatrix} 1 & 2 \\ 3 & 4 \end{bmatrix}$$

As stated earlier, the copy command is used extensively in *ArrayTools*.

CHAPTER 8

DrawTools

The *DrawTools* chapter introduces a large collection of commands created to allow easy plotting of standard geometrical shapes (e.g., circles, lines, spheres, etc.). The *draw structures* created by these commands are an extension of the standard Maple plot structures (PLOT and PLOT3D), and allow you to perform some special types of transformations and manipulations. Many of these tools are applicable directly to standard Maple plots as well.[1] There are also tools provided for traveling between draw structures and plot structures, and between two and three dimensions.

This section of *The Practical Approach Utilities for Maple* contains well over thirty new commands.

What Maple Has

The two basic commands for creating plots in Maple are plot and plot3d. The first, in its simplest form, takes an expression in one unknown and a range over which to plot that unknown.

```
> plot(sin(x), x=-5..5);
```

---

[1] So, even if you are not interested in drawing geometrical shapes, it is recommended that you read on.

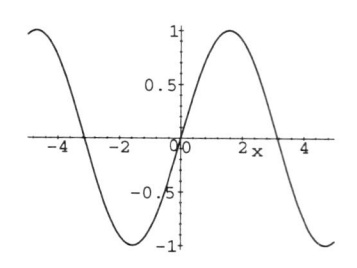

Similarly, plot3d takes an expression in two unknowns with ranges for each and produces a three-dimensional image.

```
> plot3d((x^2-y^2)/(x^2+y^2), x=-2..2, y=-2..2);
```

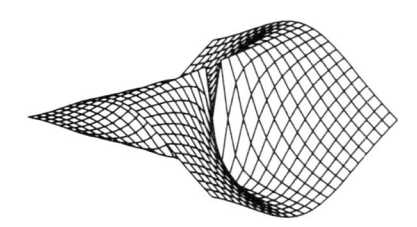

More than one function can be plotted at a time by enclosing the multiple expressions in set braces.

```
> f := sin(x);
```

$$f := \sin(x)$$

```
> g1 := convert(series(f, x=0), polynom);
```

$$g1 := x - \frac{1}{6}x^3 + \frac{1}{120}x^5$$

```
> g2 := convert(series(f, x=0, 12), polynom);
```

$$g2 := x - \frac{1}{6}x^3 + \frac{1}{120}x^5 - \frac{1}{5040}x^7 + \frac{1}{362880}x^9 - \frac{1}{39916800}x^{11}$$

```
> plot({f, g1, g2}, x=-5..5, y=-2..2);
```

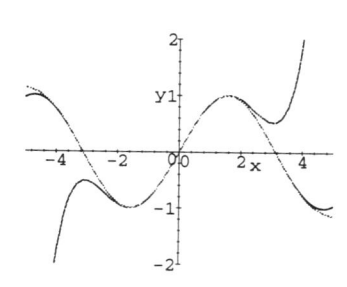

Functions to be plotted can be expressed in several other ways as well, including parametrically, as explicit lists of points, or in other coordinate systems. See the help pages for plot and plot3d, or an introductory Maple text for more information on the different methods of expressing functions.

Optional Parameters

Several optional parameters which allow you to specify aspects of the final image are available for both of these commands. Many of these optional values have nothing to do with how the function itself is displayed, but instead control other "non-essential" details, such as axes style, tickmarks, and textual labelling. Some optional parameters are specific to two-dimensional plots, some are used only with three-dimensional plots, and some are shared by both.

A few of the available options are:

- axes—FRAME, BOXED, NORMAL, or NONE
- color—red, black, green, etc., or a more specific color definition
- numpoints—a positive integer value
- orientation—a list with two numeric values
- projection—FISHEYE or ORTHOGONAL
- scaling—CONSTRAINED, NORMAL, UNCONSTRAINED, or a number between 0 and 1
- style—POINT, LINE, PATCH, WIREFRAME, etc.
- tickmarks—a list of three positive integer values
- title—a Maple string

For more information on the available options, see the help pages for ?plot,options and ?plot3d,options.

Each option has an option name associated with it and a value that can be either another name, a value, a list, etc. When included in plot or plot3d commands, each option is written as an *equation*. For example, the option to specify that a plot is drawn in blue is color=blue, and the option for a title could be title='This is my plot.'. All options are placed at the end of the parameter sequence; the order in which they appear within themselves is not important.

The following shows three options applied to a two-dimensional plot.

```
> plot(x^3+2*x^2-3*x-1, x=-3..3, axes=FRAME, style=POINT,
>    symbol=DIAMOND);
```

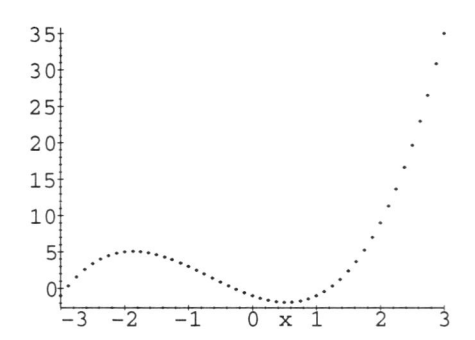

Each of the optional parameters has a *default value* that is used if you do not specify the option. However, these default values can vary from one type of Maple platform to another. To see what default values hold for your machine, enter a simple plot or plot3d command without any explicit options and see what you get.

PLOT and PLOT3D Data Structures

When you call plot or plot3d and do not assign the result to a variable name, Maple assumes that you want to display the plot on your display device, and therefore renders it. Before this can happen, though, Maple creates a PLOT (for two-dimensional plots) or PLOT3D (for three-dimensional plots) data structure. This standard structure is passed to a *plot driver* which renders it to the display device.

Now recompute the last plot, but this time assign its result to the variable A.

```
> A := plot(x^3+2*x^2-3*x-1, x=-3..3, axes=FRAME, style=POINT,
>         symbol=DIAMOND);
```

$A :=$ PLOT(CURVES([[$-3., -1.$], [$-2.880423551, .336537465015034343$],

[$-2.752450833, 1.55679583245140662$],

[$-2.623629828, 2.57817505032837602$],

[$-2.500000000, 3.37500000000000000$],

[$-2.376555171, 4.00287645436930362$],

[$-2.253476401, 4.47323652432034180$],

[$-2.126188161, 4.80810867997205804$], [$-2.000000000, 5.$],

[$-1.868796435, 5.06460465055590614$],

[$-1.753841657, 5.01869832504842073$],

[−1.624429805, 4.86433360147428662],
[−1.500000000, 4.62500000000000000],
[−1.369262195, 4.29034362402350933],
[−1.255546461, 3.94019364578360420],
[−1.120327455, 3.46508893888047176], [−1.000000000, 3.],
[−.872532391, 2.47595266526351798],
[−.754586370, 1.97289836545422670],
[−.625180891, 1.41289229794365001],
[−.500000000, .875000000000000000],
[−.373384312, .346928935734418298],
[−.255315116, −.120325957331844924],
[−.127961537, −.585462341131852915], [0, −1.],
[.119477151, −1.32817636258399063],
[.243846748, −1.59811834182458390],
[.372332710, −1.78811773933268858],
[.500000000, −1.87500000000000000],
[.619650869, −1.85309259928687942],
[.754688823, −1.69511907159365727],
[.876026430, −1.42095245480407550], [1.000000000, −1.],
[1.122975219, −.430624859068170274],
[1.251318955, .336955516800188537],
[1.372080409, 1.23205302698134300],
[1.500000000, 2.37500000000000000],
[1.621724325, 3.65992500853232983],
[1.750926719, 5.24660233396713238],
[1.875363980, 7.00352464678170250], [2.000000000, 9.],
[2.128820389, 11.3248418887358042],
[2.244786310, 13.6553976488334285],
[2.377696343, 16.6159541444796197],

[2.500000000, 19.6250000000000000],

[2.623319609, 22.9468287392268273],

[2.744632611, 26.5074583862970599],

[2.879335110, 30.8144672497755607], [3., 35.]], COLOUR(RGB, 0, 0, 0))

, AXESTICKS($DEFAULT$, $DEFAULT$, FONT($TIMES$, $ROMAN$, 24)),

AXESLABELS(x,, FONT($TIMES$, $ROMAN$, 24)),

FONT($TIMES$, $ROMAN$, 24), TITLE(, FONT($TIMES$, $ROMAN$, 36)),

COLOUR(RGB, 0, 0, 0), STYLE($POINT$), SYMBOL($DIAMOND$),

THICKNESS(3), VIEW($-3...3.$, $DEFAULT$), AXESSTYLE($FRAME$))

The image is represented by an unevaluated function call to PLOT. Within the PLOT call are other unevaluated calls containing defining information. For example, the CURVES command contains pairs of $[x_i, y_i]$ values in a list of lists. The remaining unevaluated command calls at the end of the structure define optional values for the plot. Notice that some of the optional parameters at the end of the PLOT structure were not explicitly supplied by you in the command call—the values for these parameters were automatically supplied by Maple.

The PLOT3D structure is similar to the PLOT structure in its overall organization, but has a couple of structural differences. It is not important at this time that you know the internal working of these structures intimately; it *is* important that you realize that such structures are being built and manipulated.[2]

If you have assigned a plot structure to a variable name, you can display that plot by simply evaluating the variable.

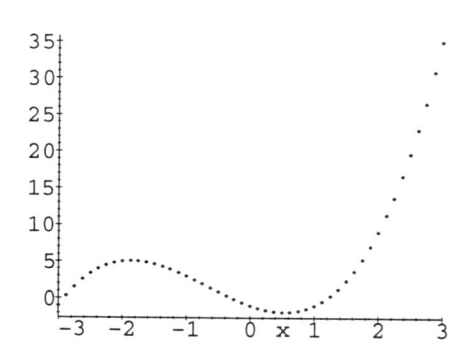

> A;

---

[2]There will be more discussion of working with these structures in the *Programming Tips* section of this chapter.

Other Plotting Commands

Of course, there are many other built-in plotting commands besides plot and plot3d, but they all eventually create a PLOT or PLOT3D structure. The majority of these commands are found in the plots package.

> with(plots);

[*animate, animate3d, conformal, contourplot, cylinderplot, densityplot, display, display3d, fieldplot, fieldplot3d, gradplot, gradplot3d, implicitplot, implicitplot3d, loglogplot, logplot, matrixplot, odeplot, pointplot, polarplot, polygonplot, polygonplot3d, polyhedraplot, replot, setoptions, setoptions3d, spacecurve, sparsematrixplot, sphereplot, surfdata, textplot, textplot3d, tubeplot*]

Two of the most useful commands in the plots package are setoptions and setoptions3d. These commands allow you to alter the default values of the optional plotting parameters for the remainder of the current session.

> setoptions(title='Hello', style=point);
> plot(cos(x), x=-10..10);

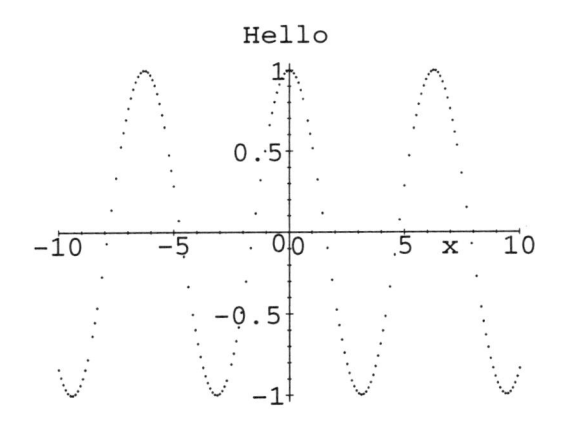

A little known (and undocumented) feature of Maple, the USERDEFAULT choice will reset any option to its *system* default value.

> setoptions(title=USERDEFAULT, style=USERDEFAULT);
> plot(cos(x), x=-10..10);

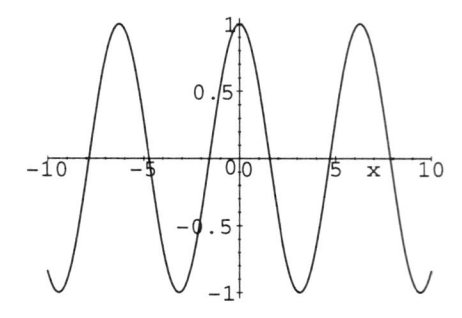

Another pair of useful commands are display and display3d. The basic functionality of these commands is to take a set of PLOT structures (display) or a set of PLOT3D structures (display3d) and display them all in one plot. In order to do this, you must make use of the "trick" detailed above of assigning the result of the plotting command to a name so that the actual plot is not rendered. In this case, and in most others as well, you do *not* want to see all the details of the plot structures, so it is advisable to use colons to terminate your commands.

```
> A := plot(6*cos(x), x=-5..5, style=POINT, axes=BOXED):
> B := plot(3*x^3-15*x^2+4*x+15, x=0..4, axes=FRAME):
> display({A, B});
```

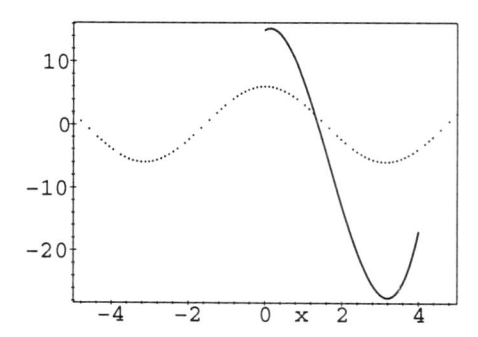

Both display and display3d have rules for dealing with conflicts among various plot structures in the areas of range, optional values, etc.

In some areas, such as range, an entirely new range is computed that encompasses the ranges of all the individual plots.[3]

With *optional* parameters, some are allowed to have different values for each individual plot (such as style), while with others (such as axes) one value is arbitrarily chosen. While it is difficult to say which optional

---

[3]This is one of the best reasons for using display instead of plot with a set of functions as the first parameter (as shown earlier). By using display, you are able to specify different options (such as range, color, etc.) for each individual function displayed.

value will be chosen by display in these cases, one rule that usually holds is that when you provide an optional parameter directly to the call to display or display3d, these values take precedence over the optional parameters in *each* individual plot.

```
> display({A, B}, axes=NONE, style=POINT);
```

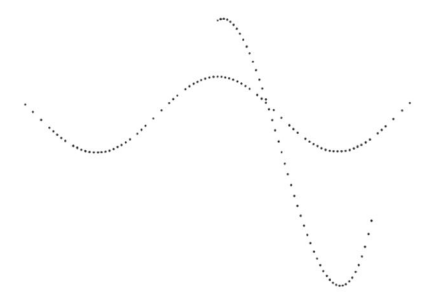

Most of the remaining commands in the plots package are for creating specific types of two- and three-dimensional plots. Some of these commands are detailed later in the *Utility Commands* section.

There are several other plotting commands scattered throughout the Maple library. Included in those are the following:

- leftbox, rightbox, middlebox, and showtangent in the student package
- dfieldplot, phaseportrait, DEplot, PDEplot, etc. in the DEtools package
- boxplot, histogram, quantile, etc. in the statplots subpackage of the stats package

For more information on any of these plotting commands, see their on-line help pages or their entries in *The Maple Handbook*.

Utility Commands

The commands provided in *DrawTools* have four basic purposes:

1. Rendering basic geometrical shapes in two and three dimensions.
2. Selecting plot structures with given characteristics from a greater collection of plots or querying individual optional values found within a single plot structure.
3. Changing plot structures through standard transformations.
4. Viewing the results of standard transformations upon the defining points of geometrical shapes.

In the following sections, each of these purposes is explained in detail and examples are given.

Drawing Geometrical Shapes
The Draw Structure Data Type

bundle(ds$_1$, ..., ds$_n$)	combine several draw structures into one
draw({ds$_1$, ..., ds$_n$})	display draw structures
type(expr, *ds*)	determine whether an expression is a valid draw structure

All the commands in *DrawTools* deal with draw structures,[4] a Maple construct that we created to hold the necessary information to represent geometrical shapes. For the most part, you will not have to be aware of the internal working of these structures or be able to *directly* manipulate them, but having an overview of how they work may help you better understand the commands that are fashioned around them.

A draw structure is always a Maple array containing *two* elements. In the simplest case, the first element is a list containing *one* PLOT or PLOT3D command for a geometrical shape and the second element is a list containing *one* list with the defining information for that same shape (called a *specifier list*).

$$\text{array([plot] [speclist])}$$

A draw structure can also contain multiple geometrical shapes. It then looks like the following:

$$\text{array([plot}_1\text{, ... , plot}_n\text{] [speclist}_1\text{, ... , speclist}_n\text{])}$$

Each element of the first list corresponds to the element of the second list in the identical position. The bundle command is provided to take multiple single-shape draw structures and create a multi-shape draw structure.

---

[4]Many of them also deal with standard Maple plot structures, but that is discussed later.

bundle does *not* allow you to mix two- and three-dimensional shapes in the same multi-shape structure.[5]

Do not think of bundle as the **Group** command you may find in other software applications; there is no hierarchal structure to multi-shape draw structures. That is, if you group together several shapes (or several multi-shape structures) with bundle there is no way to retrieve any of the individual draw structures (or individual bundles) based simply on how the larger draw structure was created. bundle does not preserve where each individual shape came from.[6]

Of course, since only a "stand alone" PLOT or PLOT3D structure is *automatically* displayed by Maple, we have also provided a basic draw command that takes a draw structure and displays the contained plot structures by calling plots[display] or plots[display3d].

In the command listing at the beginning of this section, we included a mechanism for determining whether a Maple expression is a valid draw structure. This was done by extending the built-in type command to recognize the optional typename ds. This command is mostly used internally by the commands in *DrawTools*, but may be of use to you as well. For more information on adding functionality to an existing Maple command, see the *Extending an Existing Command* section on page 266.

Examples of the use of bundle, draw, and type(, ds) are given throughout the rest of this chapter.

Two-Dimensional Shapes

point([x, y])	draw a point
line([x_1, y_1], [x_2, y_2])	draw a line segment
polygon([[x_1, y_1], ..., [x_n, y_n]])	draw a polygon
circle([x, y], rad)	draw a circle
ellipse([x, y], [rad_x, rad_y])	draw an ellipse
arc([x, y], a..b, rad)	draw an arc

All of the commands in this section create draw structures for standard two-dimensional shapes by taking defining information much in the way you would intuitively think of presenting it. For example, the circle command takes two parameters, an x, y-point for the center of the circle and a radius.

---

[5]There are many reasons for this, the least of which is that there is no way to display both PLOT and PLOT3D commands on the same set of axes.

[6]There are, however, methods available to extract a subset of shapes from a multi-shape draw structure based on the *defining characteristics* of the shapes. See the sections *Querying and Altering Internal Information* on page 210 and *Transformation Commands* on page 221 for more details.

```
> with(utility):
> draw(circle([3, -2], 6));
```

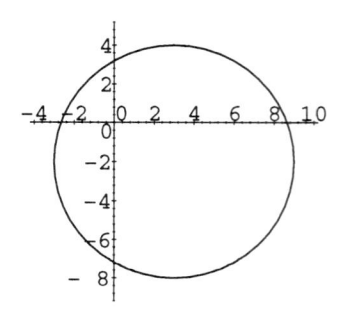

We have wrapped the call to circle in a call to draw so that the two-dimensional plot is displayed. (See the previous section, *The Draw Structure Data Type* for more information.) If we had just called circle, Maple would have printed out the rather large and cumbersome draw structure that was created. While you don't need to see all that data now, it is important at this point to realize that the defining information you provided has been saved in the second element of the draw structure. You can access this information in the following way.

```
> c1 := circle([3, -2], 6):
> type(c1, ds);
```

$$true$$

```
> c1[2];
```

$$[[SHAPE = CIRCLE, CENTER = [3, -2], RADIUS = 6]]$$

The reasons for the specific representation of defining points is detailed later.

It is, of course, possible to create the same plot using only the commands from Maple's built-in library. The *simplest* way to do so is to use the plots[implicitplot] command, but you need to remember that the implicit formula for a circle with center $[x_c, y_c]$ and radius r is:

$$(x - x_c)^2 + (y - y_c)^2 = r^2$$

The appropriate Maple call should then be:

```
> plots[implicitplot]((x-3)^2+(y+2)^2=6^2);
  Error, (in plots[implicitplot]) improper op or subscript selector
```

That didn't work, and the error message isn't much help either. You must supply the *x* and *y* ranges to plots[implicitplot]. Setting both ranges to -10..10 should encompass the entire circle.

```
> plots[implicitplot]((x-3)^2+(y+2)^2=6^2, x=-10..10, y=-10..10);
```

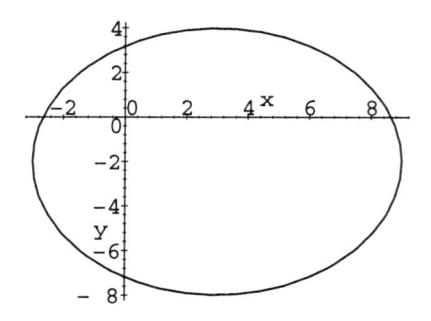

We got a plot, but why do the axes not go over the entire range we specified? plots[implicitplot] overrode the ranges that were entered and calculated the values necessary to encompass the circle. This is not how ranges are treated by other plotting commands! And, if it was going to go to all that trouble, why didn't Maple automatically produce these ranges when none were supplied? Also, because the option scaling=CONSTRAINED was not supplied, the above plot doesn't *look* very circular.

circle, on the other hand, does not require you to remember any formulae (which is even more helpful with more complex shapes like arcs, ellipses, and spheroids), computes the necessary bounds for you automatically, makes sure the scaling is constrained, and is extremely simple in its syntax. There are several other reasons for using the commands in *Draw-Tools*, as you will see throughout the rest of this chapter, so we will not dwell further on how to reproduce their results until the *Programming Tips* section.

The point command is straightforward.

```
> pt1 := point([3, -2]):
> draw(pt1);
```

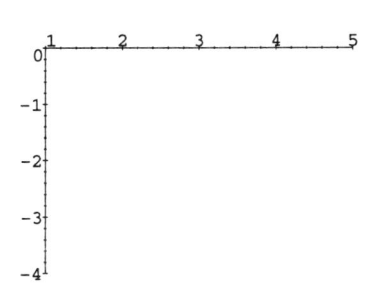

Both **line** and **polygon** connect together two or more points with line segments.

```
> l1 := line([3, -2], [-1, -2]):
> draw(l1);
```

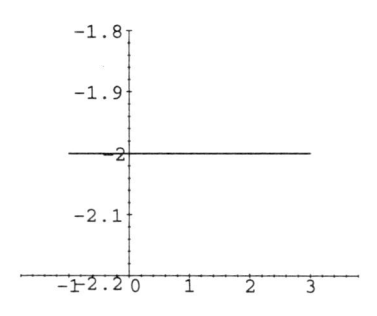

```
> poly1 := polygon([[-1, -2], [-2, -3], [-3, -2], [-2, -1], [-1, -2]]):
> draw(poly1);
```

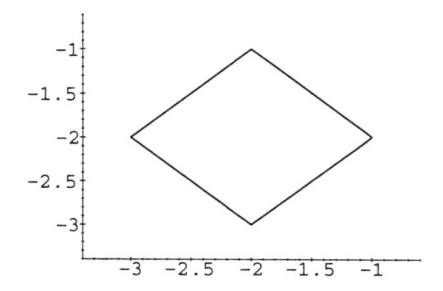

polygon does *not* automatically close up your polygon; you must supply the same first and last point to accomplish this.

ellipse is similar to **circle**, except that it takes *two* radii, one for the *x*-axis and one for the *y*-axis.

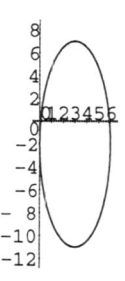

```
> e1 := ellipse([3, -2], [3, 9]):
> draw(e1);
```

arc is also similar to circle, except that its second parameter is a range (in radians) specifying which part of the related circle you wish to display.

Notice that for both ellipse and arc, as for circle, the scaling = CONSTRAINED option has been automatically appended.

```
> a1 := arc([3, -2], 3*Pi/8..5*Pi/8, 5):
> draw(a1);
```

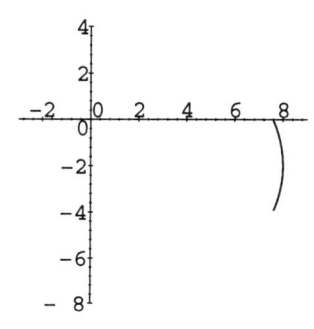

Of course, bundle allows you to draw all or any of these shapes on the same set of axes.

```
> picture1 := bundle(c1, pt1, l1, poly1, e1, a1):
> type(picture1, ds);
```

true

```
> draw(picture1);
```

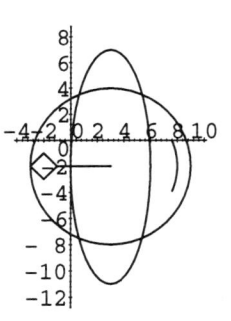

Additionally, you can explicitly enter optional parameters, as you would in a call to plot or plot3d, for *any* of the commands in this (or the next) section. The appropriate equations are just added on to the end of the parameter sequence.

```
> c2 := circle([3, -2], 6, style=POINT):
> e2 := ellipse([3, -2], [3, 9], style=POINT, symbol=DIAMOND,
> title='Shape plot'):
```

```
> picture2 := bundle(c2, pt1, l1, poly1, e2, a1):
> draw(picture2, axes=NONE);
```

Shape plot

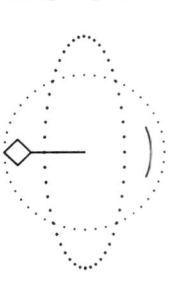

The interaction between the options of the individual plots is exactly the same as that created by plots[display]. See the section *Other Plotting Commands* on page 195 for more details.

Three-Dimensional Shapes

point3d([x, y, z])	draw a point
line3d([x_1, y_1, z_1], [x_2, y_2, z_2])	draw a line segment
polygon3d([[x_1, y_1, z_1], ..., [x_n, y_n, z_n]])	draw a polygon
circle3d([x_1,y_1,z_1], [x_2,y_2,z_2], [x_3,y_3,z_3])	draw a circle
sphere([x, y, z], rad)	draw a sphere
spheroid([x, y, z], [rad_x, rad_y, rad_z])	draw a spheroid
cylinder({[x_1,y_1,z_1], [x_2,y_2,z_2], [x_3,y_3,z_3]}, hgt)	draw a cylinder
cone({[x_1,y_1,z_1], [x_2,y_2,z_2], [x_3,y_3,z_3]}, hgt)	draw a cone
plane([x_1,y_1,z_1], [x_2,y_2,z_2], [x_3,y_3,z_3])	draw (part of) a plane

While it is a little more difficult to think of the defining information for standard shapes in three dimensions than for those in two dimensions, it is harder still to come up with their x, y, z-formulae.

Some of the commands in this section draw what are basically two-dimensional shapes in three-dimensional space. point3d, line3d, and polygon3d work exactly the same as their two-dimensional counterparts, except that each defining point also has a z-component.

```
> pt3 := point3d([3, -4/3, exp(1)]):
> l3 := line3d([-2, 0, 7], [4, 1, -2]):

> poly3 := polygon3d([[1, 1, 0], [2, 0, 0], [1, -1, 0],
>     [0, 0, 0], [1, 1, 0]]):
> draw({pt3, l3, poly3}, shading=NONE);
```

However, circle3d is not defined in the same way as its two-dimensional cousin. circle3d takes three points, and creates the *unique* circle that passes through those three points.

```
> c3 := circle3d([1, 1, 1], [2, 3, 4], [3, 2, 5/4]):
> draw(c3);
```

There are also commands in this section that create inherently three-dimensional shapes. The simplest of these is sphere, which, like the two-dimensional circle command, takes a center point and a radius.

```
> draw(sphere([4, 3, -2], 5));
```

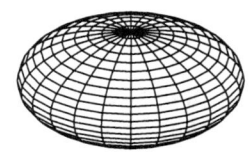

spheroid takes three radius values, representing radii parallel to the *x*, *y*, and *z* axes.

```
> draw(spheroid([4, 3, -2], [1, 5, 3]));
```

(The reason that the previous two plots look so similar is that neither is using constrained scaling, so the *x*, *y* and *z* axes are scaled to fit the window.)

The cylinder and cone commands are both defined with exactly the same combination of parameters. First, a set of three points is given to define the circular base of the shape. Then a value representing the height is supplied.

```
> cyl3 := cylinder({[1, 1, 1], [2, 3, 4], [3, 2, 5/4]}, 4):
> co3 := cone({[11, 1, 1], [12, 3, 4], [13, 2, 5/4]}, 4):
> draw({cyl3, co3});
```

The last command in this section, plane, is different than the others in that a plane is not a *contained* shape. That is, a plane goes on forever, without any specifiable "edges." Because of this, the plane command automatically computes and displays only the section of the plane that encompasses the three points given to define it.

```
> pln1 := plane([1, 1, 1], [2, 3, 4], [3, 2, 5/4]):
> draw(pln1);
```

For the special planes commonly known as the x, y-plane, x, z-plane, and the y, z-plane, the three points can be replaced by the special values 'xyplane', 'xzplane', and 'yzplane', respectively.

```
> draw({plane('xyplane'), plane('yzplane')}, style=WIREFRAME);
```

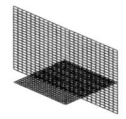

Of course, the addition of optional arguments to three-dimensional shapes works the same as for two-dimensional shapes. Any valid options from plot3d can be added at the end of each command. Also, the bundle command works the same for both two and three dimensions. (Remembering, of course, that you cannot bundle plots together from the two different dimensions.)

```
> picture3 := bundle(l3, pln1):
> draw(picture3);
```

Combining Shapes with Standard Functions

func2d(expr, var=a..b)	include a PLOT structure in a draw structure
func3d(expr, var$_1$=a$_1$..b$_1$, var$_2$=a$_2$..b$_2$)	include a PLOT3D structure in a draw structure

The practical applications of drawing and combining only geometrical shapes are limited. In many circumstances, what is desired is drawing geometrical shapes in combination with typical mathematical functions. So, how do you combine the output of the commands in the previous sections with the results from plot, plot3d, and other built-in plotting functions?

Say, for example, that you want to combine the plots of the function $f(x) = x^3 + 4x^2 - 3x - 6$ for $x = -3..3$ and the circle centered at $(1, f(1))$ with radius 2. There are two distinct ways to do this.

In the first option, you could create the plot of the function within a draw structure using func2d, create the draw structure for the circle, and display the two of them together. The func2d command passes its parameters directly to the plot command, then takes the resulting PLOT structure and wraps it inside an appropriate draw structure.

```
> f := x -> x^3+4*x^2-3*x-6:
> myfunc := func2d(f(x), x=-3..3):
> mycirc := circle([1, f(1)], 2):
> myplot := bundle(myfunc, mycirc):
> draw(myplot);
```

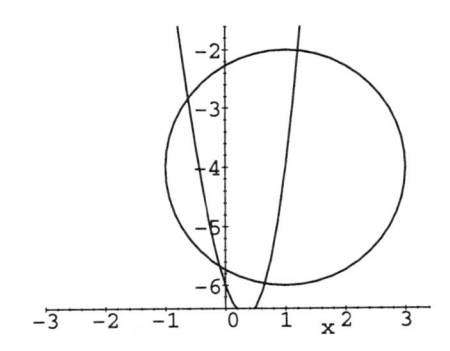

The advantage to this method is that the net result, myplot, is a bona fide draw structure which can later be manipulated with the many procedures in *DrawTools*.

In the second option, you could create the function plot using plot, create the circle using circle, extract the PLOT call from the circle's draw structure, and then display the two together with plots[display].

```
> f := x -> x^3+4*x^2-3*x-6:
> myfunc := plot(f(x), x=-3..3):
> mycirc := draw(circle([1, f(1)], 2)):
> plots[display]({myfunc, mycirc});
```

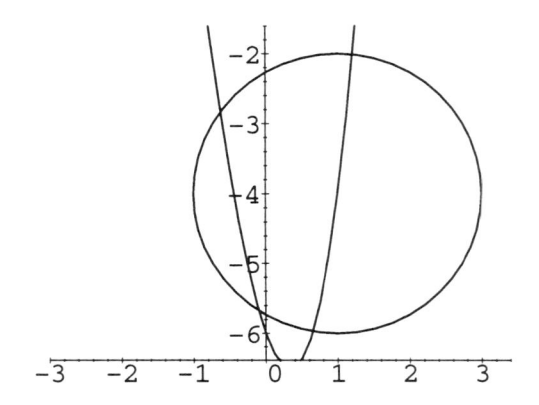

Calling circle within the draw command and assigning the result to a variable name returns the PLOT structure without the defining information found in the circle's draw structure.

The advantage to this method is that the combined plots end up in a structure with one less level of complexity. But by using this method, the resulting plot cannot be further manipulated as easily.

func3d performs a similar operation by passing its parameters to plot3d. The specifier list for a draw structure created with func2d or func3d has only one equation.

```
> func3d(sin(x*y), x=-2..2, y=-2..2)[2];
```

$$[[SHAPE = FUNC3D]]$$

Of course, optional parameters can be used in the func2d and func3d commands exactly as they would be in plot or plot3d. Also, most valid ways of defining expressions and ranges for the built-in commands (e.g., polar coordinates) can be used in the corresponding Utility commands.

Utility Commands 209

Extending Two-Dimensional Shapes

extend3d({[x_1,y_1,z_1], [x_2,y_2,z_2], [x_3,y_3,z_3]}, ds)	extend the two-dimensional shapes in ds to the three-dimensional plane defined by three points

You may have noticed that all the shapes defined in *Two-Dimensional Shapes* (with the exception of ellipse and arc) have counterparts in *Three-Dimensional Shapes*. It might be natural to assume that there is a way to extend two-dimensional shapes into three-dimensional space. To map the shapes to a *unique* representation in three-dimensional space, you must supply a plane on which to project them. This is done in the extend3d command through the use of three defining points for the plane, or by the use of one of the optional strings 'xyplane', 'xzplane', or 'yzplane'.[7]

Either a single-shape or multi-shape two-dimensional draw structure can be passed as the last parameter. Let's extend the multi-shape structure picture1 created in an earlier section, first onto the x,z-plane, and then onto an arbitrary plane.

```
> draw(extend3d('xzplane', picture1), axes=NORMAL);
```

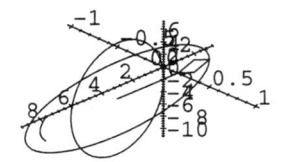

```
> draw(extend3d({[1, 1, 1], [2, 3, 4], [3, 2, 5/4]}, picture1));
```

Even the ellipse and arc were transformed. If extend3d can determine from the defining information of a two-dimensional shape that there is a related *well-defined* three-dimensional shape to be created, it will also update the defining information in the new draw structure. For example:

```
> c2d := circle([3, -2], 6):
```

---

[7]These three plane specifiers will be seen again in the *Transformation Commands* section on page 221.

```
> c2d[2];
```

$$[[SHAPE = CIRCLE, CENTER = [3, -2], RADIUS = 6]]$$

```
> c3d := extend3d('yzplane', c2d):
> c3d[2];
```

$$[[SHAPE = CIRCLE3D, POINT3D = [9, -2, 9], POINT3D = [-3, -2, -3],$$
$$POINT3D = [3, 4, 3]]]$$

Keep in mind that for circles, the defining information takes a different form depending on the dimension. If there is no direct correspondence to a well-defined shape, then the two-dimensional object is transformed to a simple three-dimensional function whose specifier list contains [SHAPE=FUNC3D], as detailed in the previous section.

Querying and Altering Internal Information

shape(ds)	display the specifier lists for shapes in a draw structure
render(speclist)	create a draw structure from a specifier list
getitem(option, ds)	return the value associated with a given optional parameter
choose([opt$_1$=val$_1$, ..., opt$_m$=val$_m$], ds)	select a specific subset of draw structures from a multi-shape structure
alter({opt$_1$=newval$_1$, ..., opt$_m$=newval$_m$}, ds)	alter the optional values of a draw structure

As you learned earlier in this chapter, a draw structure consists of a Maple array containing *two* elements. The first element is always a list containing one or more PLOT or PLOT3D commands which represent instructions on how to render the individual functions.[8] The second element is always a list of one or more (one for each element of the first list) specifier lists that provide defining information about each individual plot.

The multi-shape draw structure picture2, created in an earlier section, will help to illustrate the commands in this section.

```
> draw(picture2);
```

---

[8]If any of the shapes cannot be rendered, a PLOT() or PLOT3D() element is found in the appropriate spot in this list.

```
                          Shape plot
                        8
                        6   .......
                        4 .·       ·.
                        2·           ·
              -4 -2  0 2 4 6  8 10
                        0
                       ◇2       ─
                       -4·           ·
                       -6·         ·
                       - 8 ·.    .·
                       -10   ......
                       -12
```

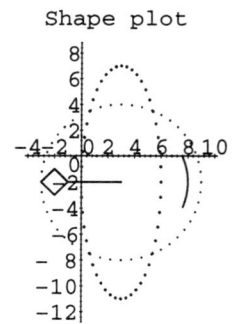

The specifier lists contained within picture2 can be used for several purposes, but at this time let's explore how to access these lists. The shape command, in its simplest form, returns the list of specifier lists for a draw structure (in other words, the second element of the draw structure's two-element array).

```
> shape(picture2);
```

$$\begin{bmatrix} [SHAPE = CIRCLE, CENTER = [3,-2], RADIUS = 6], \\ [SHAPE = POINT, POINT = [3,-2]], \\ [SHAPE = LINE, POINT = [3,-2], POINT = [-1,-2]], [\\ SHAPE = POLYGON, POINT = [-1,-2], POINT = [-2,-3], \\ POINT = [-3,-2], POINT = [-2,-1], POINT = [-1,-2]], \\ [SHAPE = ELLIPSE, CENTER = [3,-2], RADIUS = [3,9]], \\ \left[SHAPE = ARC, CENTER = [3,-2], ANGLE = \frac{3}{8}\pi..\frac{5}{8}\pi, RADIUS = 5 \right] \end{bmatrix}$$

You can see here how the shape creating commands save the defining information for the various two-dimensional shapes. A similar syntax is used for three-dimensional shapes. A more impressive use of shape comes when the optional string 'equation' is added. Then, instead of the specifier lists, the actual x, y equations of the shapes are returned.[9]

```
> shape(picture2, 'equation'):
> printlist(", 'pretty');
```

$$(\_x - 3)^2 + (\_y + 2)^2 = 36$$

---

[9] If shape is unable to compute an exact formula for a specific plot, then the specifier list for that plot is returned.

$$[SHAPE = POINT, POINT = [3,-2]]$$

$$\_y + 2 = -3$$

$$[SHAPE = POLYGON, POINT = [-1,-2], POINT = [-2,-3], POINT = [-3,-2],$$
$$POINT = [-2,-1], POINT = [-1,-2]]$$

$$\frac{1}{9}(\_x-3)^2 + \frac{1}{81}(\_y+2)^2 = 1$$

$$\left[SHAPE = ARC, CENTER = [3,-2], ANGLE = \frac{3}{8}\pi..\frac{5}{8}\pi, RADIUS = 5\right]$$

The printlist command[10] was used to display the elements of the resulting list one element per line, to improve readability.

A list of strings can be supplied as an optional third parameter if you wish to override the use of the default strings '_x' and '_y' (and '_z' for three-dimensional shapes).

```
> shape(sphere([3, 5, 6], 4/3), 'equation', ['a', 'bb', 'ccc']);
```

$$\left[(a-3)^2 + (bb-5)^2 + (ccc-6)^2 = \frac{16}{9}\right]$$

The shape command also accepts a *single* specifier list (i.e., not contained in a draw structure) as input. Typically, this is used in conjunction with the 'equation' option.

```
> myspecl := [SHAPE=CIRCLE, CENTER=[3,-4], RADIUS=5/3];
```

$$myspecl := \left[SHAPE = CIRCLE, CENTER = [3,-4], RADIUS = \frac{5}{3}\right]$$

```
> shape(myspecl, 'equation');
```

$$\left[(\_x-3)^2 + (\_y+4)^2 = \frac{25}{9}\right]$$

The render command, on the other hand, can be used to take a specifier list and create a complete draw structure from it. The draw command must then be called to display the shape.

```
> render(myspecl):
> draw(");
```

---

[10]See the *IOTools* chapter for details on printlist.

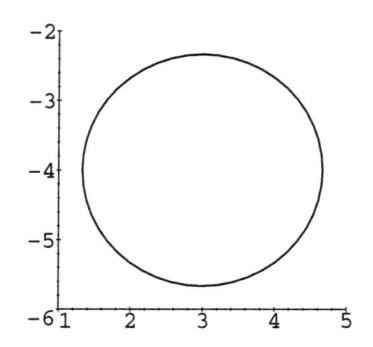

Just as for any other shape defining command, optional plotting parameters can be added to the end of the call to render.

```
> draw(render(myspec1, style=POINT, symbol=DIAMOND));
```

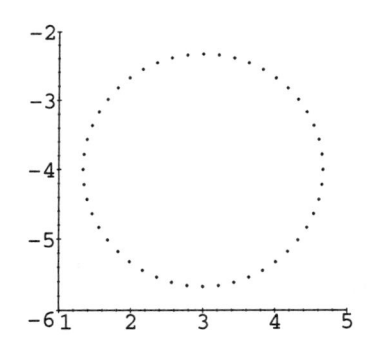

If the specifier list passed to render does not define a renderable shape, then an empty plot structure is placed in the draw structure.

```
> render([SHAPE=LINE, POINT=[a,b], POINT=[c,d]]);
```

$$[\,[PLOT(\,)]\quad[[SHAPE = LINE, POINT = [a,b], POINT = [c,d]]]\,]$$

The next command in this section, getitem, can be used to extract specific information from a specifier list that is either within a draw structure or on its own. By supplying one of the following keywords, the value on the right-hand side of the appropriate equation is returned.

- SHAPE
- POINT
- CENTER
- RADIUS
- ANGLE
- POINT3D

- CENTER3D
- HEIGHT

```
> draw(c1);
```

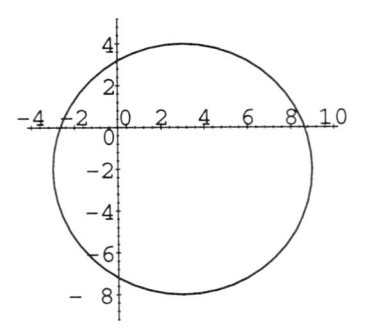

```
> shape(c1);
```

$$[[SHAPE = CIRCLE, CENTER = [3, -2], RADIUS = 6]]$$

```
> getitem(CENTER, c1);
```

$$[3, -2]$$

```
> getitem(RADIUS, c1);
```

$$6$$

This can be particularly helpful when you want to define a new shape dependent on some information from an already existing shape.

```
> e5 := ellipse(getitem(CENTER, c1), [2*getitem(RADIUS, c1),
>              getitem(RADIUS, c1)/2]):
> draw({c1, e5}, axes=NONE);
```

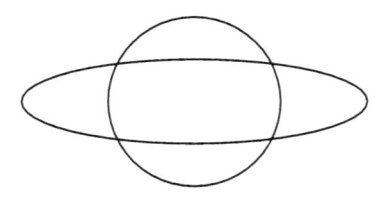

Not only can the value of specifier list options be extracted, but values assigned to standard plotting options (e.g., color, style, etc.) can also be queried. Simply supply the left-hand side name exactly as you would when using the option to create a plot.

```
> draw(e2);
```

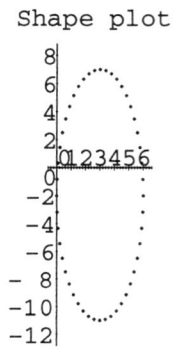

Shape plot

```
> getitem(style, e2);
```

$$\text{STYLE}(\textit{POINT})$$

```
> getitem(symbol, e2);
```

$$\text{SYMBOL}(\textit{DIAMOND})$$

The result of getitem when a plotting option is queried is not just the value you would supply in a call to plot or plot3d, but the entire related unevaluated command call from within the PLOT or PLOT3D structure.

As you might expect, such plotting options can also be extracted directly from PLOT and PLOT3D structures, without the encompassing draw structure.

```
> myplot := plot(cos(x), title='COS(X)', color=blue):

> mytitle := getitem(title, myplot);
```

$$\textit{mytitle} := \text{TITLE}(\textit{COS(X)})$$

```
> mycolor := getitem(color, myplot);
```

$$\textit{mycolor} := \text{COLOUR}(\textit{RGB}, 0, 0, 1.00000000)$$

Using this information in further plots or draw structures is a tricky thing, because the parameter sequences in the unevaluated calls do not always directly match the method of input in the plot or plot3d commands. For instance, to use mycolor in another plot, you can simply put it directly on the right of the appropriate equation.

```
> plot(sin(x), x=-2..2, color=mycolor);
```

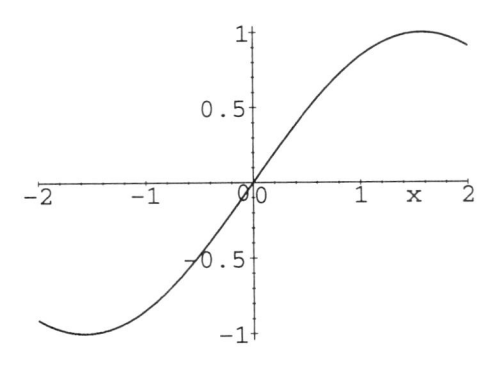

But, to use mytitle to label another plot, you must use only the single parameter of the TITLE command.

```
> draw(line([1,3], [6,4], title=op(mytitle)));
```

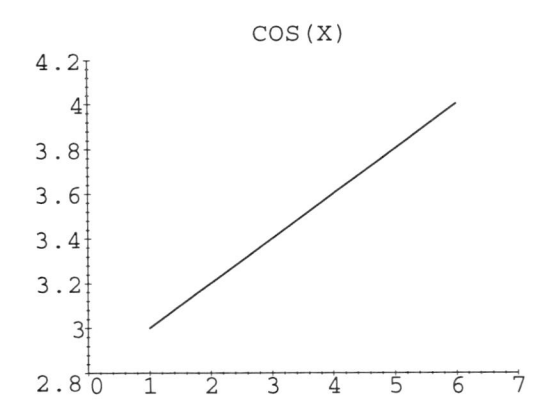

To determine what needs to be done to reuse information supplied by getitem, examine both the result of the command and the format of the appropriate option equation.

You can also extract information that wasn't directly supplied in your plotting command.

```
> getitem(tickmarks, myplot);
```

AXESTICKS(*DEFAULT*, *DEFAULT*, FONT(*TIMES*, *ROMAN*, 24))

This is because Maple automatically saves information on tickmarks in the PLOT structure.

For more information on the relationship between these two formats, see the *Using Built-In Second-Level Functions* section on page 240.

What happens when you want to extract information from multi-shape draw structures (or multi-function plots)? *All* the shapes are investigated, and the relevant values are returned in an expression sequence.

```
> centseq := getitem(CENTER, picture2);
```

$$centseq := [3, -2], [3, -2], [3, -2]$$

```
> getitem(view, picture2);
```

$$\text{VIEW}(-4.2..10.2, -9.2..5.2), \text{VIEW}(1...5., -4...0),$$
$$\text{VIEW}(-1.8..3.8, -2.2..-1.8), \text{VIEW}(-3.4..-.6, -3.4..-.6),$$
$$\text{VIEW}(-.6..6.6, -12.8..8.8), \text{VIEW}(-3.0..9.0, -8.0..4.0)$$

Now that you know how to query information from a draw structure, it will be simple to use the choose command to *select* a subset of draw structures from a multi-shape structure.

The first parameter to choose can contain *equations*[11] of the form found in the specifier lists.

So, in order to select the draw structures in picture2 that have a defining point at [1, -1], use the following command:

```
> choose([POINT=[-1, -2]], picture2):
> draw(");
```

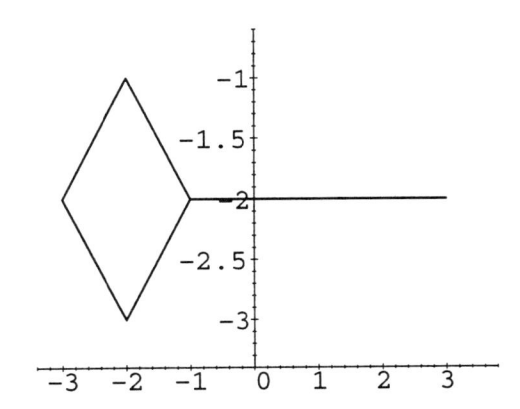

The result is a new draw structure, containing only those shapes that passed the criteria.

To narrow the selection down even further, add additional equations to the list.

```
> choose([POINT=[-1,-2], SHAPE=POLYGON], picture2):
> draw(");
```

---

[11]The lefthand sides of which were used in the getitem command.

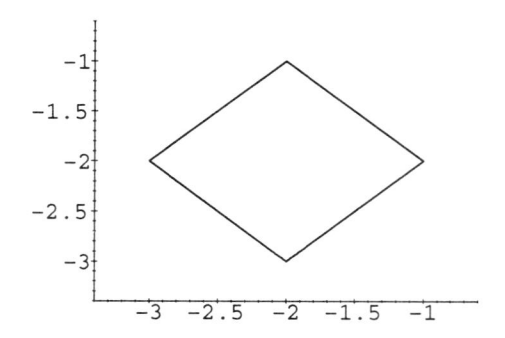

When a list is used to enclose the equations, the selected draw structures must satisfy *all* of the options. When a set is used instead, the selected draw structures need only satisfy *one* (or more) of the options.

> draw(choose({CENTER=[4, 4], SHAPE=LINE, RADIUS=6}, picture2));

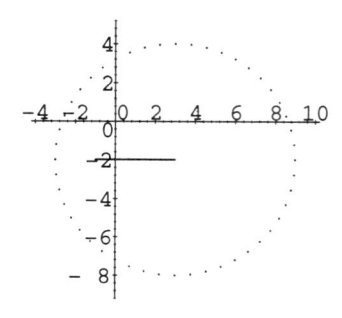

Of course, the other optional parameters (e.g., style, color) that were used when the shapes were created are also valid search candidates. To use these options as selection criteria, simply add them to the first parameter of choose as you would specify them in the plot or plot3d command call.

> draw(choose([style=POINT], picture2));

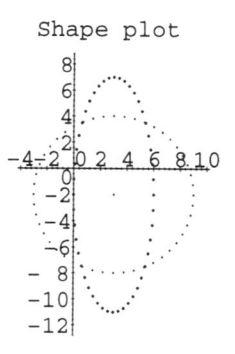

```
> draw(choose({symbol=DIAMOND, SHAPE=ARC, POINT=[123, -34]}, picture2));
```

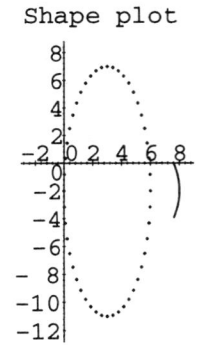

```
                                              Shape plot
                                              8|
                                              6|  .......
                                              4|.·       ·.
                                              2|·          ·
                                          -2  0| 2  4  6  8
                                              0|·          ·
                                             -2|·          ·
                                             -4| ·        ·
                                             -6|·         ·
                                             -8| ·       ·
                                            -10|  ·······
                                            -12|
```

The last example demonstrates that you can easily mix and match specifier list options and plotting options in the same call to choose.

The last parameter does not need to be a draw structure—a PLOT or PLOT3D structure works equally as well. Naturally, specifier list options do not work when searching plotting structures, and the result of such a search is the same type of structure that went in. Try a few examples of this to convince yourself of its working.

One other thing to remember is that there is not always a direct correspondence between the optional parameters passed to a plot or plot3d command and the optional values stored in the related PLOT and PLOT3D structure. Usually there are a few extra options automatically generated. As well, some of the options you specify are not stored explicitly because they are default values or because they are contained in the way the actual plotting points are represented (e.g., the numpoints option). If you want more information about what sort of options are present in plotting structures, create a few PLOT and PLOT3D structures and examine them internally.[12]

The last command in this section, alter, is like a combination of the Utility command choose and the built-in command subs. Both choose and alter take option equations as the first parameter. Instead of selecting draw structures (or plots) based on the value of these options (i.e., the right hand sides), alter changes the values in the given structure to reflect the information in these option equations.

In its simplest form, alter changes the optional values for *all* draw structures in a multi-shape structure.

```
> alter({style=POINT}, picture2):
```

---

[12]For further information, refer to the *Using Built-In Second-Level Functions* section on page 240.

```
> draw(", axes=NONE);
```

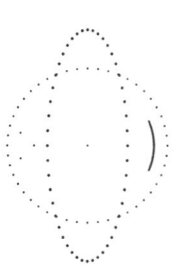

Shape plot

Of course, it doesn't make any sense to try to change all the shapes to, say, circles—the defining points don't allow it—so trying to do so produces an error message.

```
> alter({style=POINT, SHAPE=CIRCLE}, picture2):
Error, (in plot/options2d) unknown or bad argument, SHAPE = CIRCLE
```

In fact, none of the specifier list options can be used in alter.

In most of the windowing interfaces for Maple, once a plot is generated and displayed, most of its optional values can be altered through menu item choices. This only changes the representation of the plot on the screen; the internal representation remains the same. Using the alter command saves your changes internally, so that they can be called up at a later time (or session) or added to further combination plots.

alter takes an optional second parameter that adds a significant new level to its functionality. By providing a list of option equations as the *second* parameter (like you did for the first), you specify that alter should only work on those structures that would pass through choose if it were given that list as a first parameter. This concept can be hard to visualize; a simple example of its use should clear things up.

```
> draw(picture2);
```

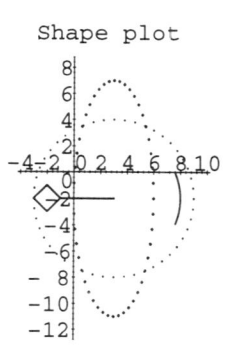

Shape plot

```
> alter({style=LINE}, [SHAPE=CIRCLE], picture2):
> draw(");
```

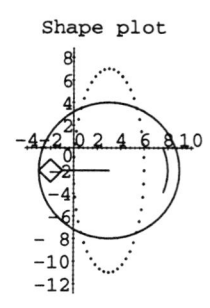

Shape plot

Of course, much more ambitious combinations of first and second parameters can be entered. The "choosing" parameter can also be a set of values, which then gets passed directly to choose.

```
> alter({style=POINT, color=green},
>       {SHAPE=ARC, RADIUS=6, style=POINT},
>         picture2):
> draw(", axes=NONE);
```

Shape plot

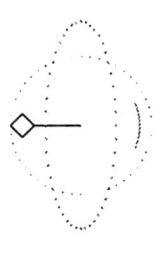

This optional second parameter can be used to act on a subset of the passed structure in several other *DrawTools* commands, including getitem and those commands detailed in *Transformation Commands*.

One more option that is common to most commands that take a draw structure as the last parameter is the ability to pass a *set* of draw structures instead. bundle is called internally to turn them into a single multi-shape structure before the computations are continued.

Transformation Commands

DrawTools contains several commands for performing standard transformations on draw structures and plotting structures. With draw structures, both the underlying specifier lists and plot structures are affected. First, however, let's examine the effect of these commands on the plots as displayed on the screen.

Two-Dimensional Functions

translate([num_x, num_y], ds)	move a draw structure
scale(num, ds)	scale a draw structure
rotate(num, ds)	rotate a draw structure about the origin
reflect({[x_1, y_1], [x_2, y_2]}, ds)	reflect a draw structure about a line
transform(M, ds)	apply a transformation matrix to a draw structure

The first of these commands is the simplest to understand. translate takes an *x*-distance, a *y*-distance and a draw structure, and moves every shape the prescribed distances.

```
> c0 := circle([0, 0], 1):
> ct := translate([3, -2], c0):
> draw({c0, ct});
```

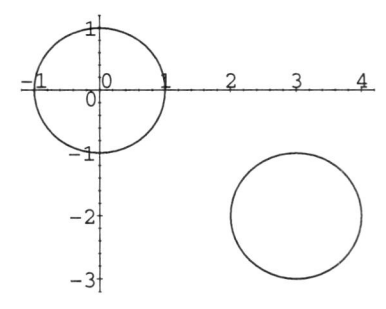

Of course, multi-shape structures can also be translated; and (as with every other command in this section) an option equation list or set can be supplied to specify which shapes get transformed.

```
> draw(picture2);
```

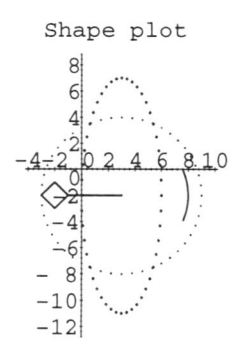

```
> draw(translate([6, 16], [style=POINT], picture2), axes=NONE);
```

Shape plot

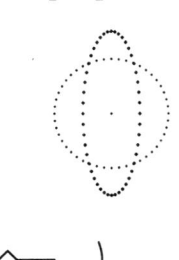

Observe that the individual shapes in picture2 that did *not* get translated are included in their original positions in the result of translate. If you want to see only the translated objects, use choose before you call translate.

```
> choose([style=POINT], picture2):
> draw({", translate([6, 16], ")}, axes=NONE);
```

Shape plot

One reason translate is so easy to use is that it affects *every* draw structure; every type of shape can be translated. scale, on the other hand, reacts differently with different shapes.

- Points, lines, polygons, and two-dimensional functions are not affected.
- Circles and ellipses keep the same center points, but their radii are scaled.
- Arcs keep the same center points and angle ranges, but their radii are scaled.

```
> draw(scale(1/3, picture2));
```

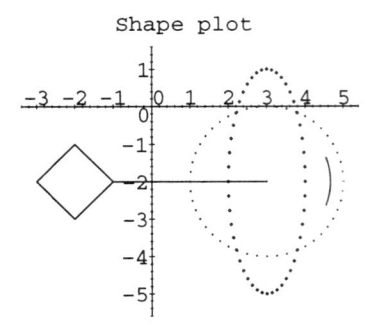

While it may look like the polygon, line, and point structures were increased in size, actually everything else was shrunk.

The rotate command works identically on every type of shape, but is a little more complicated to understand in general. If no point of rotation is supplied, the shapes are rotated about the origin ($[0, 0]$) by the given number of radians.

```
> draw({c1, rotate(Pi, c1)});
```

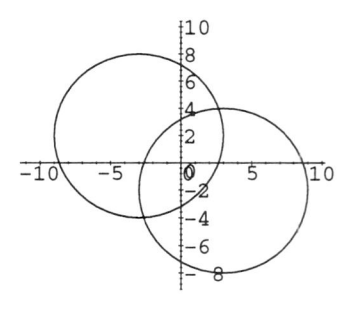

Supplying a point as the second parameter indicates that you want to rotate about that point.

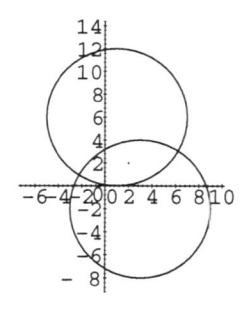

```
> draw({c1, rotate(Pi, [2, 2], c1), point([2, 2])});
```

Of course, a multi-shape structure (or selected parts thereof) can be easily rotated.

```
> draw(rotate(Pi/2, picture2));
```

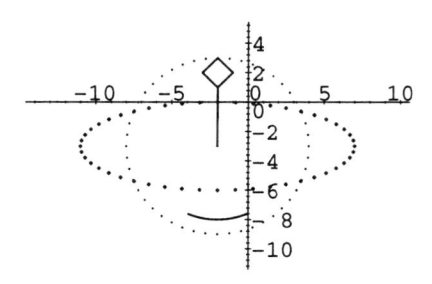

Shape plot

reflect takes two parameters. The first parameter specifies, through either a set of two points or through the special strings 'xaxis' or 'yaxis', the line about which the draw structure is reflected.

```
> draw({poly1, reflect('yaxis', poly1)});
```

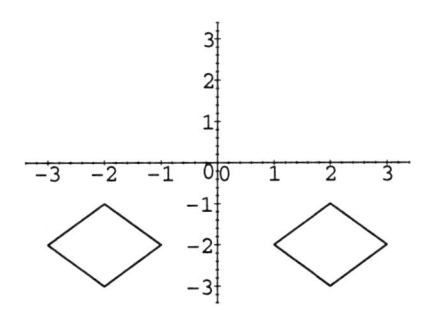

```
> draw({poly1, reflect({[-3, -6], [3, 0]}, poly1), line([-3, -6], [3, 0])});
```

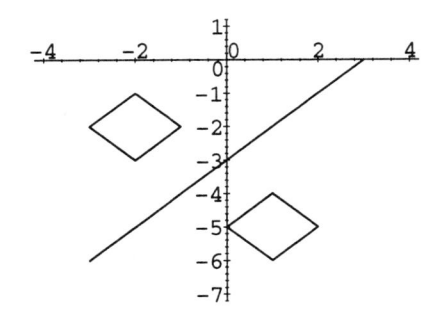

And another example of selective transformation:

```
> draw(reflect('xaxis', {SHAPE=ELLIPSE, SHAPE=LINE}, picture2));
```

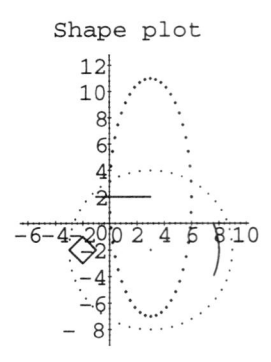

The transform command allows you to perform additional transformations. The transformation defined by the 2×2 transformation matrix supplied as the first parameter is applied to each point in the plot structures.

```
> tM := linalg[matrix](2, 2, [1, -3, 4, -5/2]);
```

$$tM := \begin{bmatrix} 1 & -3 \\ 4 & \frac{-5}{2} \end{bmatrix}$$

```
> draw({c1, transform(tM, c1)});
```

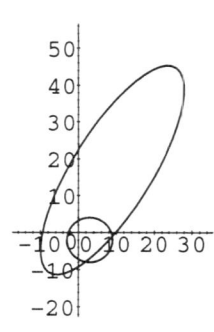

So far, only *complete* draw structures have been passed to the transformation commands. It is also possible to pass both types of structures contained in a draw structure independently.

Since all of the above commands work primarily on the points stored in the PLOT structures, they are equally useful[13] when passed such a structure.

---

[13] With the exception of scale.

```
> plot(sin(x), x=-10..10);
```

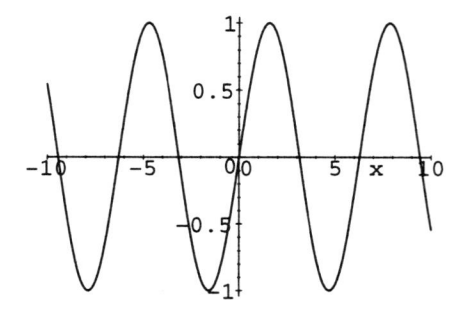

```
> translate([Pi/2, 0], ");
```

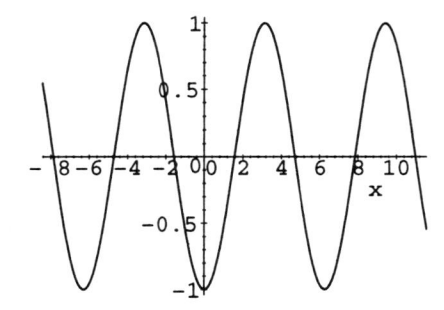

As well, when passed a *single* specifier list, the transformation routine returns a transformed list (when applicable). This can be handy when doing multiple transformation on a single shape.[14]

Three-Dimensional Functions

translate3d([num_x, num_y, num_z], ds)	move a draw structure
scale3d(num, ds)	scale a draw structure
reflect3d({[x_1,y_1,z_1],[x_2,y_2,z_2], [x_3,y_3,z_3]}, ds)	reflect a draw structure about a plane
transform3d(M, ds)	apply a transformation matrix to a draw structure

As with two-dimensional shapes, translate3d is the simplest command to understand. A *z*-distance is also provided and every shape is moved the prescribed distances.

---

[14]Specifier lists can also be passed instead of draw structures to the commands getitem and extend3d.

```
> sph0 := sphere([0, 0, 0], 1):
> spht := translate3d([3, -2, 4], sph0):
> draw({sph0, spht}, axes=BOXED);
```

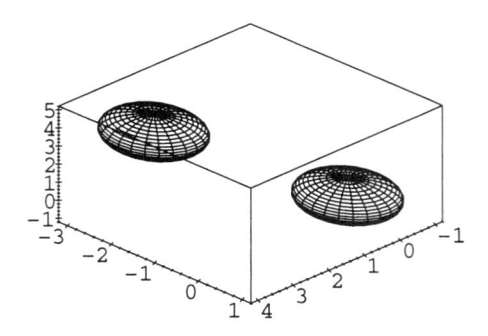

Of course, multi-shape structures can also be translated; and an option equation list or set can be supplied to specify which shapes get transformed. Similar to translate, translate3d works the same way on every three-dimensional draw structure; every type of shape can be translated.

scale3d, on the other hand, reacts differently with different shapes.

- Points, lines, polygons, circles, arcs, planes, cylinders, cones and three-dimensional functions are not affected.

- Spheres and spheroids keep the same center points, but their radii are scaled.

```
> draw(scale3d(3, sph0), axes=BOXED);
```

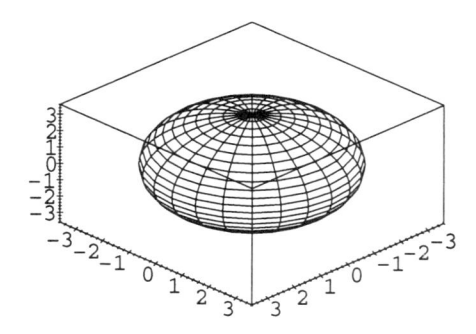

reflect3d takes two parameters. The first parameter specifies, either through a set of three points or through the special strings 'xyplane', 'xzplane', or 'yzplane', the plane about which the draw structure is reflected.

```
> draw({c3, reflect3d('xyplane', c3)});
```

```
> draw({poly3, reflect3d('yzplane', poly3), plane('yzplane')});
```

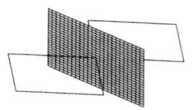

The transform3d command, like its two-dimensional cousin, allows you to perform additional transformations in three dimensions. The transformation defined by the 3×3 transformation matrix is applied to each point in the PLOT3D structures.

```
> tM3 := linalg[matrix](3, 3, [2, 1, -5, 4, 7, 0, 6, 3, -1]);
```

$$tM3 := \begin{bmatrix} 2 & 1 & -5 \\ 4 & 7 & 0 \\ 6 & 3 & -1 \end{bmatrix}$$

```
> draw({c3, transform3d(tM3, c3)}, orientation=[60,60]);
```

Of course, these commands can be applied directly to PLOT3D structures as well.

The Effect on Specifier Lists

Earlier, it was demonstrated how specifier lists (those lists contained in the second element of a draw structure) could be used to select individual shapes from a multi-shape structure. As well, the shape command was used to display precise formulae for those shapes. These are not the only reasons for saving information in specifier lists.

When standard transformations are performed upon a shape, the actual points in the PLOT or PLOT3D structures are altered *within* their structures. That is, no new invocation of plot or plot3d is made; the plot structures are simply altered within themselves.[15] In addition to this, the tools in *DrawTools* perform the same transformations on the defining points found in the specifier lists (whenever possible).

---

[15] See the *Programming Tips* section for more details.

For example, the following code creates a circle, determines its x, y equation, performs three standard transformations, then examines the new specifier list and x, y equation.

```
> mycircle := circle([-2, 1], 3):
> shape(mycircle, 'equation');
```

$$\left[(\_x+2)^2 + (\_y-1)^2 = 9\right]$$

```
> draw(mycircle);
```

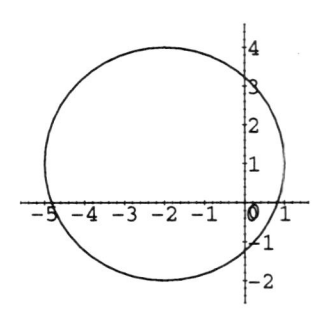

```
> newcircle := scale(2/5, rotate(Pi/2, translate([6, 5], mycircle))):
> shape(newcircle);
```

$$\left[\left[SHAPE = CIRCLE, CENTER = [6, -4], RADIUS = \frac{6}{5}\right]\right]$$

```
> shape(newcircle, 'equation');
```

$$\left[(\_x-6)^2 + (\_y+4)^2 = \frac{36}{25}\right]$$

```
> draw({mycircle, newcircle}, title=convert(op("), string));
```

$((((\_x)+(-6))^\wedge(2))+(((\_y)+(4))^\wedge(2))) = (36/25)$

This feature is useful for examining the effect of transformations on standard shapes. For more examples, see the following section, *Symbolic Shapes*, on page 232.

It must be noted that if a given transformation causes any of the elements in a specifier list to no longer make sense, then the entire specifier list is replaced with either [SHAPE=FUNC2D] or [SHAPE=FUNC3D], depending on what dimension you are working in. For example, since ellipses are defined by radial lengths parallel to the fixed (x, y, and z) axes, once a rotation by anything other than $\frac{\pi}{2}$ or some multiple thereof is performed, the axes values will have lost some of their meaning.

```
> myellipse := ellipse([4/3, -2/3], [2, 6]):
> shape(myellipse, 'equation');
```

$$\left[\frac{1}{4}\left(\_x - \frac{4}{3}\right)^2 + \frac{1}{36}\left(\_y + \frac{2}{3}\right)^2 = 1 \right]$$

```
> newellipse := rotate(Pi/3, myellipse):
> shape(newellipse, 'equation');
```

$$[\,[\,SHAPE = FUNC2D\,]\,]$$

```
> draw({myellipse, newellipse});
```

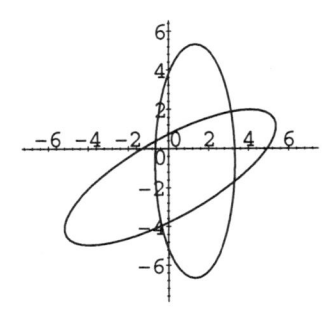

Just because a definitive equation cannot be found does *not* mean that the plot of the shape cannot be displayed.

Also, the transform and transform3d commands nullify any specifier lists containing non-point elements[16] passed through them. Those specifier lists made entirely of points are returned transformed by the given matrix.

```
> myline := line([1, 1], [3, 4]):
> tM := linalg[matrix](2, 2, [1, 5, -2, 6]):
> newline := transform(tM, myline):
```

---

[16]SHAPE equations are not counted.

> `shape(newline);`

$$[[SHAPE = LINE, POINT = [6., 4.], POINT = [23., 18.]]]$$

> `draw({myline, newline});`

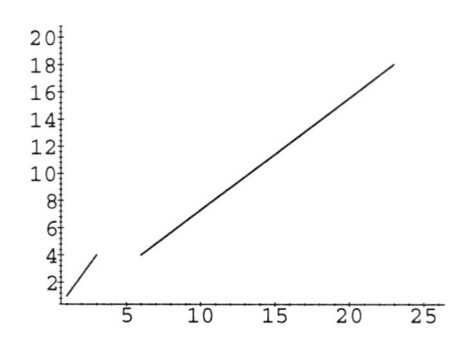

Symbolic Shapes

This last section introduces no new commands of its own, but instead shows a different way to use commands that have been already described.

In the last section, you learned how to apply standard transformations to given geometrical shapes, and how to view the effect of these transformations upon their defining characteristics. In an earlier section, it was explained that if a shape-forming command was given defining points that it could not render, PLOT() or PLOT3D() was inserted in the draw structure in the place of a more standard PLOT or PLOT3D structure. Putting these two concepts together, now explore what happens when you define shapes with *symbolic*, not numeric, attributes. This functionality can give a keen insight into the effects of transformations.

For simplicity's sake, the following example is kept to two dimensions; but it could be extended to three dimensions as well.

> `sympoint := point([xval, yval]);`

$$sympoint := [\ [PLOT(\ )]\ \ [[SHAPE = POINT, POINT = [xval, yval]]]\ ]$$

The draw structure contains a call to PLOT(), where typically a much more complex PLOT structure would be. What happens when you call draw with this structure?

> `draw(sympoint);`

`Error, (in draw) only NULL plots supplied`

But the specifier list for the structure is still there.

```
> shape(sympoint);
```
$$[[SHAPE = POINT, POINT = [xval, yval]]]$$

Now perform a simple translation on the point sympoint and see what happens to the specifier list.

```
> shape(translate([1, 1], sympoint));
```
$$[[SHAPE = POINT, POINT = [xval + 1, yval + 1]]]$$

Of course, the translation itself need not be purely numeric—symbolic distances can be used.

```
> shape(translate([xdist, ydist], sympoint));
```
$$[[SHAPE = POINT, POINT = [xval + xdist, yval + ydist]]]$$

What happens when a symbolic transformation is applied to a numerically defined shape?

```
> draw(mycircle);
```

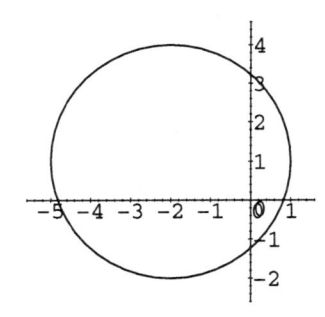

```
> stcircle := translate([xdist, ydist], mycircle);
```
$$stcircle := [[PLOT(\ )]\quad [[SHAP\backslash]$$
$$[PE = CIRCLE, CENTER = [-2 + xdist, 1 + ydist], RADIUS = 3]]]$$

```
> shape(stcircle, 'equation');
```
$$\left[(\_x + 2 - xdist)^2 + (\_y - 1 - ydist)^2 = 9\right]$$

The PLOT structure was set to PLOT() by applying a symbolic translation.

When you are performing symbolic transformations on symbolic shapes, the equations that define the shapes can get very complex very quickly. Let's re-examine the example from the last section with totally *symbolic* values.

```
> symcircle := circle([xval, yval], rad):
> shape(symcircle, 'equation');
```

$$\left[(\_x - xval)^2 + (\_y - yval)^2 = rad^2 \right]$$

```
> newsymcircle := reflect({[x1, y1], [x2, y2]},
>                         rotate(rf,
>                         translate([xdist, ydist],
>                         symcircle))):
> shape(newsymcircle, 'equation');
```

$$\Big[(\_x - (2\,x2\,y1^2 + 2\,y2^2\,x1 - 2\,x2\,y1\,y2 - 2\,y2\,x1\,y1 + 2\sin(rf)\,ydist\,y2\,y1$$
$$+ 2\cos(rf)\,xval\,y2\,y1 + 2\cos(rf)\,xdist\,y2\,y1 - 2\,x2\,y2\sin(rf)\,xval$$
$$- 2\,x2\,y1\cos(rf)\,ydist + x1^2\sin(rf)\,yval + x1^2\sin(rf)\,ydist - \sin(rf)\,ydist\,y2^2$$
$$+ 2\sin(rf)\,yval\,y2\,y1 - 2\,x2\,y1\cos(rf)\,yval - \sin(rf)\,ydist\,y1^2$$
$$- \sin(rf)\,yval\,y2^2 - \sin(rf)\,yval\,y1^2 - \cos(rf)\,xdist\,y1^2 - \cos(rf)\,xval\,y2^2$$
$$- \cos(rf)\,xval\,y1^2 - \cos(rf)\,xdist\,y2^2 - 2\,x2\,x1\sin(rf)\,yval$$
$$- 2\,x2\,x1\sin(rf)\,ydist - 2\,x1\,y2\cos(rf)\,ydist - 2\,x1\,y1\sin(rf)\,xval$$
$$- 2\,x1\,y1\sin(rf)\,xdist + 2\,x1\,y1\cos(rf)\,yval + 2\,x1\,y1\cos(rf)\,ydist$$
$$+ 2\,x2\,y2\cos(rf)\,ydist + 2\,x2\,y1\sin(rf)\,xval + 2\,x2\,y1\sin(rf)\,xdist$$
$$+ 2\,x1\,y2\sin(rf)\,xval + 2\,x1\,y2\sin(rf)\,xdist - 2\,x2\,x1\cos(rf)\,xval$$
$$- 2\,x1\,y2\cos(rf)\,yval + x1^2\cos(rf)\,xval + x2^2\cos(rf)\,xval + x2^2\cos(rf)\,xdist$$
$$+ x2^2\sin(rf)\,yval + x2^2\sin(rf)\,ydist + x1^2\cos(rf)\,xdist - 2\,x2\,x1\cos(rf)\,xdist$$
$$+ 2\,x2\,y2\cos(rf)\,yval - 2\,x2\,y2\sin(rf)\,xdist) /($$
$$y2^2 - 2\,y2\,y1 + y1^2 + x2^2 - 2\,x2\,x1 + x1^2))^2 + (\_y - (-2\,y1\,x2\cos(rf)\,xdist$$
$$- 2\,y1\,x2\cos(rf)\,xval - 2\,y2\,y1\cos(rf)\,ydist + 2\,y2\,x2\cos(rf)\,xval$$
$$+ 2\,y2\,x2\cos(rf)\,xdist + 2\,y2\,x2\sin(rf)\,yval + 2\,y2\,x2\sin(rf)\,ydist$$
$$- 2\,y2\,x1\cos(rf)\,xval - 2\,y2\,x1\cos(rf)\,xdist - 2\,y2\,x1\sin(rf)\,yval$$
$$- 2\,y2\,x1\sin(rf)\,ydist - 2\,y1\,x2\sin(rf)\,yval - 2\,y1\,x2\sin(rf)\,ydist$$
$$+ 2\,y1\,x1\cos(rf)\,xval + 2\,y1\,x1\cos(rf)\,xdist + 2\,y1\,x1\sin(rf)\,yval$$
$$+ 2\,y1\,x1\sin(rf)\,ydist + 2\cos(rf)\,yval\,x2\,x1 + 2\cos(rf)\,ydist\,x2\,x1$$
$$- 2\sin(rf)\,xval\,x2\,x1 - 2\sin(rf)\,xdist\,x2\,x1 + 2\,y2\,x1^2 - 2\,x2\,y1\,x1$$

$$\begin{aligned}
&- 2\, y2\, x1\, x2 + 2\, y2\, y1 \sin(\mathit{rf})\, xval + 2\, y2\, y1 \sin(\mathit{rf})\, xdist \\
&- 2\, y2\, y1 \cos(\mathit{rf})\, yval + 2\, x2^2\, y1 + \sin(\mathit{rf})\, xval\, x2^2 + \sin(\mathit{rf})\, xval\, x1^2 \\
&+ \sin(\mathit{rf})\, xdist\, x2^2 + \sin(\mathit{rf})\, xdist\, x1^2 - \cos(\mathit{rf})\, yval\, x2^2 - \cos(\mathit{rf})\, yval\, x1^2 \\
&- \cos(\mathit{rf})\, ydist\, x2^2 - \cos(\mathit{rf})\, ydist\, x1^2 - y2^2 \sin(\mathit{rf})\, xval - y2^2 \sin(\mathit{rf})\, xdist \\
&+ y2^2 \cos(\mathit{rf})\, yval + y2^2 \cos(\mathit{rf})\, ydist - y1^2 \sin(\mathit{rf})\, xval - y1^2 \sin(\mathit{rf})\, xdist \\
&+ y1^2 \cos(\mathit{rf})\, yval + y1^2 \cos(\mathit{rf})\, ydist) \Big/ (\\
&y2^2 - 2\, y2\, y1 + y1^2 + x2^2 - 2\, x2\, x1 + x1^2))^2 = \mathit{rad}^2 \Big]
\end{aligned}$$

Symbolically and numerically defined draw structures can be combined in the same multi-shape structure. When draw is called, only those shapes that are numerically defined are rendered.[17]

Examples

Plotting Radio Coverage

A new radio station, WPAC, wishes to broadcast over an area containing twenty cities. The station has towers in six of these cities which transmit their signal each with varying effective distances.

The following matrix, RM, has three columns. The first and second columns contain the x and y coordinates of the cities' locations, respectively. The third column contains a rational value: the effective distance of that city's transmitter if there is one, or 0 if there isn't a tower.

```
> RM := linalg[matrix](20, 3, [
> 0.534, 4.325, 2,
> -2.196, -3.736, 0,
> 1.234, 0.006, 0,
> 4.123, -1.855, 0,
> 2.134, -2.321, 0,
> -0.123, -4.486, 3/2,
> 3.021, -3.012, 0,
> -4.986, -4.123, 0,
> -3.977, 3.920, 3/2,
> -1.808, 2.231, 0,
> 0.924, -0.756, 2,
> 1.738, -3.111, 0,
> 2.009, 1.845, 0,
```

---

[17] Keep in mind that shapes that are *defined* numerically and then transformed symbolically (such as stcircle above) do not pass through draw, but instead cause an error message.

```
>   3.997,  2.068, 0,
>   4.845, -0.848, 2,
>  -0.777,  4.777, 0,
>  -1.069,  3.111, 0,
>  -4.067, -2.844, 0,
>  -3.238,  1.825, 0,
>  -4.968, -4.111, 1
> ]):
```

Using the *DrawTools*, determine whether all the cities are covered by the current system.

First of all, create point draw structures for the individual cities.

```
> cities := bundle(seq(point([RM[i,1], RM[i,2]], symbol=CROSS), i=1..20)):
```

Now create circle draw structures for the radio towers, with the appropriate cities at their centers, and their radii at the non-zero rational values in the third column of RM.

```
> towers := []:
> for i from 1 to 20 do
>     if RM[i,3] > 0 then
>         towers := appendlist(circle([RM[i, 1], RM[i, 2]], RM[i, 3]), towers);
>     fi;
> od:
```

Bundle the expression sequence create above using bundle.

```
> towers := bundle(op(towers)):
```

To create one multi-shaped draw structure with all the information, use bundle once again.

```
> coverage := bundle(towers, cities):
> draw(coverage);
```

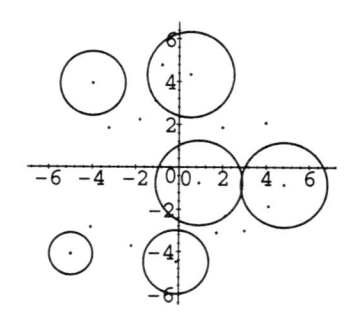

Obviously there are still some cities that are not going to get WPAC's signal. What if the station were to boost each tower's effective distance by 30%?

```
> draw(scale(1.3, [SHAPE=CIRCLE], coverage));
```

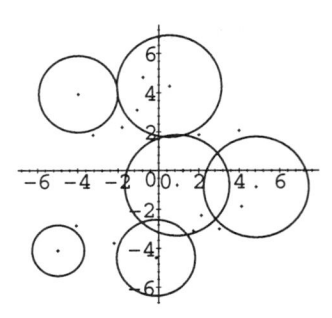

This still isn't enough. Try boosting the signal by 60% over the original values.

```
> draw(scale(1.6, [SHAPE=CIRCLE], coverage));
```

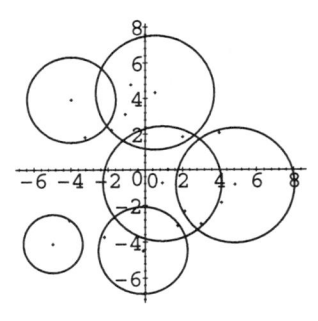

The circles now seem to take in all the cities.

Given that the cost of transmission for each tower is proportional to the effective distance squared:

1. What is the cost of the original coverage if 1 km. of effective radius costs $1,000?
2. What is the cost of the final solution above?
3. Leaving the towers in their current cities, can you adjust the individual radii to cover all the cities, yet decrease the overall cost?
4. Working with at most six towers, can you place them in another combination of cities (with possibly different effective distances), and thereby decrease the overall cost?

Framing Geometrical Shapes

Every PLOT structure has stored within it a call to VIEW() which contains the ranges over which the plot is to be displayed. The geometrical shape commands in *DrawTools* compute these values explicitly for each shape created. The getitem command can be used in conjunction with the option name view from plot to extract this information from any geometrical shape.

```
> c := circle([-4,3], 5):
> getitem(view, c);
```

$$\text{VIEW}(-10.0..2.0, -3.0..9.0)$$

Since this information is readily available, it should be relatively easy to write a command that draws a frame around any geometrical shape. The following code for the frame command calls getitem and also polygon to accomplish just that.

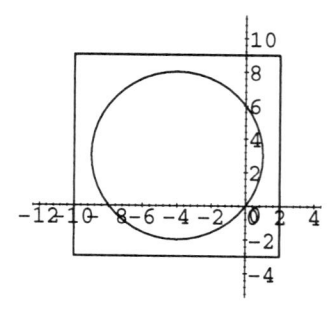

```
> frame := proc(ds)
>    local v;
>
>    v := op(getitem(view, ds));
>    polygon([ [lhs(v[1]), lhs(v[2])],
>              [rhs(v[1]), lhs(v[2])],
>              [rhs(v[1]), rhs(v[2])],
>              [lhs(v[1]), rhs(v[2])],
>              [lhs(v[1]), lhs(v[2])] ]);
> end:

> draw({c, frame(c)});
```

What about drawing frames around multi-shaped draw structures? Since each draw structure has its own view ranges, a loop must be set up to find the appropriate minimum or maximum values.

```
>
> frame := proc(ds)
>    local i, j, v, xmin, xmax, ymin, ymax;
>
>    xmin := infinity; xmax := -infinity; ymin := infinity; ymax := -infinity;
>    for i from 1 to nops(ds[1]) do
```

```
>         v := op(getitem(view, ds[1][i]));
>         xmin := min(xmin, lhs(v[1]));
>         xmax := max(xmax, rhs(v[1]));
>         ymin := min(ymin, lhs(v[2]));
>         ymax := max(ymax, rhs(v[2]));
>     od;
>     polygon([ [xmin, ymin],
>               [xmax, ymin],
>               [xmax, ymax],
>               [xmin, ymax],
>               [xmin, ymin] ]);
> end:
```

Now, create a multi-shaped draw structure to test it on.

```
> newpict := bundle(
>     circle([2,3], 1),
>     circle([-2,3], 1),
>     line([0,3], [0,-6]),
>     ellipse([0,3], [5,4]) ):
> draw(newpict, axes=NONE);
```

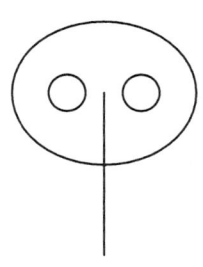

```
> draw({newpict, frame(newpict)}, axes=NONE);
```

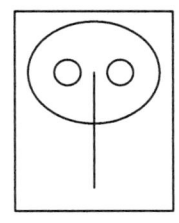

As an exercise, try adding an optional second parameter to frame that allows you to draw a frame only around *selected* shapes in a multi-shaped draw structure. For clues on how to do this, refer to the *Building Your Own Second-Level Functions* section on page 243.

Programming Tips

While there are far more individual commands provided in *DrawTools* than in any other section of the Utilities, there are relatively few unique programming techniques used throughout *DrawTools*. In fact, the same techniques are used many times for drawing different shapes and/or performing various transformations.

Using Built-In Second-Level Functions

As described earlier, the choose command allows you to select draw structures based on either the information in their specifier lists (e.g., SHAPE= CIRCLE) or standard plotting option details (e.g., color=red). In the latter case, the option is entered in choose exactly as it would be in a call to plot, plot3d, or any of the *DrawTools* shape commands (e.g., circle, plane, etc.).

Where in the draw structures is choose checking for a match with this type of optional information? If you look at a very simple draw structure, you can see where this type of information is stored.

```
> line([2, 3], [-5, 4], color=red, style=POINT, axes=BOXED);
```

$[PLOT(CURVES([[2., 3.], [-5., 4.]]),$

$\quad AXESTICKS(DEFAULT, DEFAULT, FONT(TIMES, ROMAN, 24)),$

$\quad AXESLABELS(,, FONT(TIMES, ROMAN, 24)),$

$\quad FONT(TIMES, ROMAN, 24), COLOUR(RGB, 1.00000000, 0, 0),$

$\quad STYLE(POINT), THICKNESS(3), VIEW(-6.4..3.4, 2.8..4.2),$

$\quad AXESSTYLE(BOX))]$

$[[SHAPE = LINE, POINT = [2, 3], POINT = [-5, 4]]]$

The options for color, style, and axes are stored in the PLOT structure, not as equations but as unevaluated calls to COLOUR, STYLE, and AXESSTYLE. Not only are these capitalized function names sometimes different from the lefthand side of the option equations (e.g., axes vs. AXESSTYLE), but their parameters are not always a direct match for the righthand side of the option equations (e.g., red vs. RGB,1.00000000,0,0). You'll also notice that there are some unevaluated function calls in the PLOT structure that relate to options that were not explicitly set in the call to line (i.e., VIEW and AXESTICKS).

Obviously, the choose command must translate these option equations passed as parameters into the corresponding unevaluated function calls. How can this be done? To write your own procedure would be tricky and prone to error. Every time the Maple developers update the product, they might make minute changes to how a PLOT or PLOT3D command is constructed. The most logical course of action is to look for an already existent function in Maple's built-in library. Since plot and plot3d accept options in equation form and create plotting structures in unevaluated function form, there must already be a procedure somewhere that performs the translation.

Where to look first? As you learned earlier, the interface(verboseproc= 2) command allows viewing of built-in Maple code.

```
> interface(verboseproc=2);
```

Looking at the code for plot (which is several pages in length), you can see that there are several "second-level" functions accessed. Most of these functions are named 'plot/something', where the something is descriptive of the specialized functionality. The backquotes are necessary to keep the slash character from behaving as a division sign.

The command for dealing with options is likely to have the word "options" in it, and searching on that finds the following code segment containing a call to 'plot/options2d':

```
features := readlib('plot/options2d')(features);
if dcolor <> 'NONE' then
    if has([curvseq],'COLOUR') then
        curvseq := op(eval(subs('COLOUR' = x -> NULL,[curvseq])))
    fi;
    features := features,dcolor
fi;
if hlabels <> `` or vlabels <> `` then
    features := features,AXESLABELS(hlabels,vlabels)
fi;
if not has([features],'VIEW') then
    features := features,VIEW(hrange,vrange)
fi;
if not has([features],'AXESTICKS') then
    features := features,AXESTICKS(xticks,yticks)
fi;
readlib('plots/setoptions');
defoptions := 'plots/getoptions'([features]);
```

Already some of the unevaluated function calls that make up a PLOT structure are showing up. Take a closer look at the code for 'plot/options2d'.

```
> print('plot/options2d');
```

plot/options2d

What happened to the code? It must exist, since plot calls it. Notice that when 'plot/options2d' is first called in plot, it is enclosed in a readlib command. Even though plot itself does not need to be read in with readlib, the second-level procedures it calls must be. Adding readlib to the above command makes it work:

```
> print(readlib('plot/options2d'));
```

```
proc()
local s,t,dlabels,daxes,dstyle,dtitle,dscaling,dticks,dcolor,f,aa,bb,dview,dth,
    symb,dfont,dafont,dtfont,dlfont,ddashes;
options 'Copyright 1992 by George Labahn';
    f :=
        proc(x)
        local y;
        options 'Copyright 1992 by the University of Waterloo';
            if type(x,name) and (x = 'DEFAULT' or x = 'default') then RETURN(x)
            fi;
            y := traperror(evalf(x,15));
            if type(y,numeric) then RETURN(y) fi;
            ERROR('real constants expected in ranges',x)
        end
        ;
    dlabels := NULL;
    dtitle := NULL;
    daxes := NULL;
    dstyle := NULL;
    dscaling := NULL;
    dticks := NULL;
    dcolor := NULL;
    dview := NULL;
    dth := NULL;
    symb := NULL;
    dfont := NULL;
    ddashes := NULL;
    dafont := NULL;
    dlfont := NULL;
    dtfont := NULL;
    for t in args do
        if not type(t,equation) then ERROR('bad argument',t) fi;
        s := op(1,t);
        t := op(2,t);
        if s = 'title' and type(t,'string') then dtitle := TITLE(t)
        elif s = 'axes' then
            if assigned('plot2d/axesstyles'[t]) then
                t := 'plot2d/axesstyles'[t]
```

```
            fi;
            daxes := AXESSTYLE(t)
        elif s = 'color' or s = 'colour' then
            dcolor := readlib('`plot/color`')(t)
        elif s = 'labels' and type(t,['string','string']) then
            dlabels := AXESLABELS(op(t))
        elif s = 'style' then
            if assigned('`plot2d/plotstyles`'[t]) then
                t := `plot2d/plotstyles`[t]
            fi;
            dstyle := STYLE(t)
```

Because of the length of this procedure, some of the code has been omitted from the previous printout. Looking at this segment, you quickly recognize that this is the desired translation function. The previous code from plot and the following two lines from 'plot/options2d' show that the latter takes a sequence of equations for input.

```
for t in args do
    if not type(t,equation) then ERROR(`bad argument`,t) fi;
```

Let's try calling 'plot/options2d' with the sequence of option equations from our earlier example.

> `plot/options2d`(color=red, style=POINT, axes=BOXED);

$$\text{AXESSTYLE}(\textit{BOX}), \text{STYLE}(\textit{POINT}), \text{COLOUR}(\textit{RGB}, 1.00000000, 0, 0)$$

Now that command can be incorporated into the code for choose,[18] and the user will still be able to enter options in the familiar equation format.

What about three-dimensional plot options? Try 'plot3d/options3d' as an educated guess.

> readlib(`plot3d/options3d`)(style=PATCHNOGRID, axes=NONE);

$$\text{STYLE}(\textit{PATCHNOGRID}), \text{AXESSTYLE}(\textit{NONE})$$

Now 'plot3d/options3d' can also be incorporated in choose.

Building Your Own Second-Level Functions

You saw earlier how to access "second-level" procedures already within the Maple library. If your own code is sufficiently complex, you should also implement your own second-level procedures. There are two main reasons for this:

---

[18] Remembering, of course, to use readlib the first time the function is accessed.

1. Clarity of Code: When the code for a certain command stretches for more than a few pages, it is good coding procedure to break it into smaller, more readable chunks. Each part of the code should perform a specific, well-defined task. For example, if the code for plot or int was all on one level, it would stretch for dozens, if not hundreds of pages. The standard way to notate these "subroutines" is to use second-level function names (e.g., 'plot/options2d', 'int/risch').

2. Reuse of Common Code Segments: Another reason for creating second-level procedures is to allow several commands to share a similar piece of code. In many places in the Utilities, groups of commands are similar to each other, except for a few minor differences. In these cases, second-level commands are used extensively, to optimize the size of the overall code.

A perfect example of the latter principle occurs in *DrawTools*. Most of the commands which transform shapes accept an optional second-last parameter which is either a set or list of option equations. This parameter is used to determine, within a multi-shape draw structures which specific shapes are to be transformed. This functionality is also available in alter and getitem, and is the backbone of the choose command.

The following is a simplified version (with no type-checking or error checking) of the second-level procedure 'choose/pass', which takes three parameters:

1. a list or set of option equations to test against
2. the PLOT or PLOT3D structure from a draw structure
3. the related specifier list from the same draw structure

and returns true if the draw structure passes the given test or false otherwise.

```
> 'choose/pass' := proc(test, ps, sl)
> local result, i;
>
> # Check when a list is passed.
>    if type(test, list) then
>       result := true;
>       for i in test do
>          if member(lhs(i), {SHAPE, CENTER, RADIUS, POINT, ANGLE, HEIGHT,
>             POINT3D, CENTER3D}) then
>             if member(i, sl) then
>                next;
>             else
>                result := false;
>                break;
```

```
>              fi;
>          elif type(ps, PLOT) then
>              if member(readlib(`plot/options2d`)(i), [op(ps)]) then
>                  next;
>              else
>                  result := false;
>                  break;
>              fi;
>          elif type(ps, PLOT3D) then
>              if member(readlib(`plot3d/options3d`)(i), [op(ps)]) then
>                  next;
>              else
>                  result := false;
>                  break;
>              fi;
>          fi;
>      od;
> # Check when a set is passed.
>      else
>          result := false;
>          for i in test do
>              if member(lhs(i), {SHAPE, CENTER, RADIUS, POINT, ANGLE, HEIGHT,
>              POINT3D, CENTER3D}) then
>                  if member(i, sl) then
>                      result := true;
>                      break;
>                  else
>                      next;
>                  fi;
>              elif type(ps, PLOT) then
>                  if member(readlib(`plot/options2d`)(i), [op(ps)]) then
>                      result := true;
>                      break;
>                  else
>                      next;
>                  fi;
>              elif type(ps, PLOT3D) then
>                  if member(readlib(`plot3d/options3d`)(i), [op(ps)]) then
>                      result := true;
>                      break;
>                  else
>                      next;
>                  fi;
>              fi;
>          od;
>      fi;
```

```
>     result;
> end:
```

The 'choose/pass' procedure can then be called from within all the relevant commands to decide whether an individual draw structure is to be transformed, altered, selected, etc. Imagine having a block of code of this size (and greater when error and type checking are included) repeated in command after command. By having only one occurrence of 'choose/pass', much disk space is saved, and any updates need only be made once, lessening the chance for typographical error.

A simplified version of the code for choose can now call our 'choose/pass':

```
> choose := proc(test, ds)
> local i, newps, newsl;
>
> newps := [];
> newsl := [];
> for i from 1 to nops(ds[1]) do
>     if readlib('choose/pass')(test, ds[1][i], ds[2][i]) then
>         newps := [op(newps), ds[1][i]];
>         newsl := [op(newsl), ds[2][i]];
>     fi;
> od;
> array(1..2, [newps, newsl]);
> end:
```

CHAPTER 9

StringTools

The most common use of strings in Maple is as variable names. Maple was never designed to be a high-level string manipulation product, so there are few built-in functions that focus on this area. In fact, the following Utility commands probably would not have been included if it were not for one major change in the internal handling of strings in Maple V Release 3.

Before Release 3, the maximum length of a string was 499 characters; anything longer than that caused an error message. For most users, this was a limit they never pushed, or even approached. But the fact that the limit was there made any truly complicated string manipulation impossible. In Release 3, the 499 character limit has been removed and now strings can be of *any* length. While there are much better computing languages out there for dealing with large strings (i.e., chunks of textual information), at least now, with the aid of the Utilities, some of these operations can be performed without leaving Maple.

What Maple Has

The Backquote

Typically, a string is created by placing backward quotes, or *backquotes*, around a collection of characters. These characters can be of any type, including letters (both uppercase and lowercase), numbers, blanks, underscore characters (_), and special symbols (e.g., *, !, $).

```
> `This+is a valid_string`;
```
$$This + is\ a\ valid\_string$$

> whattype(`");

string

Without the backquotes, the blanks and special characters in this string are treated as Maple operators, producing an error message.

> This+is a valid_string;

syntax error:
This+is a valid_string;

Despite this, if a string does not contain any blanks or special characters, and does not start with a number, the backquotes are not strictly necessary.

> Hello;

Hello

> top2bottom;

top2bottom

The strings you will be dealing with in this chapter are of the type found in text, so backquotes are used throughout.

To represent a single backquote *within* a string, use two backquotes one after the other.

> `Put a backquote `` here!`;

Put a backquote ` here!

> `This is a ``special`` string`;

This is a 'special' string

The Concatenation Operator

The period (.) operator has several uses in Maple. It can represent a decimal point, form part of a range operator, or be used to concatenate two values to make a string. The trick to understanding whether Maple views a single period as a decimal or as a concatenation operator is the following simple rule:

> If the object on the lefthand side of a period is a *name*, then Maple performs a concatenation.

For example, here are some valid and invalid uses of the period operator.

> `I love `.`New York`;

$$I\ love\ New\ York$$

> seq(var.i, i=1..6);

$$var1, var2, var3, var4, var5, var6$$

> 2.` good 2 be true`;

syntax error:
2.` good 2 be true`;

There is also a built-in command, cat, that does the same thing as the period operator, except in the form of a command.

> cat(`I love `, `New York `, `in the springtime`);

$$I\ love\ New\ York\ in\ the\ springtime$$

Converting Expressions to Strings

It is possible to convert any Maple expression into a string (and back again). Use the command convert with the option string.

> myexpr := a + sin(b) + 3*cos(c)^2;

$$myexpr := a + \sin(b) + 3\cos(c)^2$$

> convert(myexpr, string);

$$(a) + (sin(b)) + ((3) * ((cos(c))^\wedge(2)))$$

> whattype(");

$$string$$

The extra parentheses are an unfortunate side-effect of the conversion; but when you use the parse command to convert the string back to an expression, these parentheses are stripped away.

> parse("");

$$a + \sin(b) + 3\cos(c)^2$$

> whattype(");

$$+$$

These two commands aren't explored further in this chapter. The real importance of convert(,string) and parse shows up in the *PatternTools* chapter.

Investigating Strings

Most of Maple's built-in commands for strings deal with investigating the contents of a string. length determines the number of characters (of *all* types) contained in a string.

> length('This is a string of medium length.');

$$34$$

The commands searchtext and SearchText search for the first occurrence of a substring in a larger string. If the substring is found, the position of its first character is returned. Otherwise, a value of 0 is returned. The only difference between the two commands is that SearchText is *case-sensitive*, while searchtext is not.

> mystring := 'Most of Maple is programmed in maple.';

mystring := Most of Maple is programmed in maple.

> searchtext('maple', mystring);

$$9$$

> SearchText('maple', mystring);

$$32$$

The only other command for dealing with strings is substring which, when given a string and a valid integer range, extracts a substring.

> substring(mystring, 16..26);

s program

> substring(mystring, 18..27);

programmed

Utility Commands

Many of the commands in *StringTools* directly mirror those in *ListTools*. For example, the design of commands in the following section, *Adding and Removing Characters*, is almost identical to that in *Adding and Removing Elements* on page 54. The reason is that while lists are ordered sequences of elements, strings can be thought of as ordered sequences of *characters*. In the section *Programming Tips*, it is shown that converting strings to lists of characters is integral to how most of the commands in *StringTools* are programmed.

While there are some operations on lists that do not have logical counterparts with strings, there are also a few commands in *StringTools* that are not reflected in *ListTools*. But first, examine the commands that the two areas have in common. You may want to refer back to the related command descriptions in the *ListTools* chapter from time to time.

Adding and Removing Characters

deletestring(str, a..b)	delete substring from a string
extractstring(str, a..b)	extract substring into a new string
insertstring(str_1, str_2, n)	insert new string into an existing string
replacestring(str_1, str_2, a..b)	replace substring of an existing string
prependstring(str_1, str_2)	add a new string to the beginning of another string
appendstring(str_1, str_2)	add an new string to the end of another string

All of the above commands take an existing string and either update it with a new string or remove a selected substring from it. The first two commands, deletestring and extractstring, take an existing string as their first parameter and a range, a..b, as their second parameter. The difference in their functionality is that deletestring removes the characters of str at positions a through b to produce the resulting string, while the resulting string from extractstring contains only those b - a + 1 characters.

```
> with(utility):
> mystr := 'Maple is very, very easy to learn';
```
$$mystr := \textit{Maple is very, very easy to learn}$$

```
> deletestring(mystr, 10..15);
```
$$\textit{Maple is very easy to learn}$$

```
> extractstring(mystr, 16..length(mystr));
```
$$\textit{very easy to learn}$$

Neither of these commands has any effect on mystr.

```
> mystr;
```
$$\textit{Maple is very, very easy to learn}$$

It is *not* good design to have a command alter its input parameters. If you want mystr to be affected by the deletion, simply assign the result of the command to mystr.

By supplying a single positive integer value as the second parameter, you can work on only one character.

> `deletestring(mystr, 14);`

Maple is very very easy to learn

By supplying a list of integer values and ranges as the second parameter, you can work on several substrings.

> `extractstring(mystr, [15..20, 2..4, 12]);`

very aplr

Notice that the integer values and ranges do not have to be in ascending numeric order. Also, deletestring ignores any repeated values, while in the same situation extractstring creates multiple copies.

The next two commands, insertstring and replacestring, take strings as their first two parameters. In both commands, the characters in str$_1$ are placed into str$_2$; the only difference is the method of insertion.

In insertstring, the characters of str$_1$ are inserted into str$_2$ starting after the nth character of str$_2$. (n is provided as the third parameter.)

> `newstr := 'not ';`

newstr := not

> `insertstring(newstr, mystr, 9);`

Maple is not very, very easy to learn

In replacestring, the characters of str$_1$ replace the characters of str$_2$ at positions a through b inclusive. (The range a..b is provided as the third parameter.)

> `replacestring(newstr, mystr, 9..19);`

Maple isnot easy to learn

Notice that in replacestring, the length of str$_1$ does not have to equal the length of the substring being removed from str$_2$.

In both commands, if str$_1$ is not a string, it is first converted to a string using convert(, string).

The last two commands, prependstring and appendstring, are really special versions of insertstring which add characters either to the beginning or the end of an existing string.

> `prependstring('Can you say that ', mystr);`

Can you say that Maple is very, very easy to learn

> appendstring('?', ");

Can you say that Maple is very, very easy to learn?

Again, if the first parameter to either command is not a string, a conversion is performed.

> newstr := 'Hello there';

newstr := *Hello there*

> appendstring(3*x^3, newstr);

Hello there$(3) * ((x)^\wedge(3))$

Dealing with Character Case

uppercase(str)	convert a string to uppercase
lowercase(str)	convert a string to lowercase
switchcase(str)	switch the case of each character

The three commands in this section deal with changing characters within strings from lowercase (a through z) to uppercase (A through Z) and vice versa. uppercase converts all appropriate characters in a string to uppercase representation. Those characters already in uppercase and those that are not standard letters are left unchanged.

> mystr := 'Shout it out loud.';

mystr := *Shout it out loud.*

> uppercase(mystr);

SHOUT IT OUT LOUD.

lowercase, as you might have guessed, does the opposite.

> lowercase(");

shout it out loud.

Note, though, that the result of performing the two operations on a single string is not necessarily the string with which you started.

The third command, switchcase, changes each letter in lowercase representation to uppercase and vice versa. Applying it twice to any string *does* get you back where you started.

> newstr := 'ThIS iS a stRAnGe STRinG';

newstr := *ThIS iS a stRAnGe STRinG*

> switchcase(newstr);

> *tHis Is A STraNgE strINg*

> switchcase(");

> *ThIS iS a stRAnGe STRinG*

All three of these commands can take a range (or a list of ranges) as a second parameter. Only those characters whose positions fall within the range are altered.

> uppercase(newstr, [1..5, 14..17]);

> *THIS iS a stRANGE STRinG*

Other Commands

reversestring(str)	reverse the order of characters in a string
subsstring(str_{old}=str_{new}, str)	substitute new substring for old substring
selectstring(str, option)	select certain *classes* of characters from a string
comparestrings(str_1, str_2)	compare characters in corresponding positions

The first command in this section, reversestring, is a copy of its list counterpart, reverselist. reversestring, as its name suggests, reverses the ordering of the characters in a string.

> newstr := '?sdrawkcab siht daer uoy naC';

> *newstr := ?sdrawkcab siht daer uoy naC*

> reversestring(newstr);

> *Can you read this backwards?*

A range can be provided as an optional second parameter, allowing you to specify a subrange of the characters to reverse.

> reversestring(newstr, 12..20);

> *?sdrawkcab read this uoy naC*

The command subsstring[1] is set up very much like the built-in subs command; the first parameter is an equation relating the old substring to the new substring which replaces it, and the second parameter is the larger string in which it all takes place. One difference between subsstring and

---

[1] Note the double s in the name of this command. If you don't double the s, you get substring, a totally different, built-in Maple command.

subs is that substring only replaces the *first* occurrence of the old substring as its default behaviour.

> `mystr := 'The brown cat chased the brown rat.';`

mystr := The brown cat chased the brown rat.

> `subsstring('brown'='black', mystr);`

The black cat chased the brown rat.

In order to have subsstring replace more than one occurrence of the old substring, a third (positive integer) parameter must be provided.

> `subsstring('brown'='black', mystr, 2);`

The black cat chased the black rat.

If you want *all* appropriate substrings changed, then provide infinity as the third parameter.

One more detail about the operation of subsstring needs to be discussed. When a substitution is done, the new characters are never themselves checked for occurrences of the old substring. To illustrate, if you were to substitute the string brownish for every brown in mystr, and the above rule were *not* in effect, the end result would be a string of infinite length looking like

The brownishishishishishishishish...

because the brown in brownish would be replaced by brownish, which in turn would have its brown replaced by brown, etc., etc. Of course, this would quickly cause Maple to crash. Instead, with the rule intact, you get:

> `subsstring('brown'='brownish', mystr, infinity);`

The brownish cat chased the brownish rat.

The next command, selectstring, allows you to strip out characters from a string that match certain criteria. Each character is individually checked against the second optional argument, then either extracted if it passes or left behind if it fails.

The most commonly used option will be 'alpha', which extracts alphabetic characters (a—z and A—Z) and blanks. Use this option on charstr, a string with many different types of characters.

> `charstr := 'The special value, Pi, has a value of approximately 3.141!';`

charstr := The special value, Pi, has a value of approximately 3.141!

> `selectstring(charstr, 'alpha');`

The special value Pi has a value of approximately

The 'numeric' option chooses only numbers, blanks, decimal points (.), and + and -.[2]

> selectstring(charstr, 'numeric');

3.141

'alphanum' accepts characters from either of the two above sets.

> selectstring(charstr, 'alphanum');

The special value Pi has a value of approximately 3.141

'uppercase' and 'lowercase' extract alphabetic characters of the indicated case. (Blanks are accepted by both these options.)

> selectstring(charstr, 'uppercase');

T P

> selectstring(charstr, 'lowercase');

he special value i has a value of approximately

The 'special' option checks for characters that do not get selected by the 'alphanum' option. 'special' also extracts blanks, +, and -.

> selectstring(charstr, 'special');

, ,   !

A special feature of the selectstring command is that it allows you to supply optional filters of your own making. That is, by creating a Maple procedure 'selectstring/name' that takes a single character as input and returns true or false, you can then use name as the second parameter to selectstring.

This type of customization of existing commands is used in several places in the standard Maple library. To see how this facility is coded in selectstring, see the *Extending an Existing Command* section on page 266.

The final feature of selectstring is that a *set* of optional values can be passed instead of just a single value. By doing so, you ask selectstring to extract the characters that pass *any one* of the given filters.

> selectstring(charstr, {uppercase, numeric});

T P   3.141

The last command in this section, comparestrings, is similar to its list counterpart, comparelist. In its most basic usage, two strings are passed

---

[2]Since the contents and "meaning" of characters internal to strings can never be properly determined by selectstring, *all* occurrences of ., +, and - are extracted.

and the result is a list of position values (positive integer values and/or ranges) in which the characters in the strings differ.

> str1 := 'This is a very special, important string';

$$str1 := \textit{This is a very special, important string}$$

> str2 := 'This is a very specific type of a string';

$$str2 := \textit{This is a very specific type of a string}$$

> diffstr := comparestrings(str1, str2);

$$diffstr := [\,21..23, 25..26, 28..33\,]$$

As with comparelists, the results can be passed to commands to extract or delete the "offending" characters.

> deletestring(str1, diffstr);

$$\textit{This is a very speci p string}$$

> extractstring(str2, diffstr);

$$\textit{fictye of a}$$

An option available in comparestrings is the addition of a positive integer range as the third parameter. In this case, only those elements in that range are compared and all the resulting values fall completely within that range.

> comparestrings(str1, str2, 24..30);

$$[\,25..26, 28..30\,]$$

Examples

Comparing Digits of π

The following example was created from an article "Pi, Euler Numbers, and Asymptotic Expansions" by J. M. Borwein, P. B. Borwien, and K. Dilcher, which appeared in the *AMA Monthly*, volume 96, (1989).

In computing a decimal approximation of π, Gregory's series,

$$4 \sum_{n=1}^{N} \frac{(-1)^{n+1}}{2n-1},$$

where N is sufficiently large, can be used.

With N set to 50,000 and Digits set to 50, the related approximation for $\frac{\pi}{2}$ can be found with the Maple commands:[3]

```
> Digits := 50:
> GPiby2 := 0:
> for i from 1 to 50000 do
>     GPiby2 := GPiby2 + (-1.)^(i+1)/(2.*i-1);
> od:
> GPiby2 := convert(GPiby2*2, string);
```

$GPiby2 := 1.57078632679489761923132119163975205209 85833146897$

To see how good an approximation this really is, use the evalf command on Pi/2 to 50 digits accuracy.

```
> ePiby2 := convert(evalf(Pi/2), string);
```

$ePiby2 := 1.5707963267948966192313216916397514420985846996876$

The interesting feature of the Gregory's series approximation is that the individual digits move in and out of being correct as you progress along it. Using the Utility command comparestrings, you can find the positions of those digits which disagree.

```
> disagree := comparestrings(GPiby2, ePiby2);
```

$disagree := [\,7, 17, 27, 35..37, 44..47, 50..51\,]$

The last range 50..51 is a result of inaccuracy introduced by not having enough terms in the series, so ignore it for the present.

```
> disagree := comparestrings(GPiby2, ePiby2, 1..48);
```

$disagree := [\,7, 17, 27, 35..37, 44..47\,]$

Note that each element of disagree ends in a 7. This is not a coincidence—the approximation diverges every ten digits.

Now, take a look at the actual digits in the differing character positions indicated by disagree and compare the results between the two strings. Try extracting the digits with the Utility command extractstring.

```
> Gstrs :=  extractstring(GPiby2, disagree);
```

$Gstrs := 8712053314$

```
> estrs :=  extractstring(ePiby2, disagree);
```

$estrs := 9661444699$

---

[3]Computing this sum takes a *considerable* amount of computing time, so don't even try it unless you have a powerful computer.

extractstring has concatenated the extracted digits from the individual substrings into one larger string, which is not what was wanted. In order to compare the individual digits (and ranges of digits), the results need to be lists of five strings. Use the built-in seq command to create these lists.

```
> Gstrs := [seq(extractstring(GPiby2, disagree[i]), i=1..5)];
```
$$Gstrs := [8, 7, 1, 205, 3314]$$

```
> estrs := [seq(extractstring(ePiby2, disagree[i]), i=1..5)];
```
$$estrs := [9, 6, 6, 144, 4699]$$

What is so special about the integer values represented by these lists of strings? If you convert the strings to integers (through the parse command) and then subtract the corresponding elements from each other, you get:

```
> Gints := map(parse, Gstrs): eints := map(parse, estrs):
```
$$Gints := [8, 7, 1, 205, 3314]$$
$$eints := [9, 6, 6, 144, 4699]$$

```
> diffseq := seq(eints[i] - Gints[i], i=1..5);
```
$$diffseq := 1, -1, 5, -61, 1385$$

which is exactly the first five non-zero *Euler numbers*.

```
> seq(euler(i), i=0..15);
```
$$1, 0, -1, 0, 5, 0, -61, 0, 1385, 0, -50521, 0, 2702765, 0, -199360981, 0$$

It can then be shown that the Euler sequence can be used as an *error correction* for the Gregory series approximation of π.

Another interesting phenomenon associated with this series occurs when you take the first 500,000 terms of the series evaluated to 100 digits accuracy. Not only do the Euler numbers appear again (this time the first *seven* non-zero elements), but they occur every *twelve* digits in the approximation, starting with the sixth digit. Therefore, the formula for correcting the Gregory series approximation is also dependent on the accuracy of the original computations.

For more information about this and related series approximations, read the article quoted at the top of this example.

Stripping Digits from a Large Integer

The following problem was taken from the 1990 Bulgarian Mathematics Olympiad, and was suggested to me by Ian McGee and Ross Honsberger.

> The first 1990 positive integers are written in order in a row to form a long string of digits, S_0:
>
> $$S_0 = 12345678910112131415\ldots 198819891990$$
>
> Then the digits in all the even-numbered places (character positions) are deleted and the gaps closed up to give the string.
>
> $$S_1 = 1357901234\ldots 9990$$
>
> Next the digits in the odd-numbered places in S_1 are deleted and the gaps closed to give
>
> $$S_2 = 37024\ldots$$
>
> This thinning by alternately deleting the digits in the even- and odd-numbered places is continued until there is only one digit left. What is that last digit?

Ross Honsberger was able to come up with an answer of 9 for this problem by:

- Determining that there were 6853 digits in the initial large string.
- Using the fact that each thinning removed approximately $\frac{1}{2}$ the digits, determining that the last digit was in the 2731st position in the initial large string.
- Determining, through a sort of counting, that the digit in position 2731 is a 9.

Now create a Maple command called evenodd, which takes the value n as a parameter, to test his answer when $n = 1990$.

```
> evenodd := proc(n)
>    local i, j, largeint;
>
>    largeint := cat(seq(convert(j, string), j=1..n));
>    for i while length(largeint) > 1 do
>       largeint := extractstring(largeint,
>                   [seq(2*j-modp(i,2), j=1..ceil(length(largeint)/2))]);
>    od;
>    RETURN(parse(largeint));
> end:
```

Your version of evenodd may differ from the above. Some explanation of our code follows:

Examples • 261

- largeint := cat(seq(convert(j, string), j=1..n)) converts each of the n integers values 1 through n into their corresponding string representations and then concatenates them together.

- The loop for i while length(largeint) > 1 do starts i off at 1 and increments its value by 1 each time through the loop. The looping is stopped when the resulting string no longer contains two or more digits.

- The rather complicated call to extractstring keeps certain digits in largeint (which is really a string). The first time through the loop (i.e., when i = 1), seq(2*j-modp(i,2), ...) evaluates to seq(2*j-1, ...), therefore extracting (keeping) all the *odd* digits. The second time through the loop, the *even* digits are kept, and so on.

  ceil(length(largeint)/2) makes sure that the appropriate number of digits are removed, depending on the current length of largeint.

- RETURN(parse(largeint)) first converts the resulting string back into an integer value, then returns that integer.

Verify the suggested result for $n = 1990$.

> `evenodd(1990);`

$$9$$

This command took about a minute and a half to complete on a relatively fast 486 computer. For larger values of n, the computing time rises exponentially. Is there any way to use the "brute-force" routine, evenodd, to help us derive a general formula for n?

To start, use evenodd to compute the results for $n = 1..100$.

> `map(evenodd, [$1..100]);`

[1, 1, 3, 3, 3, 3, 3, 3, 3, 0, 0, 0, 0, 0, 0, 0, 0, 0, 0, 0, 0, 0, 0, 0, 0, 6, 6, 6, 6, 6, 6, 6, 6, 6, 6, 6, 6, 6, 6, 6, 6, 6, 6, 6, 6, 6, 6, 6, 6, 6, 6, 6, 6, 6, 6, 6, 6, 6, 6, 6, 6, 6, 6, 6, 6, 6, 6, 6, 6, 6, 6, 6, 6, 6, 6, 6, 6, 6, 6, 6, 6, 6, 6, 6, 6, 6, 6, 6, 6, 6, 0, 0, 0, 0, 0, 0, 0, 0, 0, 0, 0]

We were able to determine, after further study and experimentation, that the sequences of identical values seen above relate to a general formula (or algorithm) for computing evenodd(n) which doesn't require any actual thinning of strings. The key has to to with the values of n where the single digit changes from one value to another (e.g., at $n = 10$, the value changes from 3 to 0).

As an exercise, can you determine the following parts of that algorithm:

1. An algorithm that determines the values of *n* where these switches from one digit to another occur?[4]
2. An algorithm that takes the information from 1) and determines which digit value is switched *to* at each of the computed values of *n*?
3. A larger algorithm that takes *any* value of *n* and produces the resulting digit using 1) and 2)?[5]

Programming Tips

There is a close relationship between the commands in *StringTools* and *ListTools*. Not only is the design of many of the commands similar, but the code for these string commands often calls procedures in *ListTools*.

Converting Strings to Lists

The main reason for *StringTools*' reliance on list commands is that in order to deal effectively with multi-character strings, they must first be converted to lists. What makes this conversion necessary is that strings are stored as complete entities, not as a collection of individual characters, and that all built-in manipulations of characters *within* strings take place within the Maple *kernel* (of compiled C code) and so are not available to the average user.

Meanwhile, within the Utilities, once the appropriate computation is performed, the converted list is transformed back into a single string again. These transformations are transparent to the user, unless the source code is investigated.

How exactly is a string converted into a list? Using the built-in command **substring**, you can pick off the individual characters of any string. Let's try to write a function stringtolist:

```
> stringtolist := proc(s)
>    local i;
>    RETURN([seq(substring(s,i..i),i=1..length(s))]);
> end;

stringtolist :=

    proc(s) local i; RETURN([seq(substring(s,i .. i),i = 1 .. length(s))]) end
```

---

[4]Hint: Use the values you know from the computation of $n = 1..100$. The trick is to concentrate on the lengths (i.e., number of digits) of the initial large strings at the related values of *n*.

[5]And a new version of evenodd written in Maple that implements this algorithm?

Let's try this on a simple string.

```
> mystr := 'This is a string';
```
$$mystr := This\ is\ a\ string$$
```
> stringtolist(mystr);
```
$$[\,T, h, i, s,\ , i, s,\ , a,\ , s, t, r, i, n, g\,]$$

This seems to work, until you actually assign to some of the individual characters in the string values other than themselves.

```
> h := 22; s := z;
```
$$h := 22$$
$$s := z$$
```
> stringtolist(mystr);
```
$$[\,T, h, i, s,\ , i, s,\ , a,\ , s, t, r, i, n, g\,]$$

Things still appear to be fine, but they're really not—as you see if you evaluate this list by, for example, passing it through reverselist.

```
> reverselist(");
```
$$[\,g, n, 16, r, t, z,\ , a,\ , z, 16,\ , z, 16, 22, T\,]$$

To solve this problem, we'll prepend the characters _s to each character from the string, making each element of the resulting list a three-character string. Names starting with _ characters are reserved for variables used within procedures[6] and are very unlikely to be assigned to any other value during a session.

```
> stringtolist:=proc(s)
>    local i;
>    RETURN([seq(cat('_s',substring(s,i..i)),i=1..length(s))]);
> end:
> stringtolist(mystr);
```
$$[\,\_sT, \_sh, \_si, \_ss, \_s\ , \_si, \_ss, \_s\ , \_sa, \_s\ , \_ss, \_st, \_sr, \_si, \_sn, \_sg\,]$$
```
> rlist := reverselist(");
```
$$rlist := [\,\_sg, \_sn, \_si, \_sr, \_st, \_ss, \_s\ , \_sa, \_s\ , \_ss, \_si, \_s\ , \_ss, \_si, \_sh, \_sT\,]$$

Now all that's needed is the inverse command, listtostring, to convert the reversed list back to a string. You know that the desired character is going to be the *third* character in each element of the given list.

---

[6]This is not an enforced rule, but a general rule mentioned in all programming manuals on Maple.

```
> listtostring:=proc(l)
>     local i;
>     RETURN(cat(seq(substring(l[i],3..3),i=1..nops(l))));
> end:
> listtostring(rlist);
```

gnirts a si sihT

These types of conversions are found in most of the commands in StringTools.

Relating Values with Tables

One of the great things about Maple's table structure is that the indices for a table can be *any* value, not just an integer (as in lists and arrays). Using the index/entry relationship allows you to efficiently and effectively connect pairs of values. The Utility commands uppercase, lowercase, and switchcase need such tables to relate uppercase and lowercase letters. Program a rudimentary version of switchcase, remembering that strings are going to be converted to lists with the characters _s prepended to each element.

```
> switchcase := proc(str)
>     local i, switch, strlist, newlist;
>
>     switch := table([_sa=_sA, _sb=_sB, _sc=_sC, _sd=_sD, _se=_sE,
>     _sf=_sF, _sg=_sG, _sh=_sH, _si=_sI, _sJ=_sj, _sk=_sK, _sl=_sL,
>     _sm=_sM, _sn=_sN, _so=_sO, _sp=_sP, _sq=_sQ, _sr=_sR, _ss=_sS,
>     _st=_sT, _su=_sU, _sv=_sV, _sw=_sW, _sx=_sX, _sy=_sY, _sz=_sZ,
>     _sA=_sa, _sB=_sb, _sC=_sc, _sD=_sd, _sE=_se,
>     _sF=_sf, _sG=_sg, _sH=_sh, _sI=_si, _sJ=_sj, _sK=_sk, _sL=_sl,
>     _sM=_sm, _sN=_sn, _sO=_so, _sP=_sp, _sQ=_sq, _sR=_sr, _sS=_ss,
>     _sT=_st, _sU=_su, _sV=_sv, _sW=_sw, _sX=_sx, _sY=_sy, _sZ=_sz]);
>
>     strlist := stringtolist(str);
>     newlist := [seq(switch[strlist[i]], i=1..nops(strlist))];
>     RETURN(listtostring(newlist));
> end:
```

Try this out with mystr.

```
> switchcase(mystr);

Error, (in listtostring)
wrong number (or type) of parameters in function substring
```

What has happened here? Obviously, something has gone wrong in listtostring; but it is difficult to determine from the error message exactly what. Use a print statement in the code to determine what is getting passed as input to listtostring.

```
> switchcase := proc(str)
>    local i, switch, strlist, newlist;
>
>    switch := table([_sa=_sA, _sb=_sB, _sc=_sC, _sd=_sD, _se=_sE,
>    _sf=_sF, _sg=_sG, _sh=_sH, _si=_sI, _sJ=_sj, _sk=_sK, _sl=_sL,
>    _sm=_sM, _sn=_sN, _so=_sO, _sp=_sP, _sq=_sQ, _sr=_sR, _ss=_sS,
>    _st=_sT, _su=_sU, _sv=_sV, _sw=_sW, _sx=_sX, _sy=_sY, _sz=_sZ,
>    _sA=_sa, _sB=_sb, _sC=_sc, _sD=_sd, _sE=_se,
>    _sF=_sf, _sG=_sg, _sH=_sh, _sI=_si, _sJ=_sj, _sK=_sk, _sL=_sl,
>    _sM=_sm, _sN=_sn, _sO=_so, _sP=_sp, _sQ=_sq, _sR=_sr, _sS=_ss,
>    _sT=_st, _sU=_su, _sV=_sv, _sW=_sw, _sX=_sx, _sY=_sy, _sZ=_sz]);
>
>    strlist := stringtolist(str);
>    newlist := [seq(switch[strlist[i]], i=1..nops(strlist))];
>    print(newlist);
>    RETURN(listtostring(newlist));
> end:

> switchcase(mystr);
```

$$\left[\_st, \_sH, \_sI, \_sS, switch\_s, \_sI, \_sS, switch\_s, \_sA, switch\_s, \_sS, \_sT, \_sR, \_sI, \_sN, \_sG\right]$$

```
Error, (in listtostring)
wrong number (or type) of parameters in function substring
```

You haven't dealt correctly with characters that are not letters (in this case, blank characters). Consequently, they are left as unassigned elements of the table switch. If you check each element of strlist in order to decide whether to consult the switch table, then you cannot use the seq command, and so lose out on efficiency. There are two *efficient* methods of ensuring that non-alphabetic characters are left unchanged:

1. Extend the switch table to include *all* possible characters by adding "neutral" table entries for non-alphabetic characters. For example, the entry for the character 3 would be _s3=_s3. This method is prone to errors because different computer systems may have different character sets.

2. Find another command that can be applied to an "errant" list newlist, that converts each invalid entry into the desired form while leaving valid entries unchanged. A simple command that leaps to mind is op. What are the operands of an unassigned table entry?

```
> op(switch[_s3]);
```

$$\_s3$$

```
> op(_sA);
```

$$\_sA$$

Perfect! Using map, apply op to each element of newlist.

```
> switchcase := proc(str)
>    local i, switch, strlist, newlist;
>
>    switch := table([_sa=_sA, _sb=_sB, _sc=_sC, _sd=_sD, _se=_sE,
>    _sf=_sF, _sg=_sG, _sh=_sH, _si=_sI, _sJ=_sj, _sk=_sK, _sl=_sL,
>    _sm=_sM, _sn=_sN, _so=_sO, _sp=_sP, _sq=_sQ, _sr=_sR, _ss=_sS,
>    _st=_sT, _su=_sU, _sv=_sV, _sw=_sW, _sx=_sX, _sy=_sY, _sz=_sZ,
>    _sA=_sa, _sB=_sb, _sC=_sc, _sD=_sd, _sE=_se,
>    _sF=_sf, _sG=_sg, _sH=_sh, _sI=_si, _sJ=_sj, _sK=_sk, _sL=_sl,
>    _sM=_sm, _sN=_sn, _sO=_so, _sP=_sp, _sQ=_sq, _sR=_sr, _sS=_ss,
>    _sT=_st, _sU=_su, _sV=_sv, _sW=_sw, _sX=_sx, _sY=_sy, _sZ=_sz]);
>
>    strlist := stringtolist(str);
>    newlist := map(op, [seq(switch[strlist[i]], i=1..nops(strlist))]);
>    RETURN(listtostring(newlist));
> end:

> switchcase(mystr);
```

tHIS IS A STRING

A similar technique, with smaller tables, is used in the commands uppercase and lowercase.

Extending an Existing Command

In the *Programming Tips* section of the *DrawTools* chapter on page 239, you learned the importance of *second-level functions* in Maple, and how to create them for your own commands. Another interesting use of second-level functions is in creating new optional values for existing commands.

For example, the built-in type command has dozens of preset optional second parameters, but you can add your own typenames to this set by creating your own specially named second-level procedures.[7] Not all built-in Maple commands have this extendability, but it is a useful tool in those that do. Typically, the Maple help page for a command will tell you if this feature is available.

---

[7]The Utility command 'type/ds', which checks if an expression is a *d*raw *s*tructure, is an example of this.

This extendability mechanism works in the following way. When the first-level procedure (say myproc) is called with an optional parameter (say newopt), myproc attempts to call the second-level procedure 'myproc/newopt'. If that procedure cannot be found (through any of the normal search paths), then an error message is returned. If 'myproc/newopt' is found, then it is passed some subset of the original parameters to myproc, a value is returned to the first-level procedure, and computation continues (perhaps briefly) at that level.

Now look at how this mechanism is programmed in the Utility command selectstring. The following is simplified code for the first-level procedure.

```
> selectstring := proc(str:string, opt)
>    local i, l1, l2, cnt, fnc;
>
>    l1 := stringtolist(str);
>    fnc := cat('selectstring/', opt);
>
>    l2 := select(fnc, l1);
>    RETURN(listtostring(l2));
> end:
```

First, the string is converted to the appropriate list.[8] The second-level function name, fnc, is then created using cat. select is called to pare down that list to only those characters which pass the *boolean-valued* procedure fnc.[9] Finally, the resulting list is converted back to a string and returned.

The following is the complete code for one of the provided options to selectstring. The 'alpha' option determines whether characters belong to a – z or A – Z, or are blanks. The 'selectstring/alpha' procedure takes one "listized" (i.e., prepended with '_s') character as input and returns either true or false.

```
> 'selectstring/alpha' := proc(ch:string)
>    local goodch;
>
>    goodch := {_sa, _sb, _sc, _sd, _se, _sf, _sg, _sh, _si, _sj, _sk,
>               _sl, _sm, _sn, _so, _sp, _sq, _sr, _ss, _st, _su, _sv,
>               _sw, _sx, _sy, _sz, _sA, _sB, _sC, _sD, _sE, _sF, _sG,
>               _sH, _sI, _sJ, _sK, _sL, _sM, _sN, _sO, _sP, _sQ, _sR,
>               _sS, _sT, _sU, _sV, _sW, _sX, _sY, _sZ, '_s '};
>
>    if member(ch, goodch) then
```

---

[8] As detailed in the previous two sections.
[9] These second-level procedures do not always have to be boolean-valued, but it happens that they are in this case.

```
>         RETURN(true)
>      fi;
>      RETURN(false);
> end:
```

There are several advantages of having the second-level procedures work on only one character at a time. First, it means that the amount of work required for you or other users to extend the command's functionality is kept at a minimum. Also, it is then easier to implement in the first-level procedure, selectstring, such features as being able to pass a *set* of optional values as the second parameter,[10] without affecting how the second-level procedures are written.

How easy is it to add your own second-level procedures to selectstring? Using the code for 'selectstring/alpha' as a guide, write a second-level procedure for the new option 'vowels', which retains only the characters a, e, i, o, u, A, E, I, O, and U.

One detail that was left out of the earlier, simplified version of the code for selectstring was the check to see whether the specified second-level procedure actually exists. The following revision to the code includes a couple of important tools that are briefly described thereafter.

```
> selectstring := proc(str:string, opt)
>    local i, l1, l2, cnt, fnc;
>
>    l1 := stringtolist(str);
>    fnc := cat('selectstring/', opt);
>
>    # Make sure that fnc exists.
>    if not type(fnc, procedure) then
>       traperror(readlib(fnc))
>    fi;
>    if type(fnc, procedure) then
>       l2 := select(fnc, l1);
>       RETURN(listtostring(l2));
>    else
>       ERROR(opt, 'is an invalid option type');
>    fi;
> end:
```

The first call to type(fnc, procedure) checks to see if fnc is a second-level procedure that already exists in the current session, which is possible if it was defined when selectstring was defined (e.g., 'selectstring/alpha'), if

---

[10] See the entry for selectstring in *Other Commands* on page 254 or view the actual code for selectstring for more details.

it has already been read in from elsewhere, or if it has been directly entered into the current session.

If none of these three scenarios are true, then the call to readlib tries to read in fnc. Since unsuccessful invocations of readlib cause an error message, which completely halts execution, readlib(fnc) is enclosed in a call to traperror. traperror performs the command passed to it, but does not propagate any errors that occur.

By the nature of readlib, if the reading of the second-level procedure has succeeded, fnc will now be equal to the appropriate procedure. If readlib has failed, fnc will still be only a string. Therefore, the next call to type(fnc, procedure) determines whether the computation should proceed or an error message should be returned.

This technique should be used every time there is any doubt about whether a certain procedure that needs to be read exists.

CHAPTER 10 IOTools

Maple is rarely used in total isolation from other software packages. In many cases, data that has come from another product or that has been compiled by a non-standard process needs to be read into Maple for further computation. As well, it is often the case that results from Maple are imported into other packages. In both these scenarios, the importance of well-designed I/O (Input/Output) tools cannot be overstated.

What Maple Has

The Basic Tools

Until Maple V Release 2, only the most basic of file manipulation tools were available. These files worked fine for sharing data, *as long as the data was represented in standard Maple syntax*. That meant that if a file containing data produced with another application was to be read into Maple for further processing, it first had to be massaged into a format readily recognized by Maple. For example, imagine a file containing n lines, each line containing five integers separated by blank spaces. To import this data into Maple, the user could choose to insert a comma after every data element (except the last), place a [character before the first element and a] character after the last, and then use the **read** command to read in the data as a Maple list.

Do not, on the other hand, underestimate the basic built-in commands **read** and **write**. They are still available in Maple, and form the basis of many types of I/O activities, but almost strictly when the files being dealt with were previously created by Maple or are intended for future use by Maple itself.

The read command enters the contents of a Maple-readable file into the current session. There are two separate ways of reading in a file named filename.in.

```
> read('filename.in'):
```
$$[\,12, 34, 56, 986, -12\,]$$

```
> read 'filename.in':
```
$$[\,12, 34, 56, 986, -12\,]$$

While the former syntax is similar to how other Maple commands are used, you are more likely to see the latter syntax in other Maple works.

The results of the read command cannot be directly assigned to a variable name.

```
> mlist := read('filename.in');

syntax error:
mlist := read('filename.in');
                ^
```

If the contents of filename.ext are a list of values, use the " operator to assign them to a name.

```
> read 'filename.in';
```
$$[\,12, 34, 56, 986, -12\,]$$

```
> mylist := ";
```
$$mylist := [\,12, 34, 56, 986, -12\,]$$

When the filename presented to read ends in a .m extension (e.g., myfile.m), then Maple expects the file to be in Maple's internal machine-readable format. See the discussion of save for more information.

The counterpart of read is the save command, which creates a file containing Maple-readable information. Any file created by save can be read in with read. Every save command can also be written in two formats,

```
> save('filename.out'):

> save 'filename.out':
```

Again, the latter representation is more commonly seen. In its simplest form, as above, save writes all the information which defines the current session to the file filename.out. Even values that were not explicitly defined by you are saved (e.g., second-level library files, help pages, environment variables, etc.).

If you want to save only specific values, extra parameters can be added to save. For example, if you want to save only the values of the variables a, b, and c, call:

```
> a := 1:
> b := 5:
> c := 7/3:
> save a, b, c, 'filename.out':
```

A sequence of Maple assignment statements is written to filename.out.

As with read, when the extension for a filename is .m, save writes the information in a machine-readable Maple format. Any other extension, and the information is human-readable as well. (Information in .m format is more efficiently read into Maple.)

Another basic command that needs to be discussed here is lprint. The lprint command, while not exactly an I/O command, is important in that it displays information in the one-dimensional Maple format that is used by all the other built-in I/O commands. The following example shows how the commands print and lprint display a fairly complex expression.

```
> myexpr := int(1/(1+x^4), x):
```

```
> print(myexpr);
```

$$\frac{1}{8}\sqrt{2}\ln\left(\frac{x^2+x\sqrt{2}+1}{x^2-x\sqrt{2}+1}\right)+\frac{1}{4}\sqrt{2}\arctan\left(x\sqrt{2}+1\right)+\frac{1}{4}\sqrt{2}\arctan\left(x\sqrt{2}-1\right)$$

```
> lprint(myexpr);
```

```
1/8*2^(1/2)*ln((x^2+x*2^(1/2)+1)/(x^2-x*2^(1/2)+1))+1/4*2^(1/2)*arctan(x*2^(1/2
)+1)+1/4*2^(1/2)*arctan(x*2^(1/2)-1)
```

The lprint command is also used extensively in the commands provided by the Utilities.

There are six other basic I/O commands built into Maple: open, close, write, writeln, writeto, and appendto. All of these commands have to do with writing to a data file *a piece at a time*. The format in which the information is written is still not acceptable by other programs. It is not recommended that you rely too heavily on these commands—for more information on them, see their respective help pages.

Formatted I/O

Now that you've seen how to handle data in a Maple-readable format, how can data that is in another format be read in and/or created? Maple V

Release 2 saw the introduction of four important commands in the field of formatted I/O.

The readline command reads in a single line from a file and returns it as a Maple string. The filename is supplied as a parameter. If the file is not already open, readline opens it automatically.

The sscanf command is based on the C-language command of the same name. It takes as parameters a Maple string and a string specifying the format of the data. The result of sscanf is a list containing the information scanned from the string.

The following is a *simple* example of these last two commands.

```
> newstr := readline(myfile);
```

$$newstr := 123.456E7\ 123.45678$$

```
> newlist := sscanf(newstr, '%s %c%f');
```

$$newlist := [\,123.456E7, 1, 23.45678000000000000\,]$$

```
> map(whattype, newlist);
```

$$[\,string, string, float\,]$$

Without being an experienced C programmer, it is difficult to know how to create a format string, even one as basic as '%s %c%f'. For more information on format strings, see the help page for sscanf.

The counterpart of sscanf, the printf command outputs data to a file and is based on a C-language command of the same name. The input to a printf command consists of a format string and a sequence of values to be formatted. The following command recreates the line read in in the above example.

```
> printf('%9s %c%8.5f\n', op(newlist));
```

```
123.456E7 123.45678
```

As you can see, the format strings for printf are even more complicated then those for sscanf. See ?printf for more details.

Most Maple users should never have to use the commands sscanf and printf. Typically, non-Maple data files are in one of a set of easily predictable formats. The readdata command is the only easy-to-use built-in tool available, and it deals with one member of this set of recognizable formats. The data in a file sent to readdata must be either all integers or all floating-point values and must be separated by blank spaces (and nothing else). The result is a list of lists of numerical values, as the following example illustrates.

```
>   ##############################################################
>   # The following data is in the file integer.dat
>   # 12  345  -23  4  5
>   # 16  1    43   -1
>   # 0   0    3    0
>   ##############################################################
>   readlib(readdata):
>   readdata('integer.dat', integer, 4);
```

$$[\,[\,12, 345, -23, 4\,], [\,16, 1, 43, -1\,], [\,0, 0, 3, 0\,]\,]$$

```
>   readdata('integer.dat', integer, 2);
```

$$[\,[\,12, 345\,], [\,16, 1\,], [\,0, 0\,]\,]$$

The third parameter specifies the maximum number of data items to be read from each line of the file.

Utility Commands

The Utility commands in *IOTools* have been provided in order that formatted I/O can be performed with data in formats other than that accepted by the built-in readdata command. They are designed to allow access to a large number of often-called-for formats available from or expected by other applications, without the overhead of your having to learn the complicated syntax of C-language format strings as required by the built-in sscanf and printf commands.

Handling Charts

printchart(M, option, int)	print out a chart (matrix) of values
readchart(filename)	read in a chart (matrix) of values
makechart([expr$_1$, ..., expr$_n$],	create a chart (matrix) of values from a list of expressions

Often files of data come in a format with n lines (rows), each line with m data elements (columns). The natural Maple storage medium for such information is an $n \times m$ matrix. In this section, these matrices are referred to as *charts* because they represent information in typical chart form.

Of the three commands in this section, printchart has the most possible types of parameter sequences. In its simplest form, printchart outputs the data in a chart with each column left justified and with at least one blank space between each element.

```
> with(utility):
> mychart := linalg[band]([-1, 234, 5643, -20, 2], 7);
```

$$mychart := \begin{bmatrix} 5643 & -20 & 2 & 0 & 0 & 0 & 0 \\ 234 & 5643 & -20 & 2 & 0 & 0 & 0 \\ -1 & 234 & 5643 & -20 & 2 & 0 & 0 \\ 0 & -1 & 234 & 5643 & -20 & 2 & 0 \\ 0 & 0 & -1 & 234 & 5643 & -20 & 2 \\ 0 & 0 & 0 & -1 & 234 & 5643 & -20 \\ 0 & 0 & 0 & 0 & -1 & 234 & 5643 \end{bmatrix}$$

```
> printchart(mychart);

5643 -20  2    0    0    0    0
234  5643 -20  2    0    0    0
-1   234  5643 -20  2    0    0
0    -1   234  5643 -20  2    0
0    0    -1   234  5643 -20  2
0    0    0    -1   234  5643 -20
0    0    0    0    -1   234  5643
```

Of course, the justification can be set to 'left', 'right', 'center', or 'ragged', and the number of blank spaces between each column can be chosen.

```
> printchart(mychart, 'right', 2);

5643  -20    2    0    0    0    0
 234 5643  -20    2    0    0    0
  -1  234 5643  -20    2    0    0
   0   -1  234 5643  -20    2    0
   0    0   -1  234 5643  -20    2
   0    0    0   -1  234 5643  -20
   0    0    0    0   -1  234 5643

> printchart(mychart, 'center', 3);

5643   -20     2     0     0     0     0
 234  5643   -20     2     0     0     0
 -1    234  5643   -20     2     0     0
  0    -1    234  5643   -20     2     0
  0     0    -1    234  5643   -20     2
  0     0     0    -1    234  5643   -20
  0     0     0     0    -1    234  5643

> printchart(mychart, 'ragged', 0);

5643-2020000
2345643-202000
-12345643-20200
0-12345643-2020
```

```
00-12345643-202
000-12345643-20
0000-12345643
```

Of course, the values printed from a chart do not have to be simple integers or floating-point numbers. *All* elements of the chart are converted to strings before they are printed, in order that expressions can also be permitted.

```
> M2 := linalg[inverse](linalg[randmatrix](3, 3));
```

$$M2 := \begin{bmatrix} \dfrac{-1953}{121529} & \dfrac{-623}{121529} & \dfrac{-839}{121529} \\ \dfrac{-5665}{121529} & \dfrac{1242}{121529} & \dfrac{-5545}{121529} \\ \dfrac{9623}{121529} & \dfrac{-415}{121529} & \dfrac{10170}{121529} \end{bmatrix}$$

```
> printchart(M2, 'right');
-1953/121529 -623/121529  -839/121529
-5665/121529 1242/121529 -5545/121529
 9623/121529 -415/121529 10170/121529

> M3 := linalg[inverse](linalg[hilbert](2, x-1));
```

$$M3 := \begin{bmatrix} -(-4+x)^2(-3+x) & (-4+x)(-3+x)(-5+x) \\ (-4+x)(-3+x)(-5+x) & -(-4+x)^2(-5+x) \end{bmatrix}$$

```
> printchart(M3, 2);
(-1)*(((-4)+(x))^(2))*((-3)+(x))    ((-4)+(x))*((-3)+(x))*((-5)+(x))
((-4)+(x))*((-3)+(x))*((-5)+(x))    (-1)*(((-4)+(x))^(2))*((-5)+(x))
```

The above examples are only useful to another application that specifically wants data elements to be separated by blank spaces. What about those that want different separation characters? If an aftereach equation is supplied to printchart, then that specified string is appended directly after each data element, except the last one on the last line. The most typical alternate separation character is a comma.

```
> printchart(mychart, 'right', 2, aftereach=',');
5643,  -20,    2,    0,    0,    0,    0,
 234, 5643,  -20,    2,    0,    0,    0,
  -1,  234, 5643,  -20,    2,    0,    0,
   0,   -1,  234, 5643,  -20,    2,    0,
   0,    0,   -1,  234, 5643,  -20,    2,
   0,    0,    0,   -1,  234, 5643,  -20,
   0,    0,    0,    0,   -1,  234, 5643
```

Notice that the comma is enclosed in backquotes (it is a special character) and that it is not counted as part of the two blank spaces between each column. You can use this option to get rid of the blank spaces altogether, while still having the output make sense.

```
> printchart(mychart, 'ragged', 0, aftereach=',');
5643,-20,2,0,0,0,0,
234,5643,-20,2,0,0,0,
-1,234,5643,-20,2,0,0,
0,-1,234,5643,-20,2,0,
0,0,-1,234,5643,-20,2,
0,0,0,-1,234,5643,-20,
0,0,0,0,-1,234,5643
```

You can also supply a chart with individual row and/or column labels. This is particularly helpful when using *printchart* to output charts of data for presentation in a report. An example of the straightforward syntax follows.

```
> M4 := linalg[matrix](7, 3, [27, 19, 23.6, 31, 23, 30.1, 23, 20,
> 21.5, 25, 18, 20.1, 29, 27, 28.2, 30, 25, 29.2, 33, 27, 30.9]);
```

$$M4 := \begin{bmatrix} 27 & 19 & 23.6 \\ 31 & 23 & 30.1 \\ 23 & 20 & 21.5 \\ 25 & 18 & 20.1 \\ 29 & 27 & 28.2 \\ 30 & 25 & 29.2 \\ 33 & 27 & 30.9 \end{bmatrix}$$

```
> printchart(M4, 'center', 2,
>     rownames=['July '.(12..18)],
>     colnames=['high temp.', 'low temp.', 'ave. temp.']);
          high temp.  low temp.   ave. temp.
July 12       27         19         23.6
July 13       31         23         30.1
July 14       23         20         21.5
July 15       25         18         20.1
July 16       29         27         28.2
July 17       30         25         29.2
July 18       33         27         30.9
```

The strings themselves are factored into the computation of the spacing of the chart as if they were additional data elements. If there is not a proper number of row and/or column names provided, an error message is generated. The options rownames and colnames are used similarly in other commands throughout *IOTools*.

The last option available to printchart allows you to specify a filename to which the data should be printed (instead of to the screen).

> `printchart(M4, 'center', 2, file='m4chart.out'):`

If there is already data in that file, it is overwritten. If you want to append the data to an already existing file, use printchart in combination with the built-in command appendto.

Of course, the optional equations for aftereach, rownames, colnames, and file can be used together in one call to printchart. The order in which they are entered is not important, so long as they are at the end of the parameter sequence.

The command to *read in* a chart of data, readchart, is a little simpler to construct. In the most basic form, it very much mimics the built-in command readdata.[1]

```
> ################################################################
> # The file data1.txt contains
> # 12   34   -14   3
> # -4   10   0   15
> # 17   77   81   -91
> # 8   12   95   16
> ################################################################
> CH1 := readchart('data1.txt', integer, 4);
```

$$CH1 := \begin{bmatrix} 12 & 34 & -14 & 3 \\ -4 & 10 & 0 & 15 \\ 17 & 77 & 81 & -91 \\ 8 & 12 & 95 & 16 \end{bmatrix}$$

readchart automatically puts the data into chart (matrix) form. Unfortunately, the readchart command only accepts integer or floating-point values as input. This is because many other valid Maple statements can be represented as expressions containing blank spaces. For example:

> `lprint(f=3);`

f = 3

This expression could be interpreted as three separate data elements by readchart. This means that the data output by printchart is not always readable by readchart.

The difference between readchart and readdata is that an extra parameter can be passed to the former to strip away all occurrences of a specified

---

[1] In fact, readchart calls readdata. For examples of readdata, see the *Formatted I/O* section on page 272.

character from the raw data in the file. When a string is supplied as the last parameter, *all* occurrences of that string are removed from each line of the input file before the numerical data is retrieved from that line. This allows you to remove unwanted characters both from between data elements and within data elements. The following two examples illustrate this point.

```
> ###############################################################
> # The file data2.txt contains
> # 12,  34 , 6
> # -4, 10, 0
> # 77,  81, -91
> # 8, 12, 95
> ###############################################################
> CH2 := readchart('data2.txt', integer, 3, ',');
```

$$CH2 := \begin{bmatrix} 12 & 34 & 6 \\ -4 & 10 & 0 \\ 77 & 81 & -91 \\ 8 & 12 & 95 \end{bmatrix}$$

```
> ###############################################################
> # The file data3.txt contains
> # 12,345   456   6,789   12,000
> # 1,234,432  9  765,234,  0
> # 34  34,567   34,567,789,  4
> ###############################################################
> CH3 := readchart('data3.txt', integer, 4, ',');
```

$$CH3 := \begin{bmatrix} 12345 & 456 & 6789 & 12000 \\ 1234432 & 9 & 765234 & 0 \\ 34 & 34567 & 34567789 & 4 \end{bmatrix}$$

The final chart command is makechart. This is not really an I/O command (as it is not used directly in creating or retrieving an external file), but it is included here because of its close connection with the printchart command.

How are the charts that printchart outputs typically created? They may be results of complex matrix computations. They may be collections of data collected from some process. In many cases, however, they are the result of evaluating a number of expressions at differing values of their internal variable(s). The makechart command provides a simple syntax for creating this last kind of chart. The first parameter is a list of expressions; the second parameter is the variable being substituted for; the third parameter is the range for the value of the variable; and the fourth parameter is the step size for the variable as it moves across that range. Examine the following simple example.

```
> myM := makechart([sin(x), exp(x), sqrt(x)], x, 1..2, 1/10);
```

$$myM := \begin{bmatrix} \sin(1) & e & 1 \\ \sin\left(\frac{11}{10}\right) & e^{(11/10)} & \frac{1}{10}\sqrt{11}\sqrt{10} \\ \sin\left(\frac{6}{5}\right) & e^{(6/5)} & \frac{1}{5}\sqrt{6}\sqrt{5} \\ \sin\left(\frac{13}{10}\right) & e^{(13/10)} & \frac{1}{10}\sqrt{13}\sqrt{10} \\ \sin\left(\frac{7}{5}\right) & e^{(7/5)} & \frac{1}{5}\sqrt{7}\sqrt{5} \\ \sin\left(\frac{3}{2}\right) & e^{(3/2)} & \frac{1}{2}\sqrt{3}\sqrt{2} \\ \sin\left(\frac{8}{5}\right) & e^{(8/5)} & \frac{1}{5}\sqrt{8}\sqrt{5} \\ \sin\left(\frac{17}{10}\right) & e^{(17/10)} & \frac{1}{10}\sqrt{17}\sqrt{10} \\ \sin\left(\frac{9}{5}\right) & e^{(9/5)} & \frac{1}{5}\sqrt{9}\sqrt{5} \\ \sin\left(\frac{19}{10}\right) & e^{(19/10)} & \frac{1}{10}\sqrt{19}\sqrt{10} \\ \sin(2) & e^2 & \sqrt{2} \end{bmatrix}$$

Notice that all the resulting elements are *evaluated* as far as possible.[2]

Notice also that there are still some unevaluated function calls remaining in the above chart. This is because the *exact*[3] values substituted in for x did not always cause simplification to purely numeric values. There are three ways to force floating-point evaluation on the results of makechart.

First, you can explicitly wrap the entire call to makechart in an evalf command.

```
> myM1 := evalf(makechart([sin(x), exp(x), sqrt(x)], x, 1..2, 1/10));
```

---

[2]This is unlike the subs command, which does not automatically evaluate its results.
[3]I.e., not floating-point.

$$myM1 := \begin{bmatrix} .8414709848 & 2.718281828 & 1. \\ .8912073601 & 3.004166024 & 1.048808848 \\ .9320390860 & 3.320116923 & 1.095445115 \\ .9635581854 & 3.669296668 & 1.140175425 \\ .9854497300 & 4.055199967 & 1.183215957 \\ .9974949866 & 4.481689070 & 1.224744872 \\ .9995736030 & 4.953032424 & 1.264911064 \\ .9916648105 & 5.473947392 & 1.303840481 \\ .9738476309 & 6.049647464 & 1.341640787 \\ .9463000877 & 6.685894442 & 1.378404875 \\ .9092974268 & 7.389056099 & 1.414213562 \end{bmatrix}$$

Second, you can supply a floating-point value as one (or both) ends of the substitution range.

```
> myM2 := makechart([sin(x), exp(x), sqrt(x)], x, 1.0..2, 1/10);
```

$$myM2 := \begin{bmatrix} .8414709848 & 2.718281828 & 1.000000000 \\ .8912073601 & 3.004166024 & 1.048808848 \\ .9320390860 & 3.320116923 & 1.095445115 \\ .9635581854 & 3.669296668 & 1.140175425 \\ .9854497300 & 4.055199967 & 1.183215957 \\ .9974949866 & 4.481689070 & 1.224744871 \\ .9995736030 & 4.953032424 & 1.264911064 \\ .9916648105 & 5.473947392 & 1.303840481 \\ .9738476309 & 6.049647464 & 1.341640787 \\ .9463000877 & 6.685894442 & 1.378404875 \\ .9092974268 & 7.389056099 & 1.414213562 \end{bmatrix}$$

Third, you can supply a floating-point value as the step size.

```
> myM3 := makechart([sin(x), exp(x), sqrt(x)], x, 1..2, 0.1);
```

$$myM3 := \begin{bmatrix} .8414709848 & 2.718281828 & 1.000000000 \\ .8912073601 & 3.004166024 & 1.048808848 \\ .9320390860 & 3.320116923 & 1.095445115 \\ .9635581854 & 3.669296668 & 1.140175425 \\ .9854497300 & 4.055199967 & 1.183215957 \\ .9974949866 & 4.481689070 & 1.224744871 \\ .9995736030 & 4.953032424 & 1.264911064 \\ .9916648105 & 5.473947392 & 1.303840481 \\ .9738476309 & 6.049647464 & 1.341640787 \\ .9463000877 & 6.685894442 & 1.378404875 \\ .9092974268 & 7.389056099 & 1.414213562 \end{bmatrix}$$

Of course, the elements of the expression list do not need to have only one indeterminant. Having non-numeric expressions as elements of a chart resulting from makechart is perfectly valid.

As with printchart, labels for the rows and columns of a chart can be supplied in makechart.

```
> myM1 := makechart([sin(x), exp(x), sqrt(x)], x, 0..1, 1/10,
>     rownames=['x = 0', 'x = '.(1..9).'/10', 'x = 1'],
>     colnames=['sin(x)', 'exp(x)', 'sqrt(x)']);
```

$$myM1 := \begin{bmatrix} & sin(x) & exp(x) & sqrt(x) \\ x = 0 & 0 & 1 & 0 \\ x = 1/10 & \sin\left(\frac{1}{10}\right) & e^{(1/10)} & \frac{1}{10}\sqrt{10} \\ x = 2/10 & \sin\left(\frac{1}{5}\right) & e^{(1/5)} & \frac{1}{5}\sqrt{5} \\ x = 3/10 & \sin\left(\frac{3}{10}\right) & e^{(3/10)} & \frac{1}{10}\sqrt{3}\sqrt{10} \\ x = 4/10 & \sin\left(\frac{2}{5}\right) & e^{(2/5)} & \frac{1}{5}\sqrt{2}\sqrt{5} \\ x = 5/10 & \sin\left(\frac{1}{2}\right) & e^{(1/2)} & \frac{1}{2}\sqrt{2} \\ x = 6/10 & \sin\left(\frac{3}{5}\right) & e^{(3/5)} & \frac{1}{5}\sqrt{3}\sqrt{5} \\ x = 7/10 & \sin\left(\frac{7}{10}\right) & e^{(7/10)} & \frac{1}{10}\sqrt{7}\sqrt{10} \\ x = 8/10 & \sin\left(\frac{4}{5}\right) & e^{(4/5)} & \frac{1}{5}\sqrt{4}\sqrt{5} \\ x = 9/10 & \sin\left(\frac{9}{10}\right) & e^{(9/10)} & \frac{1}{10}\sqrt{9}\sqrt{10} \\ x = 1 & \sin(1) & e & 1 \end{bmatrix}$$

Printing Other Types of Structures

printlist(list, posint)	print elements of a list a certain number per line
printtable(T)	print index=entry pairs for a table
printstring(str, posint)	print a string divided into sections
printplot(2DP)	print the data points from a plot structure

The commands in this section deal with printing, in a format readable by other applications (i.e., using lprint), all or some of the contents of four special Maple data structures: lists, tables, strings, and plot structures.

The printlist command simply prints out the elements of a list a given number of elements per line. If a positive integer (or a list of positive integers) is not given as a second parameter, a single element is placed on each line.

```
> mylist1 := [seq(int(1/(1+x^i), x), i=0..5)]:
> printlist(mylist1);

1/2*x
ln(1+x)
arctan(x)
1/3*ln(1+x)-1/6*ln(x^2-x+1)+1/3*3^(1/2)*arctan(1/3*(2*x-1)*3^(1/2))
1/8*2^(1/2)*ln((x^2+x*2^(1/2)+1)/(x^2-x*2^(1/2)+1))+1/4*2^(1/2)*arctan(x*2^(1/2
)+1)+1/4*2^(1/2)*arctan(x*2^(1/2)-1)
1/5*ln(1+x)-1/20*ln(2*x^2-x-5^(1/2)*x+2)-1/20*ln(2*x^2-x-5^(1/2)*x+2)*5^(1/2)+
1/(10-2*5^(1/2))^(1/2)*arctan((4*x-1-5^(1/2))/(10-2*5^(1/2))^(1/2))-1/5/(10-2*5
^(1/2))^(1/2)*arctan((4*x-1-5^(1/2))/(10-2*5^(1/2))^(1/2))*5^(1/2)-1/20*ln(2*x^
2-x+5^(1/2)*x+2)+1/20*ln(2*x^2-x+5^(1/2)*x+2)*5^(1/2)+1/(10+2*5^(1/2))^(1/2)*
arctan((4*x-1+5^(1/2))/(10+2*5^(1/2))^(1/2))+1/5/(10+2*5^(1/2))^(1/2)*arctan((4
*x-1+5^(1/2))/(10+2*5^(1/2))^(1/2))*5^(1/2)
```

It is difficult to see where the larger expressions in that last result begin and end, but that is only because of their size. With smaller elements, this is not a problem.

```
> mylist2 := [seq(ithprime(i), i=1..20)]:
> printlist(mylist2, 2);

2    3
5    7
11   13
17   19
23   29
31   37
41   43
47   53
59   61
67   71

> printlist(mylist2, 4);

2    3    5    7
11   13   17   19
23   29   31   37
41   43   47   53
59   61   67   71

> printlist(mylist2, [1, 2, 3, 4, 4, 3, 2, 1]);

2
3    5
```

```
7    11   13
17   19   23   29
31   37   41   43
47   53   59
61   67
71
```

As demonstrated by the last example, when the second parameter is a list of positive integers, the different lines of the output contain the corresponding numbers of elements. The positive integers in this list must add up to exactly the number of elements in the first parameter.

Because it uses the lprint command, the printlist command produces output suitable for exporting to another application. If you want to display only the information on the screen using Maple's typographical output format, supply the optional parameter 'pretty', and the print command will be used instead.

```
> printlist(mylist1, 'pretty');
```

$$\frac{1}{2}x$$

$$\ln(1+x)$$

$$\arctan(x)$$

$$\frac{1}{3}\ln(1+x) - \frac{1}{6}\ln(x^2 - x + 1) + \frac{1}{3}\sqrt{3}\arctan\left(\frac{1}{3}(2x-1)\sqrt{3}\right)$$

$$\frac{1}{8}\sqrt{2}\ln\left(\frac{x^2 + x\sqrt{2} + 1}{x^2 - x\sqrt{2} + 1}\right) + \frac{1}{4}\sqrt{2}\arctan\left(x\sqrt{2} + 1\right) + \frac{1}{4}\sqrt{2}\arctan\left(x\sqrt{2} - 1\right)$$

$$\frac{1}{5}\ln(1+x) - \frac{1}{20}\ln\left(2x^2 - x - \sqrt{5}x + 2\right) - \frac{1}{20}\ln\left(2x^2 - x - \sqrt{5}x + 2\right)\sqrt{5}$$

$$+ \frac{\arctan\left(\frac{4x - 1 - \sqrt{5}}{\sqrt{10 - 2\sqrt{5}}}\right)}{\sqrt{10 - 2\sqrt{5}}} - \frac{1}{5}\frac{\arctan\left(\frac{4x - 1 - \sqrt{5}}{\sqrt{10 - 2\sqrt{5}}}\right)\sqrt{5}}{\sqrt{10 - 2\sqrt{5}}}$$

$$- \frac{1}{20}\ln\left(2x^2 - x + \sqrt{5}x + 2\right) + \frac{1}{20}\ln\left(2x^2 - x + \sqrt{5}x + 2\right)\sqrt{5}$$

$$+ \frac{\arctan\left(\frac{4x - 1 + \sqrt{5}}{\sqrt{10 + 2\sqrt{5}}}\right)}{\sqrt{10 + 2\sqrt{5}}} + \frac{1}{5}\frac{\arctan\left(\frac{4x - 1 + \sqrt{5}}{\sqrt{10 + 2\sqrt{5}}}\right)\sqrt{5}}{\sqrt{10 + 2\sqrt{5}}}$$

```
> printlist(mylist2, 5, 'pretty');
```

$$2, 3, 5, 7, 11$$
$$13, 17, 19, 23, 29$$

$$31, 37, 41, 43, 47$$
$$53, 59, 61, 67, 71$$

Finally, a *set* can also be provided as the initial parameter to printlist. As is typical with sets, the order the elements are stored (and therefore displayed) in is not well-defined.

```
> printlist({9,3,5,2,6,1,4,7,8}, 3);
```

```
1   2   3
4   5   6
7   8   9
```

The next command in this section, printtable, prints the contents of a table. First, create a table using the built-in table command and see how Maple displays the information by default.

```
> Tnum := table([one=un, two=deux, three=trois, four=quatre,
>    five=cinq, six=six, seven=sept, eight=huit,
>    nine=neuf, ten=dix]);
```

$$Tnum := \text{table}([$$
$$three = trois$$
$$four = quatre$$
$$two = deux$$
$$eight = huit$$
$$seven = sept$$
$$six = six$$
$$one = un$$
$$nine = neuf$$
$$five = cinq$$
$$ten = dix$$
$$])$$

What printtable does in its simplest form is mimic the equation-style output of the index/entry pairs, using the lprint command, so that the output is readable by other applications.

```
> printtable(Tnum);
```

```
three = trois
four  = quatre
```

```
two   = deux
eight = huit
seven = sept
six   = six
one   = un
nine  = neuf
five  = cinq
ten   = dix
```

The optional parameter 'titles' can be provided to specify that the table be printed in a two-column chart form (left justified) with the title 'index' added to the first column and the title 'entry' added to the second column.

```
> printtable(Tnum, 'titles');

index entry
three trois
four  quatre
 two   deux
eight  huit
seven  sept
  six   six
  one   un
 nine  neuf
 five  cinq
  ten   dix
```

As before, the optional parameter 'pretty' forces *printtable* to use the print command internally instead of lprint.

```
> printtable(Tnum, 'pretty');
```

$$three = trois$$
$$four = quatre$$
$$two = deux$$
$$eight = huit$$
$$seven = sept$$
$$six = six$$
$$one = un$$
$$nine = neuf$$
$$five = cinq$$
$$ten = dix$$

The 'pretty' option cannot be used in conjunction with the 'titles' option.

As extra functionality, if a command name which has a remember table[4] (e.g., sin, exp) is passed instead of a table, then printtable automatically accesses that remember table.

```
> printtable(sin);

0            = 0
(1/6)*(Pi)   = 1/2
(1/4)*(Pi)   = (1/2)*((2)^(1/2))
(1/8)*(Pi)   = (1/2)*(((2)+((-1)*((2)^(1/2))))^(1/2))
(5/12)*(Pi)  = (1/4)*((6)^(1/2))*((1)+((1/3)*((3)^(1/2))))
x            = sin(x)
(1/10)*(Pi)  = ((1/4)*((5)^(1/2)))+(-1/4)
Pi           = 0
(3/10)*(Pi)  = ((1/4)*((5)^(1/2)))+(1/4)
(1/5)*(Pi)   = (1/4)*((2)^(1/2))*(((5)+((-1)*((5)^(1/2))))^(1/2))
(1/2)*(Pi)   = 1
(2/5)*(Pi)   = (1/4)*((2)^(1/2))*((((5)^(1/2))+(5))^(1/2))
(3/8)*(Pi)   = (1/2)*(((2)+((2)^(1/2)))^(1/2))
(1/3)*(Pi)   = (1/2)*((3)^(1/2))
(-1)^(1/2)   = ((-1)^(1/2))*(sinh(1))
(1/12)*(Pi)  = (1/4)*((6)^(1/2))*((1)+((-1/3)*((3)^(1/2))))

> printtable(sin, 'pretty');
```

$$0 = 0$$
$$\frac{1}{6}\pi = \frac{1}{2}$$
$$\frac{1}{4}\pi = \frac{1}{2}\sqrt{2}$$
$$\frac{1}{8}\pi = \frac{1}{2}\sqrt{2-\sqrt{2}}$$
$$\frac{5}{12}\pi = \frac{1}{4}\sqrt{6}\left(1+\frac{1}{3}\sqrt{3}\right)$$
$$x = \sin(x)$$
$$\frac{1}{10}\pi = \frac{1}{4}\sqrt{5}-\frac{1}{4}$$
$$\pi = 0$$
$$\frac{3}{10}\pi = \frac{1}{4}\sqrt{5}+\frac{1}{4}$$
$$\frac{1}{5}\pi = \frac{1}{4}\sqrt{2}\sqrt{5-\sqrt{5}}$$
$$\frac{1}{2}\pi = 1$$

---

[4] A remember table is a place where previously computed or initially set values of a procedure are stored for later use.

$$\frac{2}{5}\pi = \frac{1}{4}\sqrt{2}\sqrt{\sqrt{5}+5}$$
$$\frac{3}{8}\pi = \frac{1}{2}\sqrt{2+\sqrt{2}}$$
$$\frac{1}{3}\pi = \frac{1}{2}\sqrt{3}$$
$$I = I\sinh(1)$$
$$\frac{1}{12}\pi = \frac{1}{4}\sqrt{6}\left(1-\frac{1}{3}\sqrt{3}\right)$$

The printstring command allows for lengthy strings to be printed in "sections" of a certain length. This is particularly helpful when looking at large integer values or floating-point values with many decimal digits. Create such a value and convert it to a string.

```
> bigval := 250!:
> bigstr := convert(bigval, string);
```

bigstr := *3232856260909107732320814552024368470994843717673780 66\
67479424271128237475551112094888179153710281994509285073\
53189432926730931712808990822791030279071281921676527240\
18926473321804118626100683292536513367893908956993571353\
01750405131787600772479330654023390061648255522488194365\
72586057399222641254832982204849137721776650641276858807\
15312897877672951913990844377478702589172973255150 28324\
17873206581884820624785826598088488255488000000000000000\
00000000000000000000000000000000000000000000000*

Now send this string to printstring to print it out in chunks of three characters.

```
> printstring(bigstr, 3);
```

```
323 285 626 090 910 773 232 081 455 202 436 847 099 484 371 767 378 066 674
794 242 711 282 374 755 511 120 948 881 791 537 102 819 945 092 850 735 318
943 292 673 093 171 280 899 082 279 103 027 907 128 192 167 652 724 018 926
473 321 804 118 626 100 683 292 536 513 367 893 908 956 993 571 353 017 504
051 317 876 007 724 793 306 540 233 900 616 482 555 224 881 943 657 258 605
739 922 264 125 483 298 220 484 913 772 177 665 064 127 685 880 715 312 897
877 767 295 191 399 084 437 747 870 258 917 297 325 515 028 324 178 732 065
818 848 206 247 858 265 980 884 882 554 880 000 000 000 000 000 000 000 000
000 000 000 000 000 000 000 000 000 000 000 000 0
```

The command automatically decides how many sections fit on each line.[5] If you want to supply a specific number of sections to be printed per line, use the 'eachline' option as follows.

```
> printstring(bigstr, 3, 'eachline'=8);
```

```
323 285 626 090 910 773 232 081
455 202 436 847 099 484 371 767
378 066 674 794 242 711 282 374
755 511 120 948 881 791 537 102
819 945 092 850 735 318 943 292
673 093 171 280 899 082 279 103
027 907 128 192 167 652 724 018
926 473 321 804 118 626 100 683
292 536 513 367 893 908 956 993
571 353 017 504 051 317 876 007
724 793 306 540 233 900 616 482
555 224 881 943 657 258 605 739
922 264 125 483 298 220 484 913
772 177 665 064 127 685 880 715
312 897 877 767 295 191 399 084
437 747 870 258 917 297 325 515
028 324 178 732 065 818 848 206
247 858 265 980 884 882 554 880
000 000 000 000 000 000 000 000
000 000 000 000 000 000 000 000
000 000 000 000 0
```

Another option, 'skipfirst', can be used to print the first *n* characters before beginning the sectioning.

```
> printstring(bigstr, 3, 'skipfirst'=1);
```

```
3 232 856 260 909 107 732 320 814 552 024 368 470 994 843 717 673 780 666 747
  942 427 112 823 747 555 111 209 488 817 915 371 028 199 450 928 507 353 189
  432 926 730 931 712 808 990 822 791 030 279 071 281 921 676 527 240 189 264
  733 218 041 186 261 006 832 925 365 133 678 939 089 569 935 713 530 175 040
  513 178 760 077 247 933 065 402 339 006 164 825 552 248 819 436 572 586 057
  399 222 641 254 832 982 204 849 137 721 776 650 641 276 858 807 153 128 978
  777 672 951 913 990 844 377 478 702 589 172 973 255 150 283 241 787 320 658
  188 482 062 478 582 659 808 848 825 548 800 000 000 000 000 000 000 000 000
  000 000 000 000 000 000 000 000 000 000 000 000
```

As well, another string can be provided in an optional 'aftereach' equation to specify what characters are used to separate each section (by default a single blank space). The characters are placed directly after every section except the final one.

---

[5]The value of interface(screenwidth) is used in the calculation.

```
> printstring(bigstr, 3, 'aftereach'=',');
```

```
323, 285, 626, 090, 910, 773, 232, 081, 455, 202, 436, 847, 099, 484, 371,
767, 378, 066, 674, 794, 242, 711, 282, 374, 755, 511, 120, 948, 881, 791,
537, 102, 819, 945, 092, 850, 735, 318, 943, 292, 673, 093, 171, 280, 899,
082, 279, 103, 027, 907, 128, 192, 167, 652, 724, 018, 926, 473, 321, 804,
118, 626, 100, 683, 292, 536, 513, 367, 893, 908, 956, 993, 571, 353, 017,
504, 051, 317, 876, 007, 724, 793, 306, 540, 233, 900, 616, 482, 555, 224,
881, 943, 657, 258, 605, 739, 922, 264, 125, 483, 298, 220, 484, 913, 772,
177, 665, 064, 127, 685, 880, 715, 312, 897, 877, 767, 295, 191, 399, 084,
437, 747, 870, 258, 917, 297, 325, 515, 028, 324, 178, 732, 065, 818, 848,
206, 247, 858, 265, 980, 884, 882, 554, 880, 000, 000, 000, 000, 000, 000,
000, 000, 000, 000, 000, 000, 000, 000, 000, 000, 000, 000, 000, 000, 0
```

All of the above optional parameters can be combined in one call to printstring to create exactly what you want.

```
> printstring(bigstr, 3, 'aftereach'=',', 'eachline'=8, 'skipfirst'=1);
```

```
3, 232, 856, 260, 909, 107, 732, 320, 814,
   552, 024, 368, 470, 994, 843, 717, 673,
   780, 666, 747, 942, 427, 112, 823, 747,
   555, 111, 209, 488, 817, 915, 371, 028,
   199, 450, 928, 507, 353, 189, 432, 926,
   730, 931, 712, 808, 990, 822, 791, 030,
   279, 071, 281, 921, 676, 527, 240, 189,
   264, 733, 218, 041, 186, 261, 006, 832,
   925, 365, 133, 678, 939, 089, 569, 935,
   713, 530, 175, 040, 513, 178, 760, 077,
   247, 933, 065, 402, 339, 006, 164, 825,
   552, 248, 819, 436, 572, 586, 057, 399,
   222, 641, 254, 832, 982, 204, 849, 137,
   721, 776, 650, 641, 276, 858, 807, 153,
   128, 978, 777, 672, 951, 913, 990, 844,
   377, 478, 702, 589, 172, 973, 255, 150,
   283, 241, 787, 320, 658, 188, 482, 062,
   478, 582, 659, 808, 848, 825, 548, 800,
   000, 000, 000, 000, 000, 000, 000, 000,
   000, 000, 000, 000, 000, 000, 000, 000,
   000, 000, 000, 000
```

If the first parameter passed to printstring is not a string, the expression is converted using convert(, string).

```
> printstring(expand((x+y)^20), 10, 'aftereach'=' ');
```

```
((x)^(20))    +((20)*(y)   *((x)^(19))   ))+((190)*   ((y)^(2))*   ((x)^(18))
)+((1140)*   ((y)^(3))*   ((x)^(17))    )+((4845)*   ((y)^(4))*   ((x)^(16))
)+((15504)   *((y)^(5))   *((x)^(15))   ))+((38760   )*((y)^(6)   )*((x)^(14)
```

```
)))+((7752    0)*((y)^(7    ))*((x)^(1    3)))+((125    970)*((y)^    (8))*((x)^
(12)))+((1    67960)*((y    )^(9))*((x    )^(11)))+(    (184756)*(    (y)^(10))*
((x)^(10))    )+((167960    )*((y)^(11   ))*((x)^(9    )))+((1259    70)*((y)^(
12))*((x)^    (8)))+((77    520)*((y)^   (13)*((x)    ^(7)))+((3    8760)*((y)
^(14))*((x    )^(6)))+((    15504)*((y   )^(15))*((    x)^(5)))+(    (4845)*((y
)^(16))*((    x)^(4)))+(    (1140)*((y   )^(17))*((    x)^(3)))+(    (190)*((y)
^(18))*((x    )^(2)))+((    20)*((y)^(   19))*(x))+    ((y)^(20))
```

The last command in *StringTools* is printplot, which prints out the pairs of x and y values for each point stored in a two-dimensional plot, or the triplets of x, y, and z values for each point stored in a three-dimensional plot.

For two-dimensional plots, one set of values is printed per line, using the Utility printchart with left justification.

```
> P2 := plot(sin(x), x=-5..5, style=POINT):
> P2;
```

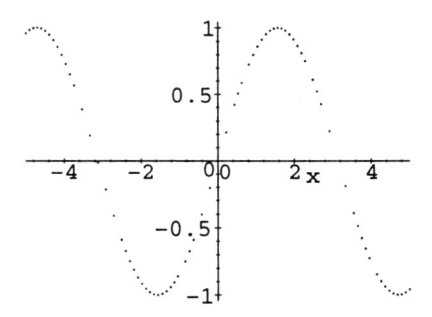

```
> printplot(P2);
-5.            0.9589242747
-4.90035296    0.98238672
-4.800705919   0.9961025934
-4.701058879   0.9999358151
-4.601411838   0.9938483544
-4.494767906   0.9764138394
-4.388123973   0.94788516
-4.281480041   0.908586464
-4.174836108   0.8589642683
-4.067485271   0.799157653
-3.960134433   0.7301502237
-3.852783596   0.6527364739
-3.745432758   0.5678076773
-3.539383046   0.38738221
-3.333333333   0.1905679625
-3.127591953   -0.01400024319
```

```
-2.921850571   -0.2179779149
-2.716719288   -0.4122054096
-2.511588004   -0.5891485149
-2.405514471   -0.6713865947
-2.299440938   -0.7460775852
-2.193367405   -0.8123818814
-2.087293871   -0.869554154
-1.982137071   -0.9165855655
-1.876980269   -0.9534907544
-1.771823468   -0.9798619994
-1.666666666   -0.9954079578
-1.557330362   -0.9999093353
-1.447994058   -0.9924692724
-1.338657754   -0.9731766223
-1.22932145    -0.942261788
-1.133525802   -0.9059108828
-1.037730154   -0.8612529646
-0.846138858   -0.7487265226
-0.7382956475  -0.6730283222
-0.630452437   -0.5895102792
-0.414766016   -0.4029757968
-0.207383008   -0.2058996899
0              0
0.217896342    0.2161761872
0.435792684    0.4221291303
0.5305557955   0.5060128074
0.625318907    0.585355865
0.81484513     0.7276193694
0.9275276355   0.8001394289
1.040210141    0.8625105858
1.152892646    0.9139417294
1.265575151    0.9537805117
1.36584803     0.9790715083
1.466120909    0.9945265289
1.566393788    0.9999903088
1.666666667    0.9954079577
1.772889675    0.9796485467
1.879112682    0.9528458303
1.985335689    0.9153019479
2.091558696    0.8674401214
2.189847048    0.8144296542
2.288135399    0.7535576405
2.484712101    0.6106495336
2.592550001    0.5218708274
2.700387899    0.4270291594
2.916063696    0.2236219556
```

```
3.333333334      -0.1905679635
3.54435948       -0.3919652644
3.649872553      -0.4866753171
3.755385626      -0.5759722341
3.853776623      -0.6534884543
3.95216762       -0.7246834931
4.148949613      -0.8454231589
4.255077596      -0.8972428633
4.361205578      -0.9389662691
4.46733356       -0.9701238809
4.573461542      -0.9903650952
4.680096157      -0.9994786321
4.786730771      -0.9972379215
4.893365386      -0.9836684184
5.               -0.9589242747
```

For three-dimensional plots, one set of values is also printed per line.

```
> P3 := plots[spacecurve]([cos(t),sin(t),t],t=0..4*Pi):

> P3;
```

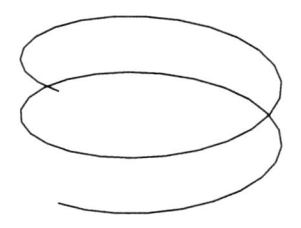

```
> printplot(P3);
```

```
1.                0                 0
0.9672948631      0.2536545839      0.2564565431
0.8713187042      0.4907175519      0.5129130862
0.7183493502      0.6956825505      0.7693696293
0.5183925688      0.8551427627      1.025826172
0.2845275874      0.9586678528      1.282282715
0.03205157847     0.9994862162      1.538739258
-0.2225209329     0.9749279124      1.795195801
-0.4625382892     0.8865993069      2.051652344
-0.6723008893     0.740277998       2.308108887
-0.8380881041     0.5455349025      2.56456543
-0.9490557465     0.3151082196      2.821021973
-0.9979453926     0.06407022178     3.077478516
-0.9815591574     -0.1911586268     3.333935059
-0.9009688688     -0.4338837372     3.590391602
-0.7614459598     -0.6482283936     3.846848145
```

```
-0.5721166621   -0.8201722532        4.103304688
-0.3453650568   -0.9384684212        4.359761231
-0.0960230286   -0.9953791127        4.616217774
 0.1595998922   -0.9871817839        4.872674317
 0.4047833404   -0.9144126242        5.12913086
 0.6234897994   -0.7818314844        5.385587403
 0.8014136199   -0.5981105331        5.642043946
 0.926916756    -0.3752670081        5.898500489
 0.9917900134   -0.1278771653        6.154957032
 0.9917900143    0.127877158         6.411413575
 0.9269167588    0.3752670013        6.667870118
 0.8014136243    0.5981105272        6.924326661
 0.6234898051    0.7818314798        7.180783204
 0.4047833471    0.9144126213        7.437239747
 0.1595998995    0.9871817827        7.69369629
-0.09602302127   0.9953791134        7.950152833
-0.3453650499    0.9384684237        8.206609376
-0.5721166561    0.8201722574        8.463065919
-0.7614459551    0.6482283992        8.719522462
-0.9009688656    0.4338837439        8.975979005
-0.981559156     0.191158634         9.232435548
-0.9979453931   -0.06407021444       9.488892091
-0.9490557488   -0.3151082126        9.745348634
-0.8380881065   -0.5455348988       10.00180518
-0.6723008947   -0.740277993        10.25826172
-0.4625382984   -0.8865993021       10.51471826
-0.222520946    -0.9749279094       10.7711748
 0.03205156212  -0.9994862167       11.02763134
 0.2845275688   -0.9586678583       11.28408788
 0.5183925497   -0.8551427743       11.54054442
 0.7183493328   -0.6956825685       11.79700096
 0.8713186904   -0.4907175765       12.0534575
 0.9672948551   -0.2536546141       12.30991404
 1.             -0.000000034359172   12.56637058
```

If the plotting points for multiple functions are included in a single plot structure, the points for each function are separated by one blank line.

By providing the optional parameter 'chart' to printplot, the points are printed out in a chart (matrix) form. The printchart command can then be used to provide further control over the output format. See the section *Handling Charts* on page 274 for more details.

For all of the commands in this section, there is one more optional parameter. As with the printchart command, a filename can be provided to output directly to a file.[6]

---

[6] As before, this option cannot be combined with the 'pretty' option.

> printstring(100!, 3, 'aftereach' = '\', file='bigstr.out'):

Examples

Viewing a Special Value

The following exercise was suggested by Ian McGee of the University of Waterloo.

In the field of Number Theory, there are often cases where you want to examine the inner structure and contents of large numerical values (typically integers or high-precision floating-point values). Maple is adept at creating these types of values, as was seen in the earlier example of 250!.

Examine the result of the following numerical computation:

> evalf(1/9^2, 30);

.012345679012345679012345679 0123

This is a repeating decimal with a pattern of 012345679. To determine any special pattern within that repeating pattern, we can use the Utility command printstring.

> printstring(evalf(1/9^2, 10), 1);

0 . 0 1 2 3 4 5 6 7 9 0 1

There is an 8 missing from this sequence. Of course, you could have "eyeballed" something this simple, but when you change the example to examine $\frac{1}{99^2}$, it's not so easy.

> Digits := 200:
> evalf(1/99^2);

.000102030405060708091011121314151617181920212223242526272829 3\

0313233343536373839404142434445464748495051525354555657 5\

8596061626364656667686970717273747576777879808182838485 8\

68788899091929394959697 9900010

Looking at the first few digits (000102030405060708 0910), a pattern seems to emerge when the digits are grouped in twos.

> printstring(", 2);

0. 00 01 02 03 04 05 06 07 08 09 10 11 12 13 14 15 16 17 18 19 20 21 22 23 24
25 26 27 28 29 30 31 32 33 34 35 36 37 38 39 40 41 42 43 44 45 46 47 48 49 50
51 52 53 54 55 56 57 58 59 60 61 62 63 64 65 66 67 68 69 70 71 72 73 74 75 76
77 78 79 80 81 82 83 84 85 86 87 88 89 90 91 92 93 94 95 96 97 99 00 01

Once you discover what's missing from that pattern, try answering the following questions on paper, then confirm your speculations using Maple.

1. What type of pattern (i.e., size of digit groupings) do you expect to get if you evaluate $\frac{1}{999^2}$?
2. What number will be missing from this pattern?
3. To how many digits will you have to evaluate $\frac{1}{999^2}$ in order to verify your prediction?
4. Can you write a formula relating the number of 9s in the fractional value to the missing pattern element? To the necessary number of digits in the expansion?

Programming Tips

Varying the Number of Parameters

A useful technique in the design of procedures is having *optional parameters* which have default values and therefore can be left out of the invocation of the procedure. In many programming languages, you must define an *exact* number of parameters to be passed to a procedure. In Maple however, you need only set the *minimum* number of parameters required.

An example of such design in the Utilities is the printchart command. This command takes up to six optional paramters, starting at the second parameter. Instead of getting into the complicated programming logic of all of these five optional parameters, a simplified version is treated where:

- The first parameter, a matrix, is required to run printchart.
- The second, third, and fourth parameters are optional, and represent a justification (just), a number of blank spaces between elements (spaces), and an equation holding the string to be inserted after each element (str), respectively. Each one has a default value associated with it, in case no value is given by the user.

The following is a simplified version of the beginning of the code for printchart, implementing the above criteria.

```
printchart := proc(M:matrix)
   local just, spaces, str;
   if nargs = 1 then
      just := 'left';
      spaces := 1;
      str := ``;
   elif nargs = 2 then
      just := args[2];
```

```
            spaces := 1;
            str    := ``;
        elif nargs = 3 then
            just   := args[2];
            spaces := args[3];
            str    := ``;
        elif nargs = 4 then
            just   := args[2];
            spaces := args[3];
            str    := rhs(args[4]);
        fi;
```

The Maple variable nargs is always set to the number of arguments passed to a procedure. This number will change from invocation to invocation of the procedure. So, in this case, if nargs=2, then the default values are assigned to spaces and str.

The Maple variable args is always set to the actual parameter sequence sent to a procedure. In this case, if nargs is equal to 2, 3, or 4, then the related parameter values can be assigned to just, spaces, and str.

If the number of parameters passed to printchart is less than one (the number specified in the proc structure), then an error message is automatically produced.

```
> printchart();
```

Error, (in printchart) printchart uses a 1st argument, M (of type matrix), which is missing

What should you do if the number of parameters sent to a command is greater than the largest number you could possibly use? Some commands (e.g., max, diff) take an unlimited number of parameters, but typically a command does have this upper bound. The two most common actions you could take are:

1. Generate an error message.
2. Ignore the extra parameters and proceed with computation.

Which response you choose is a matter of personal programming style; but make sure that you use it consistently throughout your Maple procedures.

The possible combinations of parameters for the full version of printchart is considerably more complex than what has been coded above. Not only are there more valid optional parameters, but several of those parameters can appear in any order, so long as they are grouped together at the end of the command call. To see how the complete parameter design is handled, view the code for printchart.

CHAPTER 11: MiscTools

As with most varied collections of commands, there are certain procedures within the Utilities that don't fit naturally into one of the larger functionality groupings. Instead of trying to force them into areas where they don't belong, these commands have been listed together in this chapter.

The standard Maple also has such "homeless" tools; some are available only through the readlib facility (see ?readlib for more details), while others can be accessed without readlib. For more information on these built-in commands, see the chapter *Miscellaneous* in *The Maple Handbook*.

The sections *What Maple Has*, *Examples*, and *Programming Tips* are dispensed with in this chapter. Any details about similar built-in Maple commands are provided alongside the discussion for each individual Utility command.

Utility Commands

One Expression - Many Types

listtypes(expr)	list all typenames valid for an expression

In the *ExpressionTools* chapter, several tools were introduced to perform operations (e.g., listing, locating, displaying) on subexpressions of a specified type within a larger expression. Each subexpression of the larger expression was tested against the given typename using the built-in **type** command.

```
> type(x^2+1, '+');
```
$$true$$

```
> type(x^2*z, '+');
```
$$false$$

When matches were found, the operation was performed. There is another side to the type-testing coin, however. Most Maple expressions test positive for more than one typename. The listtypes command takes an expression and tests it against *every* built-in Maple type and returns a set of all typenames for which the expression tested positive (i.e., returned true).

```
> with(utility):
> myexpr := 1 + x^2 - 5*x^3;
```
$$myexpr := 1 + x^2 - 5\,x^3$$

```
> listtypes(myexpr);
```
$$\{+, algebraic, anything, radfun, polynom, ratpoly, algfun, expanded, scalar\}$$

As you can see, both basic typenames (e.g., '+'), and structured typenames (e.g., algfun) are returned.

If more than one expression is entered, listtypes returns all the typenames for which *every* one of those expressions passes.

```
> listtypes(myexpr, x*y, Int(x,x));
```
$$\{algebraic, anything, expanded, scalar\}$$

What about user-defined (i.e., not built-in) typenames? Originally, listtypes does not check for these. For example, [1,2,3,4] is a valid locator list (typename=loclist), but doesn't show up as one in the following command.

```
> listtypes([1,2,3,4]);
```
$$\{type, list, anything, expanded, scalar\}$$

listtypes works by running the type command for each typename contained in the set assigned to the global variable _TypeNames.

```
> _TypeNames;
```
$$\{RootOf, array, series, table, taylor, type, union, +, name, integer, *, **, \hat{}, float,$$
$$numeric, indexed, list, set, string, =, and, not, or, range, .., !, ., factorial, \infty,$$

operator, fraction, rational, function, equation, algebraic, constant, procedure, relation, anything, protected, identical, specfunc, realcons, radext, radfun, radnum, square, <, <=, <>, uneval, boolean, polynom, ratpoly, radical, complex, facint, laurent, linear, logical, PLOT, radnumext, structure, algnumext, matrix, sqrt, &*, &+, anyfunc, arithop, dot, evenodd, defn, vector, surface, trig, PLOT3D, primeint, radfunext, TEXT, algext, algfun, algnum, arctrig, nonneg, nothing, posneg, argcheck, evenfunc, expanded, listlist, mathfunc, monomial, negative, positive, posnegint, point, scalar}

To check your own typenames in listtypes, simply add the appropriate information to _TypeNames.

```
> _TypeNames := _TypeNames union {loclist}:
> listtypes([1,2,3,4]);
```

$$\{ \textit{type, list, anything, expanded, scalar, loclist} \}$$

Polynomial Representation

polytovec(poly, var)	convert polynomial to vector representation
vectopoly(V, var)	convert vector representation to typical polynomial

One area where various computational products differ is in how they represent polynomials. In Maple, a polynomial is represented internally simply by a sum of the individual terms in the polynomial.[1]

```
> mypoly := 1+x-3*x^2-4*x^5;
```

$$mypoly := 1 + x - 3x^2 - 4x^5$$

```
> type(mypoly, polynom);
```

$$true$$

```
> op(mypoly);
```

$$1, x, -3x^2, -4x^5$$

---

[1] A series expansion, which looks very similar to a polynomial, is stored in another way altogether. For more information, see the on-line help page for type[series].

If a certain term has a zero coefficient (e.g., x^3 in mypoly), then no placeholder exists for that term in the internal representation. Other application packages (e.g., MATLAB) store polynomials as vectors containing only the coefficient values. The Utility command polytovec converts Maple polynomials into this form.

```
> myvec := polytovec(mypoly, x);
```
$$myvec := [\ -4 \quad 0 \quad 0 \quad -3 \quad 1 \quad 1\ ]$$

```
> whattype(op(myvec));
```
$$array$$

Note the placeholders within the vector for those terms with zero coefficients.

Note as well that the variable of the polynomial, in this case x, is not stored anywhere within the new representation, although it must be passed to polytovec if there is more than one variable in the polynomial. If your polynomial contains *only one* unknown, it is not strictly necessary to provide this second parameter.

```
> polytovec(mypoly);
```
$$[\ -4 \quad 0 \quad 0 \quad -3 \quad 1 \quad 1\ ]$$

Why provide this transformation within Maple? There are two main reasons:

1. You may want to transfer some polynomial information from Maple to another language that uses vector representation. There is an application package for MATLAB that allows you to run Maple commands from within MATLAB proper, which could make use of this Utility command.[2]

2. There are many computations with polynomials that can take advantage of vector representation of polynomials. Since Maple's built-in polynomial computations are highly efficient, it is unknown whether using such a representation will save you any computing time.

Of course, the opposing transformation is also provided.

```
> newpoly := vectopoly(myvec, x);
```
$$newpoly := -4x^5 - 3x^2 + x + 1$$

Again, note the inclusion of a variable as the second parameter. Without this, Maple could not create the polynomial.

---

[2] For more information on this application package, contact the MATLAB people at 1-508-647-4400.

Each of these commands can also convert multiple structures. Provide polytovec with a list of polynomials and a *matrix* whose rows represent the individual coefficient vectors is returned.

```
> mypolys := [seq(randpoly(x, terms=4, degree=7), i=1..6)]:
> printlist(mypolys);

50*x^7+79*x^6+56*x^4+49*x
-93*x^7+92*x^6+43*x^4-62
-61*x^5-50*x^4-12*x^2-18*x
-47*x^6-61*x^3+41*x-58
83*x^4-86*x^3+23*x^2-84
17*x^7+72*x^3-99*x^2-85

> mymatrix := polytovec(mypolys, x);
```

$$mymatrix := \begin{bmatrix} 50 & 79 & 0 & 56 & 0 & 0 & 49 & 0 \\ -93 & 92 & 0 & 43 & 0 & 0 & 0 & -62 \\ 0 & 0 & -61 & -50 & 0 & -12 & -18 & 0 \\ 0 & -47 & 0 & 0 & -61 & 0 & 41 & -58 \\ 0 & 0 & 0 & 83 & -86 & 23 & 0 & -84 \\ 17 & 0 & 0 & 0 & 72 & -99 & 0 & -85 \end{bmatrix}$$

Notice that the dimensions of the resulting matrix fit the polynomial of the highest degree. This type of matrix can be converted back into a list of polynomials with vectopoly.

```
> vectopoly(mymatrix, x);
```

$[50\,x^7 + 79\,x^6 + 56\,x^4 + 49\,x, -93\,x^7 + 92\,x^6 + 43\,x^4 - 62, -61\,x^5 - 50\,x^4 - 12\,x^2 - 18\,x,$
$-47\,x^6 - 61\,x^3 + 41\,x - 58, 83\,x^4 - 86\,x^3 + 23\,x^2 - 84, 17\,x^7 + 72\,x^3 - 99\,x^2 - 85]$

Nullifying Small Constant Values

roundtozero(exp, num)	round small values to zero

Sometimes you may want to remove miniscule real values from a larger expression because they have little or no effect on the final result. The roundtozero command examines each operand and suboperand of an expression, determines if it is of type realcons, and, if so, determines whether or not its value lies within the appropriate neighborhood of zero.

For example, create a random matrix using the built-in commands linalg[randmatrix] and rand.

```
> myrand := proc() rand(1..10)()/3000; end;

myrand := proc() 1/3000*rand(1 .. 10)() end
```

Utility Commands • 303

```
> M := linalg[randmatrix](8, 8, entries=myrand);
```

$$M := \begin{bmatrix} \frac{1}{300} & \frac{1}{375} & \frac{1}{375} & \frac{1}{300} & \frac{1}{600} & \frac{3}{1000} & \frac{1}{500} & \frac{1}{500} \\ \frac{1}{375} & \frac{1}{1500} & \frac{1}{1000} & \frac{1}{375} & \frac{3}{1000} & \frac{1}{1000} & \frac{1}{375} & \frac{3}{1000} \\ \frac{1}{375} & \frac{1}{375} & \frac{1}{600} & \frac{1}{500} & \frac{1}{375} & \frac{1}{1000} & \frac{1}{300} & \frac{1}{1000} \\ \frac{1}{600} & \frac{1}{500} & \frac{1}{500} & \frac{3}{1000} & \frac{3}{1000} & \frac{7}{3000} & \frac{1}{500} & \frac{1}{600} \\ \frac{1}{750} & \frac{1}{3000} & \frac{1}{300} & \frac{1}{1500} & \frac{1}{300} & \frac{1}{375} & \frac{1}{750} & \frac{1}{500} \\ \frac{1}{600} & \frac{1}{1500} & \frac{7}{3000} & \frac{1}{300} & \frac{1}{1500} & \frac{7}{3000} & \frac{1}{500} & \frac{1}{750} \\ \frac{1}{600} & \frac{1}{750} & \frac{1}{300} & \frac{1}{3000} & \frac{1}{3000} & \frac{1}{3000} & \frac{1}{3000} & \frac{1}{500} \\ \frac{1}{500} & \frac{7}{3000} & \frac{7}{3000} & \frac{7}{3000} & \frac{1}{1000} & \frac{1}{375} & \frac{1}{1500} & \frac{1}{600} \end{bmatrix}$$

Now round all the entries in M which are within $\frac{1}{1000}$ of zero.

```
> roundtozero(M, 1/1000);
```

$$\begin{bmatrix} \frac{1}{300} & \frac{1}{375} & \frac{1}{375} & \frac{1}{300} & \frac{1}{600} & \frac{3}{1000} & \frac{1}{500} & \frac{1}{500} \\ \frac{1}{375} & 0 & 0 & \frac{1}{375} & \frac{3}{1000} & 0 & \frac{1}{375} & \frac{3}{1000} \\ \frac{1}{375} & \frac{1}{375} & \frac{1}{600} & \frac{1}{500} & \frac{1}{375} & 0 & \frac{1}{300} & 0 \\ \frac{1}{600} & \frac{1}{500} & \frac{1}{500} & \frac{3}{1000} & \frac{3}{1000} & \frac{7}{3000} & \frac{1}{500} & \frac{1}{600} \\ \frac{1}{750} & 0 & \frac{1}{300} & 0 & \frac{1}{300} & \frac{1}{375} & \frac{1}{750} & \frac{1}{500} \\ \frac{1}{600} & 0 & \frac{7}{3000} & \frac{1}{300} & 0 & \frac{7}{3000} & \frac{1}{500} & \frac{1}{750} \\ \frac{1}{600} & \frac{1}{750} & \frac{1}{300} & \frac{1}{3000} & 0 & \frac{1}{3000} & 0 & \frac{1}{500} \\ \frac{1}{500} & \frac{7}{3000} & \frac{7}{3000} & \frac{7}{3000} & 0 & \frac{1}{375} & 0 & \frac{1}{600} \end{bmatrix}$$

If you examine M and the result, you will see that those values *exactly* $\frac{1}{1000}$ from zero are also converted.

The above is a very simple example. roundtozero works on *any* type of expression, not just matrices. You must, however, use caution when applying roundtozero on more realistic expressions. *Every* real constant value, no matter what type of element it is (e.g., coefficient, constant, exponent, parameter to an unevaluated function, etc.) is affected, as the following example illustrates.

> `myexpr := 3 + exp(x + .001)/15 + x^.03*y^3*z^(-.005);`

$$myexpr := 3 + \frac{1}{15} e^{(x+.001)} + \frac{x^{.03} y^3}{z^{.005}}$$

> `roundtozero(myexpr, .01);`

$$3 + \frac{1}{15} e^x + x^{.03} y^3$$

Now examine what happened to the third term. The value $-.005$ was rounded to 0, turning $z^{-.005}$ into z^0, which equals 1. This value was removed through the subsequent automatic simplification of the result.

In most cases, the value you supply as the second parameter will be much smaller than in the above examples. If you only supply roundtozero with one parameter, the value 1.0×10^{-10} is used.

System Commands

wait(num)	pause the session for num seconds

The only command in this section, wait, simply pauses a Maple session's computation for at least the given number of seconds. wait uses the built-in time command and, as such, tracks CPU seconds, however they are computed on your machine.

> `time();`

$$2.233$$

> `wait(5.0);`
> `time();`

$$8.216$$

If no parameter is passed to wait, the pause is one second long.

Index

!, 25
", 40
"", 40
""", 40
<, 39
<=, 39
<>, 39
\, 21
', 41
(), 26, 29
*, 25
+, 25
-, 25
->, 53
->, 45
., 248
.., 27, 51
.m format, 271
/, 22
:, 20, 81, 196
:=, 37
;, 20
=, 38, 39
?, 30
??, 34
???, 34
@, 29
[], 49
#, 119
$, 27, 52, 81
%, 70
_, 4, 263

_TypeNames, 299
{ }, 50
^, 25
`, 24, 41

abs, 25
alter, 219
anychars, 146
appendlist, 56
appendstring, 252
appendto, 278
arc, 203
array, 156
arrays, 155
    assigning values to, 157
    display form, 157
    in draw structures, 198
    querying values, 157
    ranges, 155
    special indexing, 163
    undefined elements, 156
arrow operator, 45
assignments, 37
augment, 161
automatic
    simplification, 114
automatic type checking, 125
axes, 191

backward quotes, 24, 41, 247
band, 167
banded, 167

boolean statements, 39
Borwein, J. M., 8, 257
Borwein, P. B., 257
bugs, 6
bundle, 198, 203, 221, 236

C, 19
Campbell, Colin, 8
case, 253
   sensitivity, 23
   upper vs. lower, 4
Casselman, Tom, 8
cat, 249
Catalan, 23
charts, 274
   constructing, 279
   printing, 274
   reading in, 278
Chiang, Kophu, 8
choose, 217, 240
   with transformation commands, 223
circle, 199, 236
circle3d, 205
code
   clarity, 244
   efficiency, 80
   reuse, 244
   second-level procedures, 79
   timing, 81, 83
   trapping errors, 151, 269
   viewing, 77
coefficients, 301
col, 162
coldim, 161
color, 191
column vectors, 159, 171
commands
   calling, 28
   composition, 29
   in packages, 35
   location, 30
   names, 28
   readlib defined, 35
   unevaluated, 28
comparelists, 64
comparestrings, 256, 258
composition, 29, 46
concatenation, 248
conditional statements, 42
conditions, 5, 70

cone, 205
constants, 23
constants, 23
conversion
   lists to arrays, 83
   polynomials to vectors, 301
   strings to expressions, 136
   vectors to polynomials, 301
convert, 177
convert(,string), 136, 249, 290
convert(, full), 177
convert(, sparse), 177
copy, 188
copyinto, 162
CURVES, 194
cylinder, 205

DAGs, 84, 91, 118
data
   external, 73
   from other products, 270
   in standard Maple format, 270
data types
   basic, 86, 92, 99
   extracting, 108
   finding, 108
   function, 88
   indexed, 88
   listing valid, 298
   marking, 108
   searching for, 98
   series, 88
   structured, 99
   user-defined, 299
delcols, 162
deletelist, 54, 60, 64
deletestring, 251
delrows, 162
density, 177
depth, 98
design
   intuitiveness, 1
   naming conventions, 4
   of commands, 4
   parameter conventions, 5
diag, 166
diagonal, 164
diagonal matrices, 164
Digits, 23
Dilcher, K., 257

directed acyclic graphs, 84, 118
display, 196, 199
display3d, 196, 199
Doherty, David, 7
double quotes, 40
draw, 199, 235
draw structures, 198
   altering values, 219
   are not hierarchal, 199
   choosing from among, 217
   combining with standard plots, 207
   extracting information, 213
   multi-shaped, 198
   transforming, 221
   type testing, 199

e, 23
efficiency, 27, 80, 265, 272
elif, 42
ellipse, 202, 231
empty list, 50
entermatrix, 163
entries, 160
environment variables, 4
equations, 38
ERROR, 124, 151
error checking, 126
error messages, 21, 125
errors
   checking, 79
   trapping, 151
Euler numbers, 259
eval, 77, 134, 158, 184
evalb, 39
evalf, 258, 280
evaluation, 280
   controlling, 128
   full, 128
   last name, 158, 184, 188
   tricks, 114
evenodd, 260
example, 34
exp, 23
exponential growth, 82
expression sequences, 26
expressions, 25, 84
   indivisible, 98
   large, 97
   order of operations, 26
   rational, 102

   restructuring, 114
   searching in, 98
   structure visualization, 91
   tree structure, 84
exprtree, 91, 118
extend, 162
extend3d, 209
external data, 73
extractlist, 54, 60
extractstring, 251, 258

factor, 77, 116
FAIL, 71, 153
false, 23, 39
feedback, 6
Fell, Dick, 8
file extensions, 271
findexpr, 102, 111
findpat, 138, 149, 152
findtype, 108
First Leaves, 77
flattenlist, 62, 80
flipcols, 173
fliprows, 173, 182
floating-point
   computations, 24
   numbers, 22
for/from/by/to/do/od, 43
for/from/by/while/do/od, 43
for/from/to/do/od, 81
for/in/do/od, 43
format strings, 273
forward quotes, 41, 93, 184
frequency, 99, 100
   of elements, 66
frequency, 67
func2d, 207
func3d, 208
functions, 45
   second-level, 240, 243
   unevaluated, 132

gamma, 23
geometrical shapes
   defining equations, 211
   defining information, 211
   displaying, 199
   extending to three dimensions, 209
   symbolic, 232

geometrical shapes (*cont.*)
   three-dimensional, 204
   two-dimensional, 199
getdiagonal, 167
getitem, 213, 238
global variables, 23
greatest common divisor, 75
Gregory's series, 257

has, 87
hastype, 87, 99
Heck, André, 18
Heck, André, 188
help facility, 30
   page structure, 32
hidden -1s, 89
Honsberger, Ross, 259

I, 23
if/then/else/fi, 42
implicitplot, 200
infinity, 23, 104, 255
info, 34
input prompt, 19
insertlist, 56, 60, 79
insertstring, 252
installation, 9
   system requirements, 9
   testing, 15
integers, 22
interface(verboseproc), 77, 128, 241
interfaces, 19
intersect, 65
intersectlists, 65
Introduction to Maple, 18, 188
iquo, 25
irem, 25
isleaf, 98

justification, 275

kernel, 19
keywords, 38

lasterror, 23, 151
LaTeX, 6
length, 250
libname, 23
library
   Share, 180
   standard, 19
   Utility, 11
linalg package, 159, 160
line, 202
line3d, 204
linear algebra, 155
linear growth, 82
linked lists, 117
lists, 28, 49
   accessing elements, 51
   adding elements, 54
   assigning new values, 51
   comparing elements, 64
   converting to arrays, 83
   duplicate elements, 50
   empty, 50
   frequency of elements, 66, 67
   mapping on functions, 70
   merging, 57
   ordering, 50
   processing elements, 67
   removing elements, 54
   reordering elements, 62
   replacing elements, 56
   restructuring, 62
   separating, 57
   sequential access, 82
listtypes, 299
locator lists, 102, 109, 129
looping constructs, 43
lowercase, 253
lowertri, 169
lprint, 91, 137, 272, 282, 284, 285

magic, 180
magic squares, 178
makechart, 279
map, 46, 54, 70, 124, 150, 160, 173, 266
mapcols, 172
mapexpr, 112, 128
Maple
   initialization file, 14
   interface, 19
   kernel, 262
   kudos, 2
   library, 19
   parser, 137
   platforms, 10
   programming, 3
Maple V

Release 2, 137, 270, 273
Release 3, 7, 9, 247
Release 4, 7
maplists, 70
mappat, 142
maprows, 172
markexpr, 105
markpat, 141
Mathematica, 2
MATLAB, 155, 301
matrices, 159, 274
    antisymmetric, 163
    banded, 167
    blocks, 166
    columns, 171
    copying, 187
    deleting rows or columns, 162
    diagonal, 163, 164, 169
    exchanging rows or columns, 174
    expanding, 162
    extracting rows or columns, 162
    full, 169, 176
    identity, 163
    random, 163
    rows, 171
    sorting rows or columns, 174
    sparse, 163, 169, 176
    subdiagonals, 164
    superdiagonals, 164
    symmetric, 163
matrix, 159
McGee, Ian, 8, 259, 295
member, 53, 125
minus, 65

names, 24
naming conventions, 4
nargs, 297
nchars, 146
negative exponents, 90
negative values, 89
nops, 85
numpoints, 191

on-line help, 30
op, 85, 158, 265
    nested calls, 86
operands, 84
    number of, 85
    zeroth, 88, 120, 186

operators, 84
Order, 23
order of operations, 26
orientation, 191

packages, 35, 182
parameter conventions, 5
parameters, 29
    active, 5
    args, 297
    checking validity, 123
    constant, 72
    extraneous, 297
    minimum number, 29
    nargs, 297
    number passed, 297
    optional, 5, 39, 191, 219, 296
    ordering, 5
    unevaluated variables, 59
    variable numbers of, 296
    verification, 79
parenthases
    extra, 136
parse, 137, 141, 150, 152, 249, 259
Pascal, 3
pattern, 146
pattern matching, 135
pattern ranges, 139
patterns, 138
    extracting, 141
    finding, 138
    marking, 141
    parsable, 148
    replacing, 142
    unparsable, 143
    wildcards, 146
    with unknown characters, 146
Pi, 23
π, 23
plane, 206
PLOT, 192, 210, 237
plot, 189, 238, 241
plot driver, 192
plot/options2d, 241
PLOT3D, 192, 210
plot3d, 190
plot3d/options3d, 243
plots package, 195
plotting, 189
    altering values, 219

plotting (*cont.*)
  data structures, 192
  default values, 192
  multiple expressions, 190
  options, 206
  other commands, 197
  USERDEFAULT, 195
point, 201, 236
point3d, 204
pointplot, 75
polygon, 202, 238
polygon3d, 204
polynomials
  internal representation, 300
polytovec, 301
Practical Approach
  addresses, 6
prependlist, 56
prependstring, 252
print, 158, 272, 284
  to detect errors in code, 265
printchart, 274, 296
printf, 273
printing
  directly to a file, 278, 294
  lists, 283
  plot points, 291
  strings, 288
  tables, 285
printlevel, 23
printlist, 283
printplot, 291
printstring, 288, 295
printtable, 285
proc/local/global/options/end, 44
procedures, 44
  evaluation rules, 158
prodcols, 172
proddiagonal, 167
prodrows, 172
programming
  language, 3
  procedural, 136
programming languages
  C, 19, 273
  Maple, 42, 77
projection, 191
protect, 38

quotes, 40

raiselist, 63
rand, 302
randmatrix, 302
randvector, 163
rational
  numbers, 22
  values, 90
read, 73, 271
readchart, 278
readdata, 273, 278
readlib, 35, 242, 269, 298
readline, 273
recursion, 79, 118
  infinite, 185
reflect, 225
reflect3d, 228
related, 34
relatively prime numbers, 75
relprime, 75
remember tables, 287
render, 212
replacelist, 56, 75
replacestring, 252
RETURN, 119
reverselist, 62
reversestring, 254
rotate, 224
rotatelist, 62
roundtozero, 302
row, 162
row vectors, 159, 171, 180
rowdim, 161

saddle plot, 75
save, 271
scale, 223, 236
scale3d, 228
scaling, 191, 201
scrolling the screen, 91
search
  breadth-first, 118
  depth-first, 100, 118
searching
  an expression tree, 118
  for a type, 87
SearchText, 250
searchtext, 250
second-level functions, 266
  building your own, 243
  built-in, 240

select, 53, 267
selectstring, 255, 267
   extending its functionality, 256
seq, 27, 52, 259, 265
   speed of, 81
setoptions, 195
setoptions3d, 195
sets, 28, 50
   duplicate elements, 50
   operators, 65
   ordering, 50
shape, 211, 229
Share Library, 180
showexpr, 103, 108
showpat, 141, 149
showtype, 100, 118
simplification, 183
   automatic, 114
simplify, 116
solve, 39
sortbycol, 175, 181
sortbyrow, 174
sorting, 174
   non-numeric, 175
specifier lists, 198, 210
   no longer valid, 231
   symbolic transformations, 233
   transforming, 229
sphere, 205
spheroid, 205
sscanf, 273
stack, 161
status, 23
step size, 280
strings, 24, 247
   adding characters, 251
   character case, 253
   comparing, 256
   converting from expressions, 249
   converting to lists, 262
   investigation, 250
   lengthy, 288
   maximum length, 247
   removing characters, 251
   reversing, 254
   storage, 137
   substitutions, 254
style, 191
subexpressions
   accessing, 101

   extracting, 103
   finding, 102
   marking, 105
   of elements of lists, 68
   replacing, 109
subs, 109, 128, 254
subsexpr, 110, 128
subsop, 110, 128
subspat, 142
subsstring, 254
substitution
   first-level operands, 110
   for operands, 87
   in strings, 254
   multiple, 129
   of expressions, 110
   patterns, 142
   subs, 109
substring, 250, 262
sumcols, 171, 178, 183
sumdiagonal, 167, 179
sumrows, 171, 178
swapcol, 174
swaprow, 174
switchcase, 253, 264
syntax errors, 21

table, 285
tables, 52, 264
   evaluation rules, 158
   indices, 264
terminators, 20
The Maple Handbook, 161, 298
tickmarks, 191
time, 81, 304
title, 191
transform, 226, 231
transform3d, 229, 231
transformation matrix, 226, 229
transformations, 221
   three-dimensional plots, 227
   two-dimensional plots, 222
translate, 222
translate3d, 227
transpose, 159, 183
traperror, 151, 269
tree structure, 91
true, 23, 39
type, 124, 185, 266, 298
type checking

type checking (*cont.*)
  automatic, 125
type(,ds), 199
type(,procedure), 268

underscores, 4
unevaluated functions, 132
  returning as output, 182
unevaluated variables, 59
union, 65, 118
unionlists, 66
uniquelist, 67
unziplist, 59
updates, 7
upgrade offer, 7
uppercase, 145, 253
uppertri, 169
usability, 1
usage, 34
users
  advanced, 3
  new, 3
  responsibility, 2

variables
  environment, 4
  global, 23
  temporary, 178
  unassigning, 41
vectdim, 161
vectopoly, 301
vector, 159
vectors, 159
  random, 163

wait, 304
whattype, 86, 99
whattypes, 99
whichelement, 68
wildcard characters, 146
with, 15, 35

xaxis, 225
xyplane, 228
xzplane, 228

yaxis, 225
yzplane, 228

zeroth operands, 93
zip, 58
ziplists, 57, 74
zipper, 57

Upgrade Your "Utilities" To Release 4.0
Available in Spring 1996

In order to make it easier to keep up with the latest
software updates, we are offering the purchasers of this book
an upgrade to the 4.0 version of Darren Redfern's
"The Practical Approach Utilities for Maple" at the special price of $49.00.
(A savings of $20.00)

This is not simply an additional diskette, but a
software upgrade as well as a revised 4.0 text !

*In order to participate, simply complete and mail the attached
postage-paid reply card with your payment.*

Offer valid only in North America

✓ Please enter my order for *"The Practical Approach™ Utilities for Maple™, Maple V, Release 4.0"*
(ISBN 0-387-14225-8) at the special upgrade price of $49.00 each.

Name_____

Institution_____

Address_____

City/State/Zip or Post Code/Country_____

Methods of Payment: *(Check One)*
☐ Check or Money Order *(Payable to Springer-Verlag New York, Inc.)*
Charge my: ☐ Visa   ☐ MC   ☐ AMEX   ☐ Discover

Card #_____ Expiration Date_____

Signature_____ Date_____

Subtotal $_____

Sales Tax* $_____   ***Sales Tax:** CA, IL, MA, NY, NJ, PA, TX, VA, and VT, residents add state sales taxes; Canadian customers please add 7% GST.

Shipping** $_____   ****Shipping:** $3.00 for the first book, $1.00 for each additional.

Total $_____

FOLD ON DOTTED LINE
LEAVING "BUSINESS REPLY MAIL" PANEL EXPOSED
CLOSE WITH TAPE

NO POSTAGE
NECCESSARY
IF MAILED
IN THE
UNITED STATES

BUSINESS REPLY MAIL
FIRST CLASS MAIL   PERMIT NO. 119   SECAUCUS, NJ

POSTAGE WILL BE PAID BY ADDRESSEE

SPRINGER-VERLAG NEW YORK, INC.
P.O. BOX 2485
SECAUCUS, NJ 07096-9812